Bloggers Guide To Arctic Finland

Bloggers Guide To Arctic Finland

DISCOVER THE REAL ARCTIC ENVIRONMENT

VICTOR LEINONEN

Bloggers Guide To Arctic Finland Copyright © 2019 by Victor Leinonen. All Rights Reserved.

Contents

	Introduction Victor Leinonen	1
	Table of Content	4
	Municipalities of Lapland Finland	7

PART I. MAIN BODY

1.	Travel Tips to Fennoscandia Country - Finland	13
2.	When and Where to Go in the Arctic Finland?	22
3.	List of Holiday Destinations	27
4.	Winter Nordic Flavors	53
5.	History, Tradition and Culture	72
6.	Natural Nordic Nutrition Exploration	82
7.	Bilberries in Finland	87
8.	Nordic Cuisine	91
9.	Finland National Flower Kielo	103
10.	Wild Lemmings	113
11.	Picture Gallery	116

12.	Historical View of Lapland	120
13.	Kilpis Lake Holiday Destination	130
14.	Ylläs Tundra Mountain	138
15.	Saariselkä Holiday Destination	140
16.	Skiing and Snowboarding in the Arctic Finland	144
17.	East Border Tundra Town Named Salla	148
18.	Arctic Freshwater Source	158
19.	Aurora Borealis	161
20.	Arctic Treaty Success Model	163
21.	The Land	168
22.	Fennoscandia People Victor Leinonen	171
23.	Vihta or Vasta?	177
24.	Finland Access to the Arctic Sea	180
25.	PRESIDENT OF FINLAND NEW YEARS DAY SPEECH 1940	192
26.	Santa Comes To Town	196
27.	Swans in Finland Mythology and Antiquity	202
28.	Christmas in Lapland	204
29.	Arctic Ocean Port of Finland	211
30.	The Early Pioneers	219
31.	Castle Hills and Fortresses	226

32.	Municipalities that were Extorted by USSR between 1940-1945	236
33.	Petsamo Municipality A Vital Part of Finland	240
34.	Bothnia Ice Lake	253
35.	Finland Borders of Independence	256
36.	The Arctic Sea Route to the Arctic Sea Port of Liinahamar	262
37.	Opening Up a New Arctic Sea Route	269
38.	German Soldiers Cemetery In the Arctic	277
39.	Being Logical: A Guide to Good Thinking.	284
40.	A Worldview and A Life philosophy	290
41.	Websites and YouTube Channels.	297
42.	Finland Centenary 1917-2017	300

PART II. **BOOKS BY THE AUTHOR**

About Author	323
Bibliography	328

VICTOR LEINONEN

WELCOME TO BLOGGERS GUIDE TO ARCTIC FINLAND

(Leinonen, 2018)

This book content is a compilation of my blog articles, from blogs that started way back in 2009. My first blog was named Nordic Cuisine Focus. The blog content covered many areas of the Arctic Finland region that I really enjoyed to visit, photograph, and write content on and publish. The articles were focused mainly on the natural Nordic environment, Finland, regional produce, ingredients, nature, traditional culture, and cuisine.

During the winter season, I often worked in the Arctic Finland region and later on started several other blogs with the Arctic Finland theme. Most of the articles and content that is used in this book was created while I was traveling, working, and living in the West Coast of Finland or Lapland. The content cover's Nordic environment, natural food products, and seasonal changes.

From the Spring wild berry flowering season to the summer berry harvest season and the farmer's markets. To the autumn mushroom season to the Lapland winter snow wonderland and the traditional winter activities that are common standard on the winter snow and ice. With the season's change to autumn and winter, come the work tasks, preparations, and the traditional recreational activities. Summer season activities are more user-friendly and accessible to almost everyone in natural environments. For the winter seasons in Lapland, I have covered a dozen locations in Lapland, and briefly described their situation, features, and the highlights.

Nordic Cuisine Focus blog delivers information on the Nordic region, with lots of digital images of the natural environment with various impressions of the regional ingredients. Summer season farmers markets and the berry foraging, mostly bilberries, lingonberries, and cloudberries. The Nordic summer season is fantastic for nature photography, foraging for berries, and a photo session of the yields is really a rewarding pleasure.

The Equinox occurs in mid-winter, beyond it the days move on from shadow/night dominated seasons to a day/light dominated seasons. Quickly the seasonal change is being felt and is both audible and visible. The thermometer moves from the – (negative) to the + (positive) side. Many migrating birds return to the north, seagulls, and swans, and many small birds start their singing in the trees of the forest. The snow melts from roads and pathways, and the water streams along the roadside when the afternoon sun is out.

At the end of the book, I have also added some content from my other two books.

- A Claim For A True Worldview, 2020.
- The Nemesis, 2018.
- Inkeri Land, 2010.

Those articles go more in-depth to the 500-year history of Finland, and how the people of Finland have often found themselves between a rock and a hard place. Sweden kings military crusades coming across Finland, heading East to punish the Russian imperialists. And the Russia Tzar military coming across Finland and heading West to punish the Swedish Imperialists, back and forth they went to some 400 years. In the last 200 years that has changed, the Russians no longer went to contact the Swedes, they just stayed in the Finland territory, and fought on the Finland territory against the Finns, the Karelians, and the Ingrians.

WATCH AND LISTEN TO THIS NORDIC CUISINE FOCUS VIDEO .

Visit Nordic Cuisine Focus website for the video.

Nordic Cuisine Focus has many interesting articles on tradition, culture, and ingredients. www.nordiccuisinefocus.com

Thank you for visiting the Nordic Cuisine Focus website and reading about the seasonal changes in Arctic Finland.

Table of Content

Content:

WELCOME TO BLOGGERS GUIDE TO LAPLAND FINLAND.

TABLE OF CONTENT

MUNICIPALITIES OF LAPLAND

1. Travel Tips to Fennoscandia Country – Finland
2. Where and When to Go to Arctic Finland?
3. List of Holiday Destinations?
4. Winter Nordic Flavours
5. History, Tradition & Culture
6. Natural Nordic Nutrition Exploration
7. Bilberries in Finland
8. Nordic cuisine
9. Finland National Flower, Kielo
10. Wild Lemmings
11. Picture Gallery

12. Historical view of Lapland
13. Kilpis lake holiday Destination
14. Ylläs Tundra Mountain
15. Saariselkä Township Holiday Destination
16. Skiing and Snowboarding in the Arctic Finland
17. East Border Tundra Town Named Salla
18. Arctic fresh water source
19. Aurora Borealis
20. Arctic Treaty success model
21. The Land
22. Fennoscandia people
23. Vihta or Vasta?
24. Finland Access to the Arctic Sea
25. President of Finland New Years Day Speech 1940
26. Santa Comes To Town
27. Swans In Finland Mythology And Antiquity
28. Christmas in Lapland
29. Arctic Ocean Port of Finland
30. The Early Pioneers
31. Castle Hills and Fortresses
32. Municipalities that were Extorted by USSR between 1940-1945
33. Petsamo Municapality A Vital Part of Finland
34. Bothnia Ice Lake
35. Finland Borders of Independence
36. The Arctic Sea Route to the Arctic Sea Port of Liinahamari

37. Opening Up a New Arctic Sea Route
38. German Soldiers Cemetery In the Arctic
39. Being Logical: A Guide to Good Thinking.
40. A Worldview and A Life philosophy
41. Websites and YouTube channels.
42. Finland Centenary 1917-2017

OTHER BOOKS BY THE AUTHOR

BIBLIOGRAPHY

Municipalities of Lapland Finland

EASTERN LAPLAND SUB-REGION

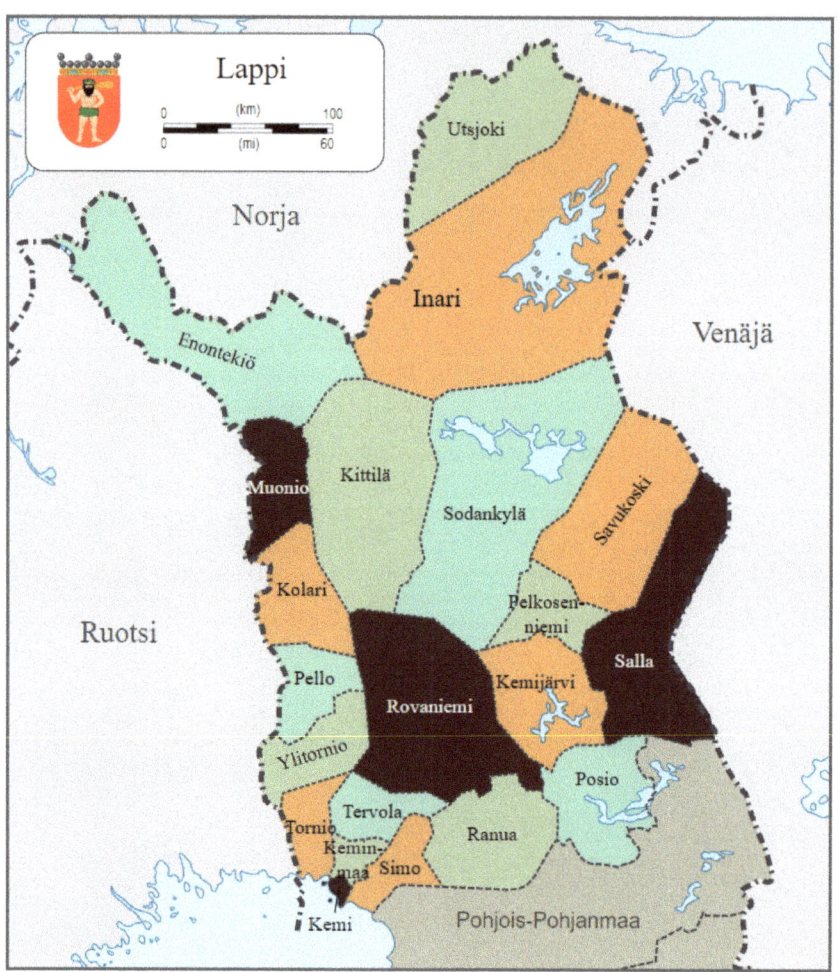

Municipality map by Oona Räisänen. Wikipedia.

- Kemijärvi
- Pelkosenniemi
- Posio

- **Salla**
- Savukoski (Northern Sami: Suovvaguoika)

KEMI-TORNIO SUB-REGION

- Kemi (Northern Sami: Giepma)
- Keminmaa
- Simo
- Tervola
- Tornio (Swedish: Torneå, Northern Sami: Duortnus)

NORTHERN LAPLAND SUB-REGION

- **Inari** (Inari Sami: Aanaar, Northern Sami: Anár, Skolt Sami: Aanar, Swedish: Enare)
- **Sodankylä** (Northern Sami: Soađegilli)
- **Utsjoki** (Northern Sami: Ohcejohka, Skolt Sami: Uccjokk)

ROVANIEMI SUB-REGION

- Ranua
- Rovaniemi (Northern Sami: Roavvenjárga)

TORNE VALLEY SUB-REGION

- Pello
- Ylitornio (Swedish: Övertorneå)

FELL LAPLAND SUB-REGION

- **Enontekiö** (Swedish: Enontekis, Northern Sami: Eanodat)
  Kittilä (Northern Sami: Gihttel)
- **Kolari**
  Muonio

PART I

MAIN BODY

CHAPTER 1

Travel Tips to Fennoscandia Country - Finland

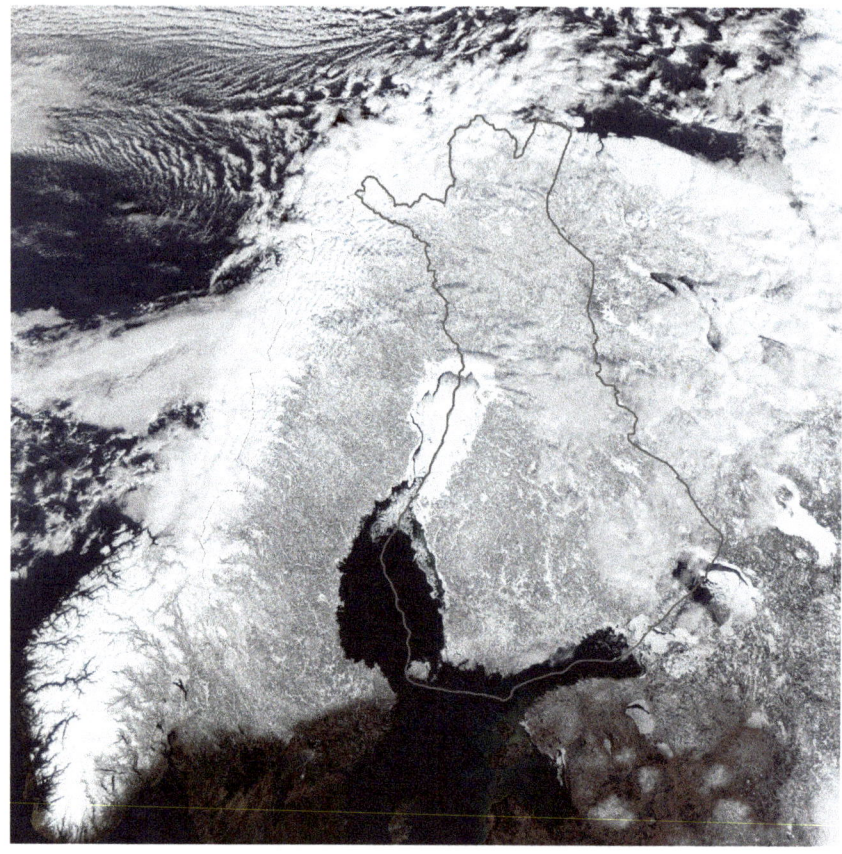

(Commons)

Travel tips to Fennoscandia country – Finland article post is an introduction to this book with important information for planning when visualizing Finland and the Lapland region with intent to visit the Nordic Lapland of Finland

ABOUT THE COUNTRY

Finland is a country of islands, lakes, and forests. The modern capital city of Finland is Helsinki and is filled with museums and galleries. In summers, the sun never sets here and vice versa in the winters.

FINLAND CULTURE

While in Finland, greet the locals by a handshake. The people here are quite reserved and don't open up quickly. Leave shoes outside the house when going over to someone's home. It is customary to wait until the toast is being raised at the dinner table. Host raises the toast by saying 'kippis' or 'skol.' People dress most of the times casually.

FINLAND TRAVEL

FINNAIR is the national airline of Finland. Other airlines that fly to Finland are Air France, Air Canada, Cathay Pacific, American Airline, British Airways, KLM, Swiss airline, Lufthansa, and United Airlines. The major airport in Finland is Helsinki airport. It is 19km away from the city, and it takes about 25 minutes to get to the city from the airport. Finnair provides buses for passengers. Taxis and hotel coaches are also available. The facilities offered at the airport are duty-free shops, car hire, bank, hotel reservation service, conference room, restaurant, and a multimedia center. Other than Helsinki airport, there are about 22 different airports, and Blue 1 is the domestic airline which operates within Finland. Times to time reasonable offers are being announced by the airlines. Prior checking of such proposals will prove to be of great help.

    If deciding to go by sea, ferry services are provided, and the major ports are Naantali, Vaasa, and Turku. These ferries connect to Rostock, Kapellskär, Grisslehamn, and Travemünde. Some of the cruises offer small cabins along with the provision of meals if staying aboard overnight.

FINLAND TRAINS

Trains from St Petersburg and Moscow can also be boarded. All the passengers are clean and very comfortable. Car-carrier trains also operate in Finland. Traveling by rail proves to be inexpensive and efficient and even great options for enjoying sightseeing. Avail the unlimited train travel offer of Inter-Rail pass or Eurailpass. There are offers for elderly people and children, check them out.

FINLAND ROADS

Remember to drive on the Right-hand side (opposite direction of the left-hand side traffic). When traveling by road at night, early morning or evening, or even on overcast days, there are chances of running into an elk or reindeer. In such cases, the police should be reported immediately. Blowing horn for small reasons should be avoided. Keep your car on the right-hand side lane. Gas stations accept credit cards. Laws about seat belt and drinking while driving should be strictly followed. Extra precautions must be taken if taking caravan along. National driving license or International Driving Permit and car insurance must be there with you at all times. Coach Service is also available and connects to even the remote places. Taxis can be hired at the airport and railway stations, and tipping is considered offensive here. Check out agents in Helsinki who run a rent-a-car business for hiring cars.

DUTY-FREE ITEMS

1. 200 cigarettes or 50 cigars or 250g of tobacco or 100 cigarillos
2. 50g of perfume and 250ml of eau de toilette
3. 2litre of alcoholic beverages of less than 22 percent by volume or 1litre of alcoholic drinks of more than 22

percent by volume, 2litre of sparkling wine and 16litre of beer

4. 100g of tea or 40g of tea extract and essence and 500g of coffee or 200g of coffee extract or essence

Tobacco and alcohol can be carried out by people over 18 years of age. Agricultural and food items should be avoided. Certain medicines require a doctor's prescription for verification. Firearms and sharp objects are strictly prohibited.

Thank you for visiting www.fennoscandia.net website and reading this Information on Travel Tips to Fennoscandia Countries – Finland article post. We hope this was helpful and useful to you. Please do share this link with your friends. Thank you.

VISITING FINLAND VIA NORWAY

Traveling to Finland from Norway. This is a fast guide to what to expect when visiting the land of Norway. Norway is unique in the geographical sense, covering the coastline of the Arctic ocean and the Fennoscandia region.

ABOUT THE COUNTRY

Norway, a Nordic country lying on the western portion of the Scandinavian Peninsula, is located in Northern Europe. It also borders Sweden, Finland, and Russia. Norway is an outstandingly beautiful country with a long coastline, stunning snow-covered peaks and mountain chains, between breathtaking fjords. Oslo is the capital of Norway and the largest city. Norway is bestowed with lots of natural beauty encompassing wild forests, high tundra plateaus, historic towns, and beautiful fishing villages of the Norwegian Sea of the Arctic Ocean. The country is very hospitable to the tourists and people are very friendly too. Many tourists are attracted by the famous midnight sun of the Arctic. All three big cities of Norway offer different experiences to visitors. Norway is a place to be for nature lovers and for cultural enthusiasts. Norway is indeed one of the most fabulous variation landscapes, as a tourist destination of Europe, with the clean natural resources of the Arctic Ocean.

NORWAY POPULATION & LANGUAGES

The population of Norway is only 4.6 million and the official languages being spoken are Bokmal Norwegian and Nynorsk Norwegian. Other languages that are also spoken in Norway include Sámi and Finnish.

NORWAY ELECTRICITY

The voltage is 230 V, and the frequency is 50 Hz. The types of plugs used are Round pin attachment plug and "Schuko" plug and receptacle with side grounding contacts.

GEOGRAPHIC LOCATION

It is a Nordic country lying on the western portion of the Scandinavian Peninsula and located in Northern Europe. It also borders Sweden, Finland, and Russia. About two-third area of Norway is mountains, has around fifty thousand small islands along its coast. It also has one of the longest coastlines in the world.

NORWAY CLIMATE

The climate of Norway can be termed as Temperate with hot summers and cold overcast winters. The highlands of interior Norway have an arctic-like climate with snow, severe wind chill and frost. Most of the rain is along with the coastal areas and comes down in winter quite heavily and frequently. Winters are mild too along with the coastal areas.

LOCAL CUSTOMS

Like any other country, Norway has its own customs too. It is customary not to drink until the host makes a toast. It is customary for guests to offer gifts to the host of a meal. Smoking is prohibited in most public areas. Casual dress is acceptable for everyday wear. Tipping taxi drivers is not customary. Tipping up to five percent is customary for service in restaurants. Porters at railway stations and airports charge per piece, while porters at hotels generally charge around NOK5-10 depending on the number of bits of luggage.

ATTRACTIONS

- **Bergen** – Numerous museums, galleries, aquarium, medieval age buildings, cable car to the top of Bergen's hills and boat trips to fjords.
- **Oslo** – Old medieval buildings, churches, modern architecture, museums like Edvard Munch Museum and the Norwegian Folk Museum, art galleries, Vigeland Park, and Akershus Fortress
- **Fjordland** – Geirangerfjorden is known for tiny S-shaped fjord,
- **Sognefjord** – the longest and the deepest fjord, beautiful villages such as Balestrand and Flam, old stave churches,
- **Nærøyfjord** – Narrowest branch of the Sognefjord and Plateau of Jostedalsbreen glacier
- **Tromsø** – Arctic cathedral, Polaris and Tromsø Museum

TRAVEL BY AIR

Many airlines operate to Norway like Braathens SAFE (BU) and SAS Scandinavian Airlines (SK), a Scandinavian airline, Air France, British Airways, Finnair, Icelandair, KLM, Lufthansa, Northwest Airlines, Norwegian Air Shuttle, Ryanair and Swiss Airlines. Oslo International Airport (OSL) (Gardermoen) (website: www.osl.no) is the biggest airport in Norway, which is located 30 miles north of Oslo.

SEA

The important passenger ports are Bergen, Kristiansand, Larvik, Oslo, and Stavanger. The main sea routes from the UK, operated by Fjord Line and DFDS Seaways respectively, are from Newcastle to Bergen and to Kristiansand.

RAIL

The country is part of the extensive network of trains connecting the European cities. If you are coming from the UK, the connections are from London via Dover/Ostend (via Denmark, Germany, The Netherlands, and Sweden) or Harwich/Hook of Holland, or from Newcastle to Bergen via Stavanger. It is also connected to Sweden through two routes, with daytime and overnight trains from Copenhagen, Malm, and Stockholm.

DUTY-FREE ITEMS

1. 200 cigarettes or 250g of tobacco products and 200 leaves of cigarette paper for EU countries.
2. 400 cigarettes or 500g of tobacco products and 200 leaves of cigarette paper for Non-EU countries.

3. 1liter of spirits and 1liter of wine or 2liter of wine and 2liter of beer for EU countries.
4. 1liter of spirits and 1liter of wine or 2liter of wine and 2liter of beer for Non-EU countries.
5. 50g perfume or 500 ml eau de toilette
6. Gifts, Food, fruits, medications and flowers for the personal use of value up to 3,500 km

PROHIBITED ITEMS

Un-canned goods, meat or dairy products, Narcotics, firearms, ammunition, weapons, eggs, plants, endangered species, fireworks and alcoholic beverages that contain more than sixty percent alcohol.

Thank you for visiting http://fennoscandia.net and reading this Information on vitamins and supplements article post. We hope this was helpful and useful to you. Please do share this link with your friends. Thank you.

CHAPTER 2

When and Where to Go in the Arctic Finland?

WHEN AND WHERE TO GO IN THE ARCTIC FINLAND? 23

(Nordic Art Images.com)

WHEN AND WHERE TO GO IN THE ARCTIC FINLAND, REALLY DEPENDS ON THE INTENTION.

A first-time visit to Finland ever?
   First-time visit in the winter season?
   First-time visit in the summer season?
   Recreational activities?
   Winter back-country skiing, downhill skiing, snowboarding, snowshoe trekking, snowmobile safaris or other?

Summer natural landscapes, spring season, summer season?
Autumn season for photography and video of Lapland?
Wild-berry foraging for bilberries, wild strawberries, raspberries, lingonberries, cranberries, and cloud-berries?
Bird watching during the peak migration periods?
Freshwater fishing at the lakes and rivers?

FINLAND DOES OFFER SPECIFIC ENVIRONMENTS SEASONS FOR SPECIFIC NATURE EXPERIENCES.

The continues four changing seasons revolve differently to other parts of the world. Summer in Finland starts in Kuly, and is relatively short 3 months, with temperatures averaging around + 10 to + 20 C during day time. There is variation from region to region, understandably, when the South region to North is approx. 1000 kilometers and 300 km (1/3) of Finland is inside the arctic circle. The extreme recorded temperature of Finland is + 37.2 °C at Liperi, on July 29, 2010. The extreme lowest is , −51.5 °C at Kittilä, on January 28, 1999.

Every region of the world for visitor attractions have their strengths and weaknesses on the global expectations of the weather climates and environments. Long winter season in the Arctic circle for skiing, ice skating, snowboarding, fat bikes, reindeer sleigh rides, snowshoe trekking, and snowmobile safaris provide some of the best conditions and environments available. Finland is a robust competitive winter sports country, skiing, snowboarding, mountain biking, and ice hockey. It is the proximity to the northern hemisphere that sets the stage for the characteristics of the region and culture.

Other countries have attributes for summer sports and recreational activities. That is the reason Hawaii is known as the place for the pipeline big surf. Similarly, West coast of American California and Australian East coast for sun surf and sand. You won't find good surf waves in the Gulf of Bothnia, but you do find excellent skiing and snowboarding conditions with a long season in the Lapland tundra environment. Clear skies and sunshine are limited to the spring season, that starts around February and ends in April-May. Also, the unique aspect of the Nordic region is the summer season. Nordic environments are lush with natural ingredients, wild berries, and mushrooms in the summer and autumn seasons. Nordic Lapland offers fantastic trekking opportunities in the open rolling hills of Tundra.

Info for trekking. Visit www.nationalparks.fi/ website.

ARCTIC PHOTOGRAPHY

The Arctic environment is excellent for photography, and a fantastic way to share the unique natural Arctic environment with friends and family the rest of the world, that may not have the opportunity to physically experience the Arctic environment. The Arctic environment goes through extreme changes of the seasons, and each season is uniquely stunning to experience.

SUMMER TO AUTUMN EXPERIENCE

The climate in the Nordic Lapland summer season temperature is temperate for trekking, with open views of rolling tundra hills, bubbling fresh arctic freshwater springs, drizzling creeks, running rivers and still lakes. Brilliantly vivid colors of the ground cover in the Autumn season. There is an enormous splash of colors over the landscape, from the conifers and the deciduous trees, various deciduous wild berry shrubs, and the moss-covered ground cover. The autumn colors of Lapland are an array of green, Auburn, blue, orange, red and yellow.

WINTER EXPERIENCE

Snow covered winter wonderland, dark days of the midwinter

solstice. Calm weather and constant snowfall that may go on for days. Spring season around February opens up with longer days and sunlight. Occasionally apparent night skies with twinkling stars and at times the Northern lights show with freezing frosty mornings. Morning clear blue skies and glistening white snow with a snow crust on top that lasts for several hours.

SPRING SEASON EXPERIENCE

The spring season sunshine is a pleasure to experience while back country skiing along rolling tundra hills and open country. The summer season is also fantastic in the natural environment, with the new life that springs up from a long cold winter. Bird migration is often a sure sign of the coming summer, also the new growth on deciduous trees that springs up

ARCTIC PHOTOGRAPHY AND SEASONAL CHANGES

Northern photography of the seasonal changes is a rapid sequential activity in the Arctic region, life moves very fast into a quick gear during the spring and summer seasons. There are time constrained windows of opportunity during these seasonal changes.

CHAPTER 3

List of Holiday Destinations

(Leinonen, 2011)

HERE IS A SAMPLE OF 12 REGIONS THAT ARE A HUB OF ACTIVITY DURING THE HOLIDAY SEASONS.

1. Rovaniemi.
2. Salla
3. Pyhä / Luosto
4. Saariselka.

LIST OF HOLIDAY DESTINATIONS

5. Karigasniemi
6. Ivalo
7. Inari
8. Ylläs
9. Äkäslompolo
10. Lewi
11. Pallas.
12. Kilpisjärvi

The above list is not in any particular order, I have listed them because they are the places where I spent the most time in, mostly in the winter season. Each regional location is unique with its own history, culture, facilities, and cultural traditions. In order of the size of the city or town and the facilities, then the order could start from Rovaniemi to Lewi, Ylläs to Saariselkä, Pyhä to Luosto, Kilpisjärvi to Inari and Pallas. This is not a complete list of all the interesting locations in Lapland. The general idea of the location varies in size, and the urban modernization of the facilities, holiday centers, and Ski Resorts. Rovaniemi is a small city, not a ski resort. There are many services to activities, safaris and ski resorts from there. Pallas Tundra is a remote national park, with very little development made there, in comparison to other locations like Lewi and Saariselkä. Rovaniemi is a city, while Salla, Karigasniemi, Ivalo, and Inari are towns. Ylläs Tundra lakeside is the only one with a big Gondola to the summit.

KNOW YOUR HOLIDAY DESTINATION AS MUCH AS POSSIBLE

To know your holiday destination in advance much as possible does provide many benefits, it can eliminate the loss of your valuable time, loss of resources, and loss of the holiday expectations that you may have had before departing on a memorable exotic location holiday of a lifetime.

SERVICES AVAILABLE

The available Services can make or break a holiday, not only if one has false expectations in their thinking. E.g., a guest visitor projecting the standard services available at a modern city with many conveniences of their own hometown to a remote Nordic Arctic location. Alternative it can also backfire in reverse, having expectations of a quiet, remote snow-covered Arctic backcountry location to the noisy racket of screaming snowmobiles and yelping dog sleighs. This is one of the many key reasons why Arctic Suomi Directory website has been established to provide relevant information on Arctic Finland from the customers perspective.

LOCATIONS PRESENTED

The broad range of potential holiday locations of Arctic Finland presented here at this Directory, covers possible holiday destinations from the South Lapland to the North Lapland, and from the Far East to West Finland.

- Rovaniemi City
- Saariselkä Township
- Inari Lake district
- Äkäslompolo Township
- Ylläs Tundra Mountain Ski Resorts
- Levi Ski Resort town
- Pallas Tundra Wilderness reserve
- Kilpisjärvi mountain plateau lake town

LIST OF HOLIDAY DESTINATIONS

- Norway is a very close distance away from the Kilpisjärvi township.
- Sweden shares the West border of Finland.

Google maps.

ROVANIEMI

(Google Maps, 2019)

Coordinates: 66°30'N 025°44'E.

Rovaniemi is 811 kilometers North of Helsinki, via E75.

Is the administrative capital and commercial center of Finland's northernmost province, Lapland. It is situated about 10 kilometers (6 miles) south of the Arctic Circle

Pop: 61,329

SAARISELKÄ. (ISLAND RIDGE).

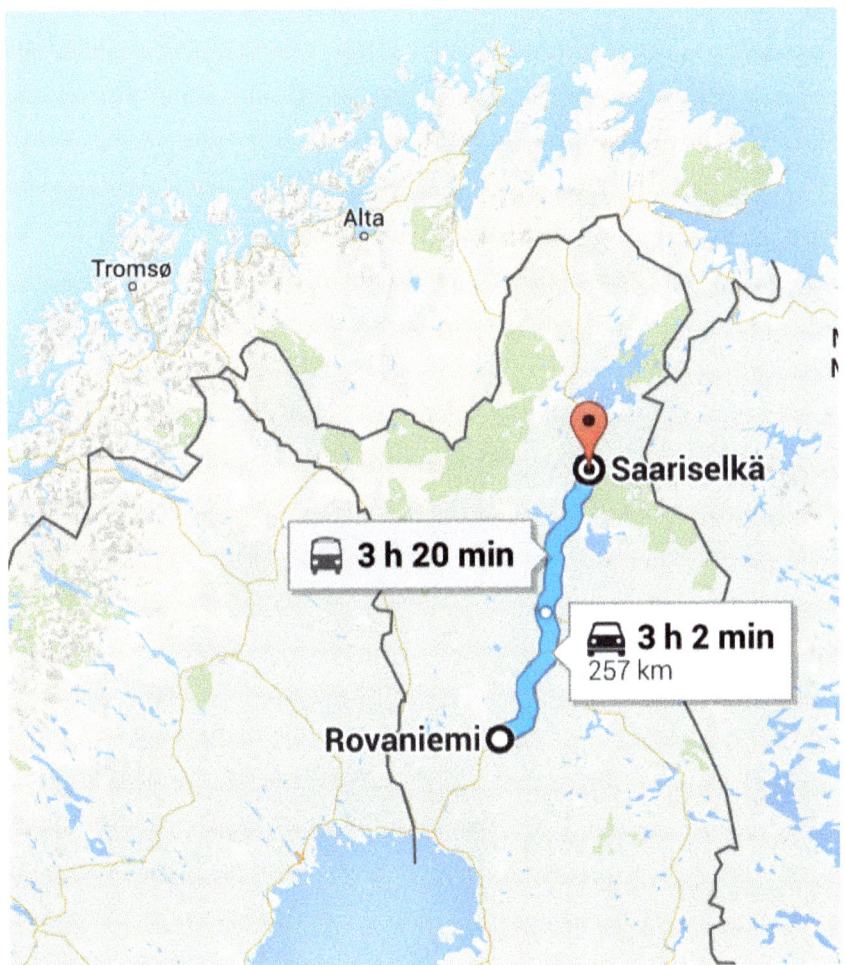

(Google Maps, 2019)

Coordinates: 68°25.25'N 27°25.03'E.

Saariselkä Township is at 300 meter altitude. It is 260 kilometers

North of Rovaniemi.

Saariselkä is a part of the municipality of Inari, which has some 7,700 inhabitants (including some 2,200 Sámi) on 17,321 square kilometers of land.

Saariselkä (Northern Sami: Suoločielgi, Island ridge) is a village located in a mountainous area in northern Finland. It is a popular tourist destination, providing activities such as skiing, hiking, and spa treatments. It is located in Northern Lapland and belongs to the Inari municipality.

UTSJOKI

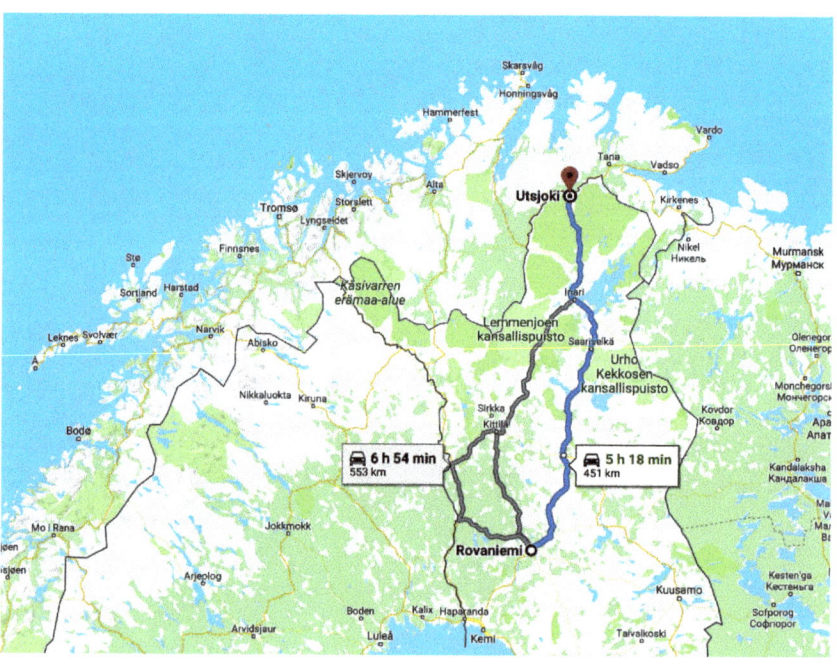

(Google Maps, 2019)

LIST OF HOLIDAY DESTINATIONS

Coordinates: 69°54'N 027°01'E

Utsjoki (Northern Sami: Ohcejohka, Inari Sami: Uccjuuhâ, Skolt Sami: Uccjokk, Swedish: Utsjoki) is a municipality in Finland, the northernmost in the country. It is in Lapland and borders Norway as well as the municipality of Inari. The municipality was founded in 1876. It has a population of 1,235 (31 January 2019)[2] and covers an area of 5,372.00 square kilometres (2,074.14 sq mi) of which 227.51 km2 (87.84 sq mi) is water.[1] The population density is 0.24 inhabitants per square kilometre (0.62/sq mi).

INARI

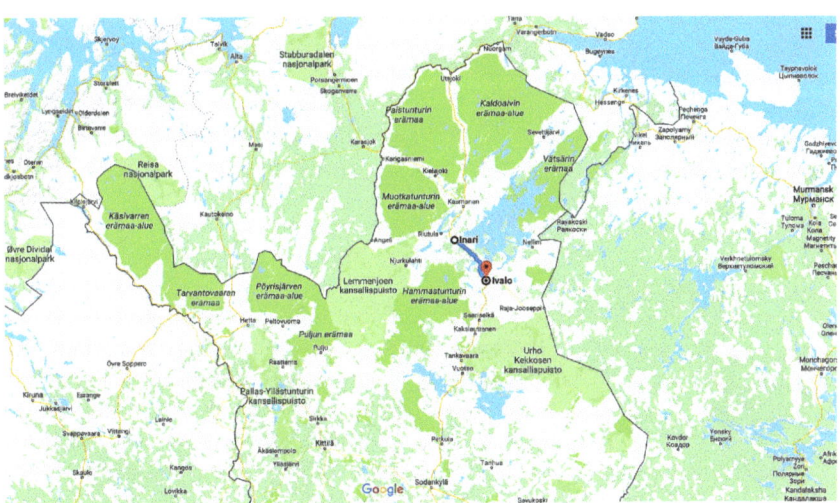

(Google Maps, 2019)

Coordinates: 68°54'20"N 27°01'40"E.

Ivalo (Inari Sami: Avveel, Northern Sami: Avvil, Skolt Sami: Â´vvel; Russian: Ивало) is a village in the municipality of Inari, Lapland, Finland, located on the Ivalo River 20 kilometres (12 mi) south of

Lake Inari. It has a population of 3,998 as of 2003 and a small airport. 30 kilometres (19 mi) south of Ivalo is a very popular resort named Saariselkä.

The township of Inari has a population of over 500 (2011).

The village of Inari was initially established along the water routes running along a swift River named Juutuan River. It ran the water away from many Tundra mountains and hills along the shores of the Lake Inari.

During the many hundreds of years, the Inari village developed into a bustling commercial and marketplace. When the municipality of Inari was founded in 1876, the village became the center of the municipality itself rightly.

LIST OF HOLIDAY DESTINATIONS

IVALO

(Google Maps, 2019)

Coordinates: 68°39'N 027°33'E

Ivalo (Inari Sami: Avveel, Northern Sami: Avvil, Skolt Sami: Â´vvel;

Russian: Ивало) is a village in the municipality of Inari, Lapland, Finland, located on the Ivalo River 20 kilometres (12 mi) south of Lake Inari. It has a population of 3,998 as of 2003 and a small airport. 30 kilometres (19 mi) south of Ivalo is the resort hub of Saariselkä.

NELLIM

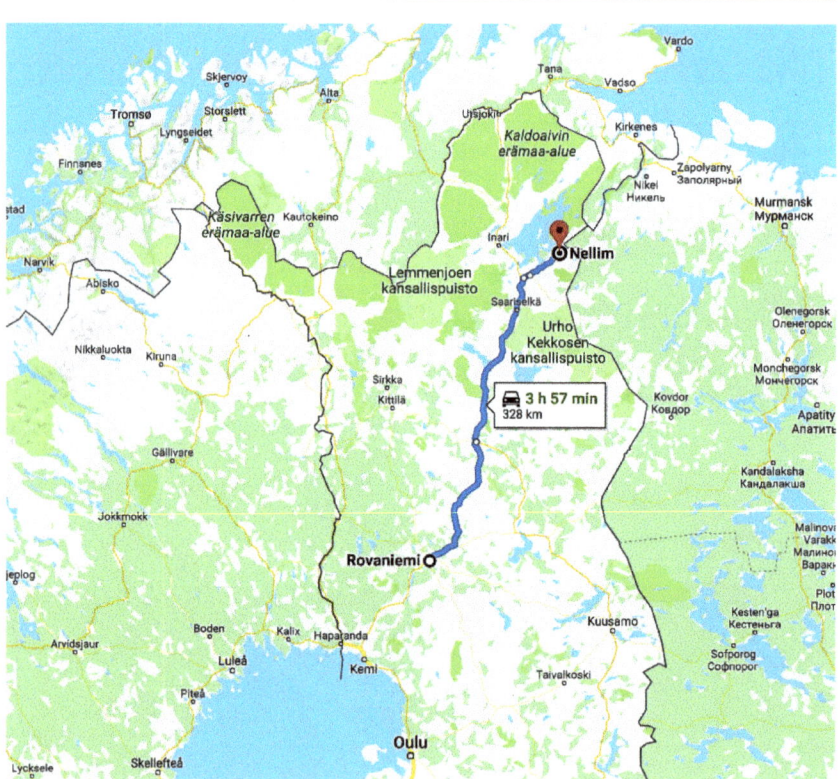

(Google Maps, 2019)

Coordinates: 68°51'N, 028°19'E

Nellim (Finnish: Nellim or Nellimö; Inari Sami: Njellim; Skolt Sami:

LIST OF HOLIDAY DESTINATIONS

Njeä'llem) is a village on the shore of Lake Inari in Inari, Finland that has three distinctly different cultures: Finns, the Inari Sámi and the Skolt Sámi. Nellim is approximately 42 kilometres (26 mi) northeast of Ivalo and approximately 9 kilometres (6 mi) away from the Russian border.

KILPISJÄRVI

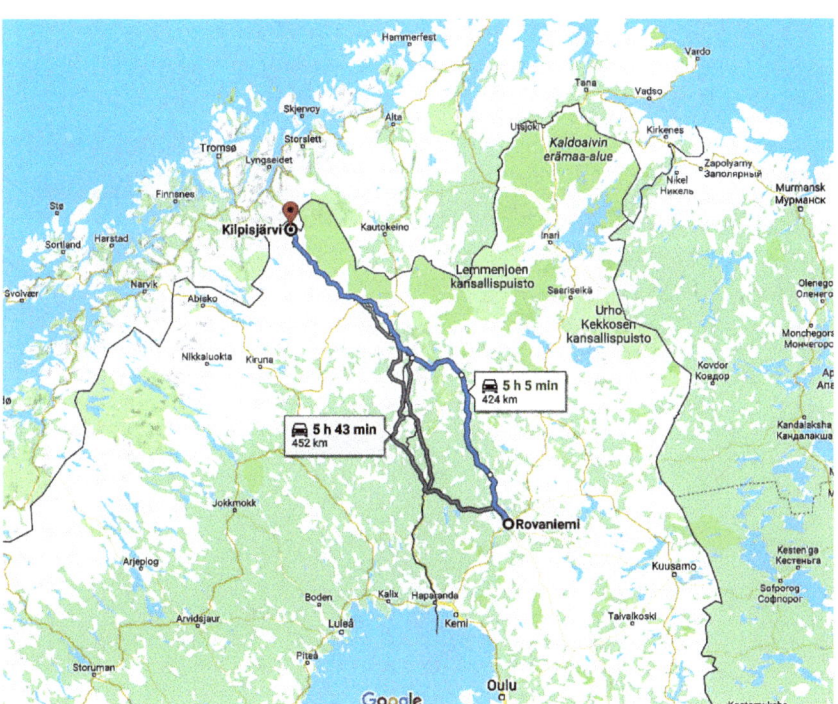

(Google Maps, 2019)

Coordinates: 69°02'50"N 20°47'50"E

Kilpisjärvi (Kilpis-lake) is a village in the municipality of Enontekiö, Lapland, Finland. It is located in Finland's northern "arm" near the very north western point of Finland. Kilpis-lake has its own school and a hotel, and the northernmost research station of the University of Helsinki is situated there, as well as the KAIRA research facility.

The most obvious monumental landmark at Kilpis-lake is the Saana fell, that stands 1000 meters above sea level tall. And about 500 meters up from the base of the Tundra mountain.There are very high tundra mountains visible on the Norway side, and also in Sweden that are visible from Kilpis-lake. Kilpis-lake is along a major road that runs from South all the way through to the Barents Sea in Norway. According to the visible map, the major road E8, is called the Finland Arm Road, or the Finland Four Winds Road.

The other unique feature of Kilpis-lake is the Finland, Sweden and Norway three-country border point monument at the border point. It is a unique feature that guest and visitors go out to see when they visit Kilpis-lake.

LIST OF HOLIDAY DESTINATIONS

YLLÄS TUNDRA

(Google Maps, 2019)

Coordinates 67°33'52"N 24°13'28"E

Ylläs, or Yllästunturi in Finnish, is one of the highest Tundra peaks at 718-metre (2,356 ft). Located in the municipality of Kolari in Lapland Province of Finland. There are two villages around the Ylläs

Tundra: The closest being Ylläs lake on the south side, and the other is Äkäslompolo on the north side. They are connected by a road that winds around the Tundra mountain (Fell).

ÄKÄSLOMPOLO

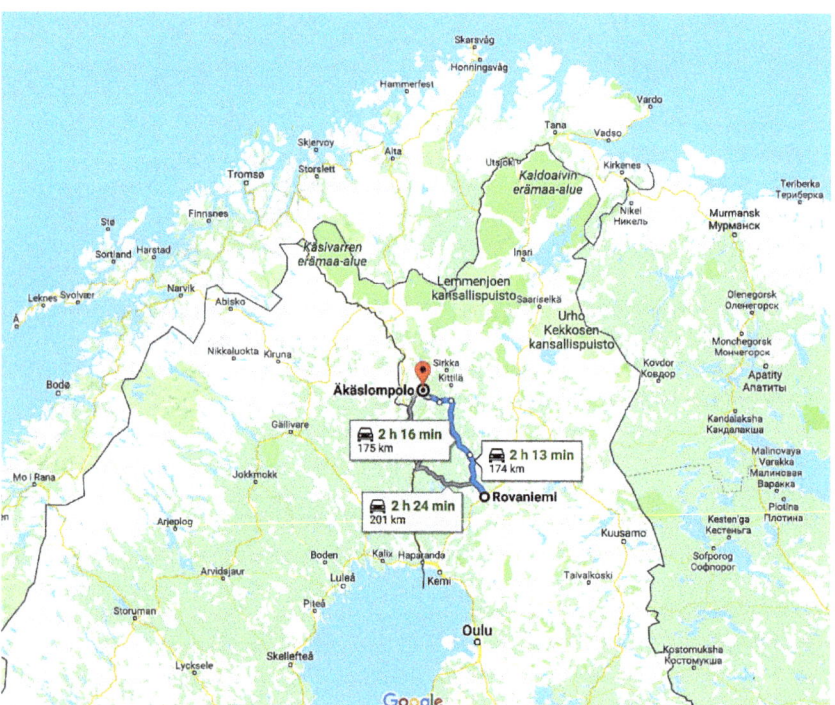

(Google Maps, 2019)

Coordinates: 67.604311°N 24.155451°E

Located 174 kilometers North West of Rovaniemi.

Äkäslompolo Township is located on the North West side of the high Tundra Mountain named Ylläs (718 meters altitude), and the many facilities and infrastructure that become a well-known ski resort town of Ylläs tundra. Alpine skiing, snowboarding, mountain bikes and snowmobile safaris.

The Ylläs ski area has a vast network total of cross-country ski tracks, covering some 330 km in total, with rest huts, shelters and some fireplaces available. There are also a large number of Alpine ski slopes (61) with 29 ski lifts operating during the peak winter months.

LEVI TUNDRA

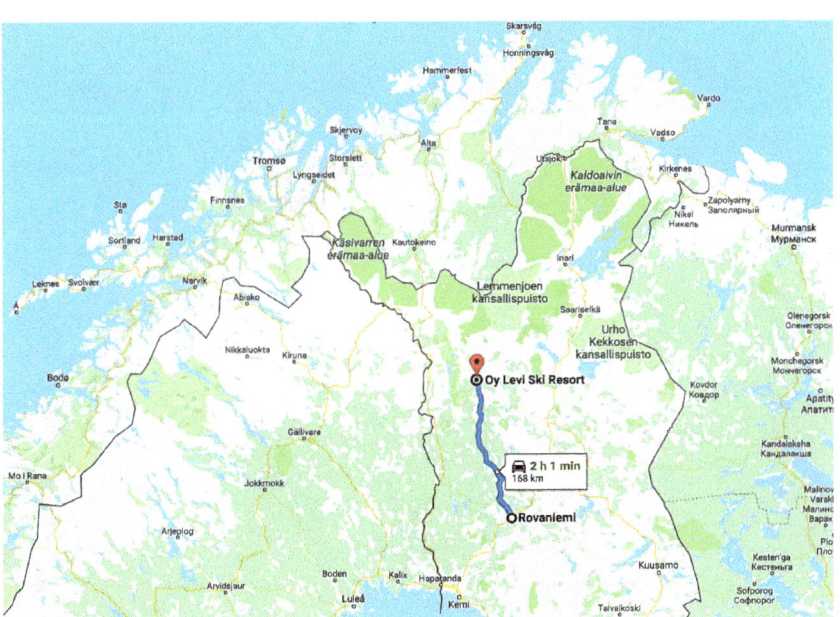

(Google Maps, 2019)

Coordinates 67.805°N 24.802°E

Levi is a Tundra mountain located in Lapland, it is more established as a township with a lot of facilities, Hotels and Ski resort. The resort is located in Kittilä municipality and is served by Kittilä Airport and Kolari railway station. It is located approximately 170 km (110 mi) into the Arctic Circle.

PYHÄ – LUOSTO NATIONAL PARK

(Google Maps, 2019)

LIST OF HOLIDAY DESTINATIONS

Coordinates 67°03'59"N 26°58'25"E

Pyhä-Luosto National Park in Lapland, Finland. It was established in 2005 when Finland's oldest national park, Pyhätunturi National Park (established in 1938) was joined to Luosto. This makes Pyhä-Luosto Finland's oldest but at the same time newest national park. The new park covers 142 square kilometres (55 sq mi). The most important features are geological specialities, old forests and wetlands.

The name Pyhä is derived from the word sacred. The Fell was regarded as being a sacred mountain.

> Forest Sámi who lived in the Pyhä-Luosto area in olden days considered Pyhä Fell sacred. They went to the seita at Uhriharju to ask the gods for good fortune during their hunt. Body parts of game such as wild forest reindeer and reindeer were sacrificed. Pagan sacrificial rituals ended at the end of the 17th century, because the Sámi were baptised into the Christian faith between 1620 and 1680.

https://www.nationalparks.fi/en/pyha-luostonp/history

PALLAS -YLLÄS TUNDRA NATIONAL PARK

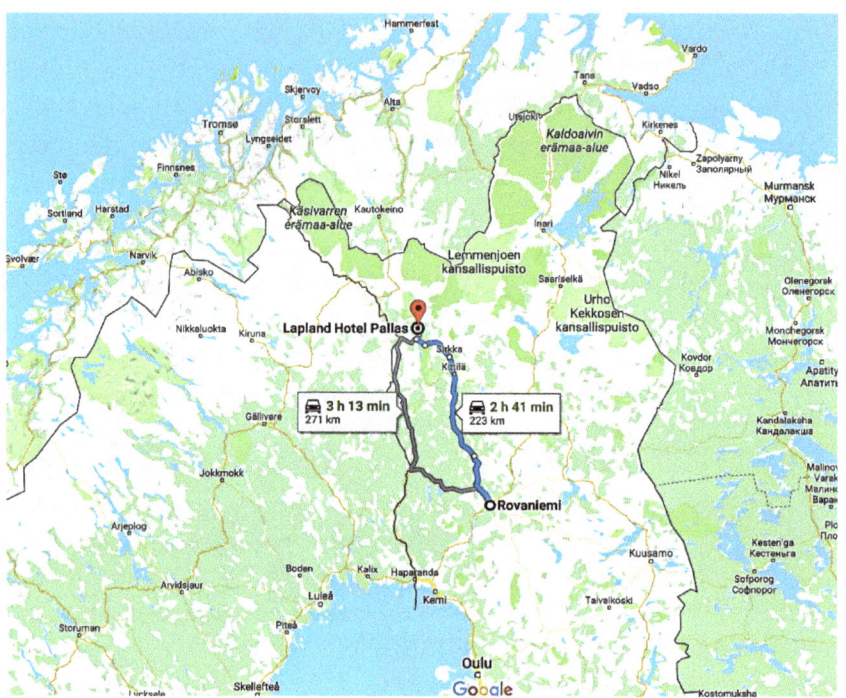

(Google Maps, 2019)

Coordinates 68°09'32"N 24°02'25"E

Pallas-Yllästunturi National Park (Finnish: Pallas-Yllästunturin kansallispuisto) is the third-largest national park in Finland, covering 1,020 square kilometres (394 sq mi). It is by far the most popular national park in Finland being visited almost 550000 times in 2018.

> Pallas-Yllästunturi National Park (Finnish: Pallas-Yllästunturin kansallispuisto) is the third-largest national park in Finland, covering 1,020 square kilometres (394 sq mi). It is by far the most

popular national park in Finland being visited almost 550000 times in 2018.

Pallas-Yllästunturi National Park has around 350 kilometres (220 mi) of marked hiking trails. The most popular hiking trail is 55 kilometres (34 mi) long Hetta–Pallas Trail, which goes mainly high up in the fells and takes 3-4 days to complete. It is also possible to hike Pallas-Ylläs Trail (69km) and Ylläs-Levi Trail (50km).

-Wikipedia.

SALLA

(Google Maps, 2019)

LIST OF HOLIDAY DESTINATIONS

Coordinates: 66°50'N 028°40'E

> Salla (Kuolajärvi until 1936) is a municipality of Finland, located in Lapland. The municipality has a population of 3,501 (31 August 2018)[2] and covers an area of 5,873.08 square kilometres (2,267.61 sq mi) of which 142.73 km2 (55.11 sq mi) is water.[1] The population density is 0.61 inhabitants per square kilometre (1.6/sq mi). Neighbour municipalities are Kemijärvi, Kuusamo, Pelkosenniemi, Posio and Savukoski. The nearby settlement of Sallatunturi is home to the Salla Ski Resort.
> -Wikipedia.

www.en.wikipedia.org/wiki/Salla

KARIGASNIEMI

(Google Maps, 2019)

Coordinates: 69°23'54"N 25°51'18"E

Karigasniemi (Northern Sami: Gáregasnjárga) is a village in the municipality of Utsjoki in Finland. It lies at the foot of Mount Ailigás.

> The village is situated on the border between Norway and Finland

LIST OF HOLIDAY DESTINATIONS

18 kilometres (11 mi) south-east of the Norwegian village of Karasjok. It lies on the banks of the river Inarijoki (Anarjohka), which, downstream of Karigasniemi, joins the river Karasjohka to form the famous salmon fishing river Tana.

Karigasniemi lies on the road between the Finnish town of Ivalo and Lakselv in Norway. The Red Line bus between Ivalo and Lakselv makes a 15 minutes' stop in front of the Kalastajan Majatalo (Fisherman's Inn).

Karigasniemi is home to about 300 people, of which more than half are Sámi. There are three shops, two petrol stations and five bars and restaurants, mostly because of a lot of border traffic from the Norwegian side. There is also a post office, a school and a small health care center in the village.

Karigasniemi is also a junction point where travellers can choose the road to Nordkapp or other places at the Arctic Ocean.

-Wikipedia.

(Leinonen, 2010)

CHAPTER 4

Winter Nordic Flavors

(Leinonen, 2016)

Winter Nordic flavors are well suited for the freezing winters, that can last at times for about six months, meaning that the temperatures during the day dip or stay below -10' Celsius, therefore an excellent time to prepare body warming foods that are healthy and have those unique Nordic flavors. Here are some fun canapes ideas that have the right tasting ingredients that are also used traditionally for serving main size meals at dinner/lunch table.

WINTER NORDIC FLAVORS IN HERRING AND POTATOES RECIPE

Boiled potatoes, cured herrings, and an egg topper, very simple to prepare, they are also rich with flavors. Herrings can be quickly prepared or purchased from a grocery store in a jar, ready-made. With readily cured herrings, it should only take approx 45 min to prepare and ready to serve canapes for 4-6 people.

Boil the potatoes with skin on for approx 20min, boil the eggs in hot water for 9 min, dunk the boiled eggs in cold water, for 5 min, then peel.

Remove the herrings from a curing liquid and cut into nice portions, approx the same size as the potato portions.

Remove potatoes from the simmering water (after 20 min), allow to cool a bit, then peel and slice into canape size medallions.

Place the potato portions on a plate, top with the herring. The egg portions may be placed on top of the potato/herring or combined with either of the two as a different taste combination required. Season according to taste, along with the cured herring flavors.

SERVING WINTER NORDIC FLAVORS CANAPE STYLE

Winter Nordic flavors and ingredients served canape style can be a natural process, it does not have to be complicated. Ideally, natural ingredients that have delicious Nordic flavors and are an exciting combination of color, texture, shape, and natural ingredients to work. Canapes can be decorated using a herb garnish, a sauce or cracking some pepper on top for extra zing.

NORDIC FLAVORS

Winter Nordic flavors are an essential part of the Nordic regional cuisine experience, a smorgasbord table of the Natural wild flavors of the Nordic cuisine focus, enjoy. Thank you for visiting the Nordic Cuisine Focus website and reading these blog posts.

FENNOSCANDIA REINDEER

Fennoscandia reindeer in the far north region are well suited and adjusted to that environment just like Kangaroos are well adapted to the environment of Australia. Fennoscandia reindeer has been farmed in larger numbers since the 16 century. Before that Reindeer naturally had many useful applications to help the original pioneers to stay alive and to protect against the extreme elements of nature in the Fennoscandia reindeer region.

UNIQUE QUALITIES OF THE FENNOSCANDIA REINDEER

The Reindeer fur is unique, it has excellent insulation properties against the extreme winter cold, the fur fiber is hollow, making it lighter and a better insulate. The antlers were used for necessary household tools, and for handles, e.g., knife. The meat of a Reindeer is typical game meat, somewhat similar to a small deer or an antelope, but nothing like a kangaroo. It was used/prepared in several ways, e.g., by hanging the meat outside in the freezing winter climate (freeze-drying) and allowing it to dry, it could take several days before it was eaten. The meat cuts were about 1/2 to 1kg size, they were usually the prime cuts, and also the heart was sometimes used/consumed by some. This style of meat preparation was/is common in the Fennoscandia reindeer, and its use was readily accessible when, e.g., when traveling, hunting/herding in the wild tundra areas, it was a protein source which was low a maintenance, quick to prepare and lasted well. It could be consumed as a snack or eaten with bread and other condiments.

The free roam style of farming of reindeer is also unique to the Fennoscandia region, the reindeer have been marked either with a neckband or an ear tag. They roam free and breed during the summer /winter time. Then in springtime, they are herded to holding pens, sorted according to the markings, and the new calves are marked according to the adult markings. The Springtime in the Nordic region still has plenty of snow and ice, so the herding is done with the use of snowmobiles and trained dogs. Within the Fennoscandia there is the Salla region on the east border of Finland, it is one of the original pioneers of reindeer farming and the reindeer meat industry.

In the Salla region, there is a reindeer meat plant that is a major producer/exporter of Reindeer meat products, within Finland and abroad. The most common reindeer meat dish in Finland is the Reindeer saute (but not literally a saute-a la minute), served with mashed potatoes, pickled cucumbers and crushed lingonberries. Its a highlight is within the natural flavors found in the reindeer meat, butter, potato puree, lingonberries, and the pickled cucumber. These are the elements of the sweet and sour, within the condiments that match the saute game meat with the mashed potato.

The preparation of the reindeer cut for the saute is done by freezing the rump and then slicing the meat into 5mm slices. The sliced rump is packed and stored in a freezer for later use. The meat is thawed according to quantity/need, then tossed in a hot pan with butter, and a brown stock and seasoning are added, and poached until the meat is tender. Traditional plating of the reindeer saute is by making a nest with the potato puree, and placing the reindeer saute in the middle of the nest (200-300g). Pickled cucumbers and the crushed lingonberries are placed on the edge of the potato nest, then served to the customer as "Poron käristys" (in Finnish).

There are also gourmet cuts/products available for restaurant use in our modern times, e.g., Smoked reindeer, tenderloins, heart, kidney, neck, shoulder, saddle, etc. Fennoscandia reindeer is highly valued as a high-quality ingredient, it is trendy among the Hotel and Restaurants of the Lapland region. Fennoscandia reindeer is also widely used in the southern parts of the Nordic region as well as in East Europe. Fennoscandia reindeer is a Natural product that goes back a long way into the traditional culture and ethnic cuisine customs in Finland.

LAPLAND REGIONAL FLAVOURS

Lapland regional flavors g are uniquely specific ingredients that have evolved over a long time, they now live and grow there in that natural Nordic Arctic environment.

Lapland regional flavor ingredients often can be on a single serving plate, that is called a Lapland region tasting plate. The purpose of the tasting plate is to showcase some of the unique regional ingredients.

THE PROXIMITY OF THE POLAR ENVIRONMENT

There have been significant changes in the estimated 10,000 years in Lapland, and as the global climate temperatures went through changes. Flora and fauna of Lapland went through many changes, one of them was the warm period after the Ice Age, the most predominant trees in Lapland were birch trees and very few pine trees. The reverse is true today, there are very few birch trees, most common trees are pine trees, and the Tundra areas are above the tree line, therefore no trees at all.

CHANGES IN THE ARCTIC ENVIRONMENT

The landscape of Lapland would have looked very different around 8000 years ago than what it looks like today. Lichen usually grows in the clean Nordic region environment, it is a major part of the reindeer died. Lichen that grows on the trees requires clean air, a pollution free environment. Where lichen used to grow on the tree branches in south Finland, it is no longer found there due to the increased urban population and motor vehicle traffic that pollutes the natural clean air.

NORDIC MUSHROOMS

Nordic mushrooms in the natural environment need to be viewed very cautiously. There are extremely toxic poisoned mushrooms in the natural environment. That can kill or destroy the internal organs permanently. There are also many harmless mushrooms in the wild, it requires guidance with the right information with experience to be able to detect which mushrooms are poisonous and which ones are harmless.

There are a variety of mushrooms like the milk-caps and Ceps. Picking mushrooms in the wild require an experienced guide, to point out the edible mushrooms from the toxic/poison ones. Inexperienced/tourists to the natural Nordic region environment sometimes pick mushrooms that appear to be harmless, e.g., white mushrooms (Amanita virosa), but they are extremely toxic.

The toxins stop the kidney from functioning, which often leads to death in a matter of days. Then there are also brown colored mushrooms like the: Paxillus involutus, they are also toxic. And the common red colored mushroom with its white dots: Amanita muscaria, that too is a toxic mushroom.

The color of a mushroom can be really misleading, especially when traveling from one region of the world to another. A white colored mushroom can be safe in one region of the world, and at another, it can be extremely toxic. Mushrooms are usually identified by 3-4 identity characteristics: Shape, color, texture (on top and under the cap), stem, and also the scent of the mushroom. Some mushrooms can be eaten after blanching them and rinsing out the toxins, but there are also mushrooms that by blanching/boiling them, the toxins remain in the mushroom, therefore inedible, e.g., the Amanita virosa.

LEARNING TO IDENTIFY THE MUSHROOMS OF THE NORDIC REGIONS AND OF LAPLAND IS CRITICAL

Mushroom identification can be learned, it is a logical process, requires a sharp eye, and patience, to follow scientific facts that are currently known about certain types of mushrooms. Just like learning the meaning of symbols in written instructions, mushrooms also have details that reveal their identity. Reindeer's love to eat mushroom during the autumn season when mushrooms are plentiful, in fact, they indulge in eating mushrooms to fatten themselves up for the long cold winter months ahead, mushrooms are a real delicacy for the Reindeer's in the Nordic region of Lapland.

LAPLAND REGIONAL TASTING PLATE INGREDIENTS:

- Unleavened potato flatbread portion (Peruna Rieska).
- Rye bread portions, grilled (Ruis leipä).
- Smoked Inari lake Char fish (Nieri).
- Salt cured salmon Gravelax (Suola lohi).
- Mushroom salad, mushrooms and onions diced (sieni salatti).
- Aura Blue cheese (sinijuusto).
- Smoked reindeer (Savustettu poron liha).

- Wildberry compote (metsän marjat).
- Ground black pepper and sea salt (musta pippuri, meri suola).

Lapland regional tasting plate is an excellent sample of the natural Nordic ingredients flavors that will be a delight to the taste buds to sample.

(Leinonen, 2009)

LOIMULOHI: GLOW BAKED SALMON

Loimulohi: glow baked salmon (loimu=glow, lohi=salmon) or glow baked salmon of the Nordic region is another fantastic unique menu item in Finland, it is so natural and relatively easy way to cook a salmon without the need for cooking facilities.

When preparing to cook the Loimulohi in this "Slow-Glow-Method" the basic requirements are; a good size salmon 1-10kg, a sharp knife (relative to the fish size), a clean wooden blank , and 8 x 2inch nails per fillet, or chicken wire netting, big enough to sandwich the open fish fillets inside the netting (approx 1m x 1m).

Leinonen 2012.

HOW TO GLOW BAKE SALMON

Start a reasonable size fire with sufficient firewood to last half hour (relative to the fish size), build a fire to create a sufficient amount of hot glowing coals that will radiate heat. If it is a windy day, then you need to use common sense where the fire is placed, some wind protection/shelter is needed so the radiated heat will be focused on the cooking of the fish, e.g., make use of the land contours, boulder, rocks, log, etc. Whether using the chicken wire or the wooden blank, the fish needs to be cleaned and filleted, and it may be sprinkled with salt and allowed to season for 1-2 hours in a 0-4'C cool area if so desired. The salmon fillets are then either nailed to the wooden blank or sandwiched inside the chicken wire so that the fillets stay flat, the flesh side facing the fire heat.

The distance between the fire and the salmon is critical, cooking a Loimulohi is not meant to be a quick method of cooking. This is a slow method of cooking, and the result is a fantastic golden color of the cooked salmon surface. To get the distance right, make sure the fire has sufficient coals that will continue to radiate heat for 30 min, you may add some wood to the fire, but it's not the only source of heat. Check the temperature at where the salmon fillets are going to be placed by placing your hand there, and hold it there for about 15 seconds, you should be able to hold it there without burning your hand. Use a natural boulder/rocks to prop the wood blank/chicken wire frame, place it almost vertical facing towards the fire, make sure it is stable and secure.

WHAT IS SO SPECIAL ABOUT LOIMULOHI?

Firstly it a classic Nordic cooking method that has been used for many thousands of years. It is a traditional menu item on the Nordic menu. Secondly the experience of catching an excellent fresh Salmon fish caught in the wild. Secondly, the slow cooking method of Loimulohi works well with a large Salmon filet that has a high-fat content, it caramelizes the flesh to a golden color. Thirdly the golden caramelized salmon flesh is absolutely delicious taste to experience when hungry after a day of physical activity. Thirdly the glow baked method was used for cooking large quantities of salmon by the fishmongers that went north for the specific purpose of catching and cooking salmon and transporting the cooked fish south to the markets. The cooking of the salmon preserved it longer, because the fat melts off the flesh, and the more or less dry meat is kept in the cold temperatures of the Arctic. The heat will continue to build gradually and caramelize the surface of the Loimulohi fish fillet, after about 1 hour – 1 1/2 hours. Salmon fillet has a lot of fat, it will start to melt, so make sure you turn sides (top-down) occasionally, so the natural fat runs back onto the fillet to moisten and caramelize the flesh.

When the surface of the Loimulohi filet is a golden color, and the aroma is delicious, then is the time to enjoy. There are many combinations that you can serve the glow baked salmon with. If you are camping at Lakeside in Lapland, then perhaps you brought some new potatoes along to your camp, if not then enjoy the delicious flavors of the Nordic salmon with a garden salad. Include some fresh greens, cucumbers, tomato and maybe a splash of olive oil and lemon juice or your favored dressing that you enjoy, with some unleavened potato flatbread (traditional potato Rieska), or some wholesome fresh rye bread. The best traditional cooking method. The traditional Loimulohi caught and prepared in the heart of the Nordic Nature in Finland is really a fine sample of how the food was prepared and enjoyed after it was caught many hundreds of years ago, there is no pretense or pedantic facade in this cooking method.

HERRING (CLUPEA HARENGUS).

Herring fish have been caught around the world for many thousands of years. The most abundant species belong to the genus Clupea, there are about 200 species of various herring. They are found in the shallow, temperate waters of the North Pacific, also North Atlantic oceans, the Baltic Sea, and the west coast of South America.

In the Scandinavian and the Nordic region, the Baltic Herrings were a very important food source along with the Herring and the sprats (Sprattus sprattus). Herring's were salted in wooden drums for the coming winter, an oily fish similar to anchovies and sardines that could also be pickled, smoked and cooked as a casserole with potatoes, bacon, and onions. Oily fish are a good source of vitamin A, D, and Omega 3. Oily fish and forage fish also can contain contaminants like mercury and dioxin.

BISMARCK HERRINGS

Pickled herring, also known as Bismarck herrings, it has been a delicacy in Europe for centuries. The pickling of Baltic herrings is prepared usually in 3 stages: 1. Cleaning and gutting. 2. Soaked in a salted pickle overnight, drained and finally the third stage placing the herring fillets into the final pickle that was briefly brought to boil containing vinegar with spices, onions, peppers and flavor giving vegetables. The traditional preserving and cooking method of herring used essential ingredients at the time, salt for smoking with various wood types, e.g., apple tree or aspen. For pickling, the ingredients used were; white vinegar, onions, dill, peppers, spice, salt, and maybe at better days red wine or sherry. As the food culture grew and experimented with ingredients from other cultures, then spices, herbs, and vegetables from other cultures got acceptance and became more widely used. The following recipe uses fennel, ginger and kafir lime for a broader flavor range. Enjoy.

WINTER NORDIC FLAVORS

(Leinonen, 2014)

PICKLED SPICY HERRING RECIPE: GINGER, LIME, AND FENNEL.

Ingredients:

- Baltic herring.   1kg.
- Red onion.   400g.
- Fennel.   1.
- Dill.   1 bunch.
- Ginger.   25 gram.
- Dill seeds.   1 tbsp.

- Lime Peel.   1 lime.
- Kafir leaves.   4.
- Schezuan pepper. 1 tbsp.

STOCK A.

- White wine vinegar.   200ml.
- Water.   100ml.
- Salt.   1 tbsp.

STOCK B.

- White wine vinegar.   100ml.
- Water.   500ml.
- Sugar.   150g.
- Salt.   4 tbsp.
- Lime juice.   4 limes.

Method: Clean the Baltic herrings from both ends.

2. Combine the ingredients for the first marinade, place the fish fillets in a glass jar, pour the first marinade into the glass jar over the fish, close and allow to marinate in the refrigerator for 6-12 hours, until the color of the fish has changed to white color.

3. Prepare the vegetables by cutting into fine slices or dice and the other flavor adding ingredients and the second marinade.

4. Drain the first marinade off the fish fillets well in a strainer.

WINTER NORDIC FLAVORS

5. Add some flavor adding ingredients to the jar, followed by a layer of fish fillets, and keep alternating the fish filets with the flavor ingredients until the jar is full.
6. pour the second marinade into the jar over the fish.
7. Refrigerate for a couple of days, every now and then turn the jar upside down and shake to mix the vinegar with the flavor adding ingredients and to distribute the marinade well over the fish fillets.

Serve with crisp rye bread, butter, cheese, and a suitable beverage.   Recipe source: **SILLI & SILAKKA. Book**. Leif Mannerstrom. Atena.

Happy Spring & Summer seasons and many prosperous Farmers markets and fish market herring endeavors shortly during the summer season.

BERRIES: VEGETABLE MUSHROOMS

The Nordic region environment has provided fruit, berries, and vegetables for thousands of years. Nature provision has been a vital source of food with vitamins, minerals, and life-sustaining goodness for the people that pioneered and found their home early in the Nordic wilderness. Seasonal changes were predictable, and sometimes also with variations of the fruit yields and temperatures. Nature, with its a diverse range of fruits, berries, grains, mushrooms, lentils, and vegetables is an essential food source for all the fauna that roam wild in the environment.

Birds and bears enjoy eating berries when they ripen during the summer time. The berries in the Nordic region don't appear/ripen all at the same time, Nature has it's own time pace, e.g., there is a considerable time delay between, e.g., strawberries-bilberries and Lingonberries. The flowering of the Bilberry and Lingonberry happens at a similar time frame, at least within the same 3-4 week period of each other (my observation), the wild strawberries flower very early in summer.

Nature also with the mushrooms in autumn time, the many different types of mushrooms appear in their own time frame, often when one type of mushrooms appear and stay for 3-4 weeks, then wilts and dissolves, then other types of mushrooms appear for about the same time duration (depending on the conditions at the time). The pacing that appears in the growing seasons in nature is very practical for the space available and from the fresh "provisions" aspect. Berries: vegetable mushrooms everywhere.

Nature supplies many types of berries in the Nordic region of Finland, e.g.; wild strawberry, raspberry, bilberry, Lingonberry, buck-thorn berry (Hippophaë rhamnoides), rowan berry, Cloudberry, Redcurrant, blackcurrant, and juniper berries, just to name the most common ones.

Traditional cultural custom is to gather and harvest berries and mushrooms during the summer/autumn season, as Nature provides. The Lingonberries are very acidic and have their own preservative qualities, they can be crushed and stored in a clean tub with a lid without any additives/added sugars, and it keeps well throughout the autumn, winter, spring season (8 months). Traditionally cellars were dug underground on a sloping hillside, with sufficient dirt over the top, and a double door to stop the fruit and vegetables freezing up during the winter time. Also, the snowfall on top (50-100cm) is very effective insulation against temperatures dropping below -'C. Underground there is constant heat, rarely will the winter frostbite down below 1-2m depth. Hessian bags were also used to cover the potato bays, carrot could be covered with clean river/lake sand, and beetroots, turnips, peas and other were also stored in separate compartments of the cellar. Root vegetables usually survived well, especially if the cellar was made/designed using the knowledge and experience from the accumulated wisdom of the previous generations.

Strawberries, Bilberries, red currants, black currants were made into jams and into concentrated fruit juice which were bottled and stored in cellars. Mushrooms were often preserved, the mushrooms could be blanched, sliced and with salt added they would keep well. The use of salt as a preservative goes back a long time, it is universal in practice, preserving fish, meat, and vegetables. Berries were used extensively later on, in our recent modern times; added to baked products, desserts, and frozen goods, or sold as frozen products. Berries: vegetable mushrooms are a great source of minerals, vitamins and general nutrition, as well as making the Natural outdoors world a brighter and more exciting place to explore and to discover, at times with real fruit incentives waiting around the corner.

WINTER FOOD STORAGE

Winter food storage is one thing that we as humans have developed more than any other types of animal, fish, and insects on the planet Earth, we are the most dependent and skilled in storing food.

The spring arrived here in April 2011. The migrating birds have started returning from their winter trip down south, their idea of storing food is in the seasons and regions where they know from experience that the environment in the right season will deliver to their satisfaction. Seagulls, ducks, swans, and many other birds are gradually moving up towards the north as the snow melts and the ice recedes from the seashore and the many lakes. Many of the small birds that fly all the way from Africa to the Nordic region is because the mosquitoes are so plentiful in the far north marshes and swamps, they are not concerned with the concept of storing food, but instead going where the food is abundant in the peak of the season. The ducks are protected during the Spring season. The shooting season for particular species of duck opens in late autumn. Swans are protected species, they were a threatened species in the 1940s with only about 14 families of swans in the

Finland area. Since then they have increased, and today there are hundreds of swan families that return each year, reputably they have the same mate for life. The white swan's appearance on calm water is symbolic of grace and purity.

UNDERGROUND CELLAR

After the long winter the household supplies in the cellar, storing food: berries, juice concentrate, fruit, and vegetables may be dwindling, and not much more stores left in the freezer.

There is still a long wait before the summer fruits are ready and the mushroom appears in autumn. Four to five months to go until the berries appear in August, and five to six months for the mushrooms that grow in August-September-October.

HARVEST SEASON

Late Summer and Autumn, traditionally in Finland people prepare their own berry juice (red currants, black currants, bilberry), fruit jams (strawberry, raspberry, etc.), and also store mushrooms, it is all about storing food when the fruits and vegetables are in season. During the mushroom storing food season in September-October there are mushroom displays usually in the local farmer's markets called the "Tori," in Finland.

A seasonal mushroom displays are often put up by the local Mushroom Club or by the Martta (Martha) association. Last year at the mushroom display at the West Coast of Finland Pori, during the Herring festival markets in September, there was a display with 50-60 different types of mushroom, several samples of each type on a paper plate with a name and symbols, whether it was edible (stars) or inedible (a death cross).

The rating was from 1 star to 4 stars (good to excellent), and 1 cross to 4 crosses (poison to the extreme). Staff volunteers that attend the mushroom displays are very knowledgeable about the local mushroom here in Finland, volunteering staff does also advise on storing food. People that are new to the area or just starting to identify mushrooms can bring mushrooms that they have picked, and ask the staff to identify them. Use precaution when picking mushrooms in a remote foreign region, often the innocent looking mushrooms (e.g., white color) are the toxic ones, even by handling them with bare hands can lead to poisoning, use rubber gloves for protection.

Here are some of the most sought after mushrooms in the Nordic region:

- Boletus edilus.
- Leccinum versipelle.
- Leccinum aurantiacum.
- Chanterelles.
- Cantharellus tubaeformis.

CHAPTER 5

History, Tradition and Culture

HISTORY, TRADITION AND CULTURE

(Leinonen, 2010)

FAMINE BREAD FLOUR EXTENDERS

At times of severe famine in Finland late 1500-1600, the bread flour was extended with the use of wheat chaff, straw and the inner layer of pine tree bark. The ratio would usually start at about 10:1 (flour: bark meal). The bread was called Pettu bread in Finnish.

The harvesting was done in the springtime, the method of collection was done by making a vertical cut on the tree bark, then cutting a line across the top, and the bottom. The tree bark would then be gently levered open until access to the 2mm thick white flesh of the inner tree bark was made. Then it was removed, and the tree bark returned to the original position. I guess it was tied tight with some string, to ensure that the tree bark grew back close against the tree trunk and protected it. If not then it would almost be like "ring barking (360')" a tree, meaning a slow death of the tree.

The inner layer of the bark was dried and later milled as bread flour. The bread bark meal has a high mineral content in the following; zinc, magnesium, calcium, and iron. Also contains vitamins and high in fiber, the energy content is very low. The "Pettu" bread is still made in some places for important and tourism purpose. One such place is the Kilen Museum.

www.sydaby.eget.net/swe/kindex.html

Another place where the bread can be purchased is at the Salla War Museum. When I visited the War Museum at Salla in 2011, I did actually purchase some "Pettu" bread. This particular bread was made into thin, crisp bread 20cm disks. The bread package contained some 20 rounds of crisp Pettu bread. There were a slight aroma and flavor of a pine tree, other than that it was like eating regular crackers with a cheese plate, the cost was about 5€ per package. It was a novelty experience tasting and eating "Pettu" bread, knowing that in the severe famines of late 1500-1600. Many improvisations were made at that time to extend food ingredients to save lives and to avoid hunger. Despite the improvisations and food extensions, many thousands of people died of starvation.

For more information on the Salla Museum, click on the link below.

www.sallaregion.com/salla-museum-lapland.html

ONIONS HISTORY

I decided to explore more on the subject of Onions because if you lived in the Nordic region during the 19 century, then at this time of the year (spring) there would be an abundant supply of onions left in the cellar storage. Onions keep well if the storage area is not too moist for mold to grow. They are naturally well packaged with layer upon layer, and also the dry outer layer, sealing the core from intruders. They are a hearty root vegetable from the Allium family, similar to the leeks and garlic.

ORIGINS

Onions are known to have originated from the Asian region, and transported to Greece and Egypt.

There are ancient drawings and hieroglyphics using onion symbols in Egypt, they were also used as medicine to cure ailments, virus, sickness, and disease. Onions were given high regard in many different ethnic cuisines. In ancient Rome it was trendy, also in Turkey-Constantinople it was prepared for gough ailments, a concoction was boiled using: leeks, sugar, and honey.

SCANDINAVIAN ONION OF THE FAMILY.

In Scandinavia, Onions is also used to describe an older wise person of the family, as the onion of the family. In Iceland, there is the Poetic Edda is a collection of Old Norse poems, that give high regard to onions. In Norway, the expression of joy with in the community is referred to as the onion of the community. In Finland some of the earliest household recipe books record the use of onions in the 18 century.

In India the Brahmins taught that if one wants to get wise, they should eat more of onions, and in Tibet, they were instructed to eat garlic as a preventative against cancer and to chew garlic would cure any gum infections. The nutrition value of an onion; Vitamin A, C, Calcium, phosphorus, potassium, sodium, calories 60/150g, and also fiber.

When growing onions, it is vital to change the seed stock every 4 years, to avoid stock loss through vegetable disease, onion fly, fungi and molds.

Onions were consumed raw in salads, they were used in soups and sauces, they were used in the stuffing of game meat and game birds. Some of the most popular use of raw onions in the Nordic region of Finland was the mushroom salad and the Baltic herring salad. Also, the ever popular Gravlax salmon (salt-cured salmon) onion was a popular condiment, raw onions and cured salmon on rye bread.

POTATOES

As the days get warmer int eh spring season, and the piles of snow are receding, then is the time take some vegetables out of the cellar into the daylight, by placing them on a damp hessian sack they will start to sprout within one week. As a precaution, you can keep them under cover, or cover them with suitable material during the night while the frost is still likely to strike the sprouting potatoes.

Preparing the garden soil for planting potatoes.

Prepare the garden by turning the soil, this is also usually done in the previous autumn. Use a rake to even out any clumps of dirt, and remove sticks and large rocks. Form/shape straight line furrows about 50 cm apart, and about 10 cm deep and 10 cm wide. The length in proportion to the potato yield required.

There are also other options for growing potatoes in pots and containers.

Once the seed potatoes have sprouted (sprouts about 3 cm long) place them in the furrows by pushing them in at various depths (that way there is more space for them to grow). Then build up a mound over the planted potatoes, from both sides of the furrow, a raised potato furrow, it drains well of excess water, and warms up

HISTORY, TRADITION AND CULTURE

quick during the sunny morning. The planted potatoes need about 10-15 cm of soil over them, to keep them out of direct sunlight and to maintain moisture during the growth of roots and the shoots.

Water the newly planted potato furrows, and maintain the moisture level according to the weather and the soil structure. After a while, the raised furrows tend to sink under the watering, therefore continue to build/raise dirt to the center from both sides of furrows.

Protecting the potatoes from green feeding animals.

If the garden is located in the Nordic wilderness, then a boundary fence is needed. Wild animals will dig up the furrows and help them selves to the newly planted potatoes, sooner or later.

SHEEP

Sheep have been a valuable resource in human history. The use of felt began early in the East-Turkey area, early as 4000 BC. Also in the Ancient Roman culture, clothing and felt hats were worn by the males.

Sheep wool for clothing felt boots and blankets were discovered to have fabulous insulation properties to retain the low human body temperatures and keep out the bitter cold of the Nordic winters. Thick felt boots are very effective against extreme cold weather, even as low as -40'C. Boots are very light to walk in, they were used both indoors and outdoors. Wool was spun and used for items like; socks, jumpers, pants, gloves, mittens and other textiles.

Animal husbandry sheep and wool textiles industry in the Nordic region dates back to the Viking era, there is real evidence and finds of the early wool textile industry.

Finn sheep and Swedish Mountain cattle and the Icelandic horse, date back to the prehistoric animal husbandry.

It is very likely that in many families/small tribes sheep were viewed as too valuable to be killed for the dinner table until the numbers had increased sufficiently to a large level. Sheep wool products are still regarded as valuable natural resources, both in spun wool products and in felt products, and it's not likely to change any time soon.

TRADITIONAL EASTER FOOD (MÄMMI)

Mämmi (Maam-me) is a traditional Easter dish that was eaten in Finland as early as the 12 century. It is also mentioned in cookbooks that date back to the 16 century.

It first appeared in the South West and on the West coast of Finland, where the Catholic church was established. It was not until the 17 century when mämmi made it's a way to the north and central Finland. There are divided opinions about mämmi also in Finland, some enjoy it, others loath it.

It was a food dish used in the Catholic church during the Easter fasting, meat and dairy products were not consumed on Fridays, so Mämmi became the Easter Friday food and part of the Easter cultural tradition in Finland.

It is said to symbolize the unleavened bread that the Jews eat during the Passover. Mämmi is made by using rye flour, rye malt, water and sweetened with molasses, and seasoned with salt. When the mixture is prepared, it is allowed to mature and sweeten naturally for many hours. It is like a wet rye porridge sweetened with molasses, then the final stage is made by baking it an oven like a pudding/casserole. It is consumed either hot or cold, with milk/cream like a pudding.

Mämmi has a long history, and it is part of the Finnish Easter food culture, it is also healthy to eat, it was part of religious discipline in fasting during the Easter time. Despite its innocent history, and cultural significance, Mämmi is often discriminated and scoffed at similar to the Vegemite in Australia. Vegemite and Mämmi are very similar in color, they are both dark brown.

HISTORY, TRADITION AND CULTURE

Crossing cultural borders do often bring surprises in ethnic cuisine discovery, and without the necessary knowledge, and the story/beginning/tradition, then it just may seem odd to have brown porridge that is baked in an oven. Rye has been very much part of the Finnish culture, there are many good reasons for that, one of them is the health benefits of eating wholemeal rye bread in their farming/forestry/agricultural communities during meal breaks.

The Christian Easter tradition is also celebrated in Finland, the word "Pääsiäinen" (Easter), meaning the end of fast, the 40 days before Easter Sunday. Palm Sunday to Good Friday, and the celebrated Easter Sunday. In the Christian church as the most important celebration day is the Resurrection Sunday.

EASTER DECORATIONS

There are many types of traditional Easter decorations e.g.; Easter rye-grass, painted eggshells, willow baskets, decorated flowering willow branches with bunny tails.

Young Children (4-12yrs) in some areas go door knocking to bless their neighbors for the coming spring/year, they are rewarded usually with some lollies/biscuits or a few cent donations.

Two opposed traditions during the Easter weekend.

It is the opposite of what the custom of the Trolls was back in the dark ages, apparently the story goes that there were witches that went around during the time between Good Friday and Easter Sunday. There was a belief that during that time landowners pets and livestock were susceptible to curses, so they gave it their best to punish the landowners pets and livestock. Mostly they were outcast single women on the fringe of society and also often bitter of their misfortune.

THE WHITE SWAN

The White Swan (Cygnus cygnus), is the national bird of Finland.

It is a large white water bird, with yellow color visible on the peak, the young swans are grey in color. They have also identified from their "whooping" or "Tooting" trumpet sound. Adult swan weighs approx 6.5-11.5 kg, their wingspan is about 2.3-2.4 meters apart. They make their nest in the reeds on water, or it can be on dry land also. They lay their eggs in May-June, 4-6 eggs, the female hatches them for 40 days. The newly hatched swans are able to fly in 45-60 days, the swan adults live in pairs and relatively private during their nesting time and fend off other swans/birds aggressively.

In the 1950 white swans almost became extinct in Finland, they became protected, and their numbers have increased rapidly since then. It is estimated that there are 4500-6000 pairs of swans during the summer, most migrate to and fro from Finland each year. However, some stay the winter depending on the winter conditions and available water free of ice cover.

Source of information. www.Luontoportti.com

The white Whooper swans can be seen at quiet bays of the seashore paddling in pairs, they are apparently planning ahead for another successful egg hatching summer. They constantly swim/feed what seems to be some kind of seaweeds/tubers/grass.

KALEVALA

"In the Finnish epic Kalevala, a swan lives in the Tuoni river located in Tuonela, the underworld realm of the dead. According to the story, whoever killed a swan would perish as well. Jean Sibelius composed the Lemminkäinen Suite based on Kalevala, with the second piece entitled Swan of Tuonela (Tuonelan joutsen). Today, five flying swans are the symbol of the Nordic Countries and the whooper swan (Cygnus cygnus) is the national bird of Finland".- Wikipedia.

WHITE SWANS IN MYTHOLOGY AND ANTIQUITY.

In the rock art of Karelia, there are pictures of swans, those people are sometimes called the "water bird nation"(vesilintukansa). According to the belief of the Karelian people, the white swans should not be harmed if they were harmed the same fate would return on that person as the injured swan. Because when swans are feeding their heads are submerging under the surface of the water, therefore it is believed that swans have access to the underworld/hades as well. Artists, Musicians, and Poets were inspired by the white swans.

CHAPTER 6

Natural Nordic Nutrition Exploration

NATURAL NORDIC NUTRITION EXPLORATION   83

(Leinonen, 2010)

Natural Nordic Nutrition journey in life is full of new discoveries, this web site attempts to explore the geographical location of the Nordic region, and seek out the features that are unique to the northern hemisphere. The proximity of the far north to the Arctic has evolved over time to create its unique environment, flora, and fauna. The local biodiversity with food ingredients have developed over a long period, they exist there naturally for a reason, and they support the inhabitants of the area. The early pioneers were a nomadic people; they grazed, traveled, hunted, and fished to stay alive as nomadic people do. There was deep respect to their environment; the land, the soil, the vegetation, the trees, the climate, seasons, their elders, and their beliefs and mythology.

Life on our planet has changed dramatically over the last 5000 years, even more so in the previous 500 years and also with the current extreme push of technology during the last 100 years. Some things are constant; the need for food and nutrition, good health and lifestyle are one of them, the importance of knowing Which Food is Good is critical. A noticeable change that has occurred in the last 5000 years is how people found food, and how and when they consumed the diet that they found. The nomadic people often traveled and grazed during their travels. More so during the summer season, food was much more plentiful during the spring, summer, and autumn season. They would have taken advantage of that natural supply; the bright berry season only came around once in a year similar to other ingredients and food items that peaked at a certain various time of the year.

The modern day lifestyle is a stark contrast to the above, the food supply today is artificially manufactured, stored, and supplied. People are no longer reliant on the natural cycles and natural provisions, the original work, and the seasons. This can be confusing to the human mind at a deep level, and also to their physical being. Artificially fed food, supplied artificially to large storage areas (shops), food created for the pleasure of the experience that diet can provide (restaurants), and not for the nutritional needs and health, that food can supply. Also, the physical activity as being necessary for strength and stamina for everyday travel on foot, and to burn the fuel that is stored on the human body as fat.

Food has always been part of social events and annual celebrations, e.g., as a community, the spring festival and the autumn harvest festival. Also other festivals during the summer, they could have been around anything; the berry festival, the Cod festival, the Baltic Herring festival, the salmon festival, the crab festival or the summer solstice. There has always been the event, occasion, and the pleasure associated with consuming food. It has ballooned exponentially in the last few hundred years, if you consider the contrast between a nomadic tribe feasting on a whole roasted deer, to the indulgence of the French Cuisine aboard the ship Titanic.

The point is this, the essential Nutritional requirements of the human body, with the need for all of the 7 nutritional types. When food was being fished and hunted, picked and foraged, planted and grown, there was a personal investment of time and effort in the involvement of finding, planting, preparing, cooking and storing of food items, and they were also handed down from parents to children. It was very much ingrained in the culture and tradition from one generation to another.

In today's society there are supermarket shelves full of sugar-loaded insulin spiked items, with bright artificial colors and additives, they are colored bright to attract and fool the naive, inexperienced young, and hungry person, that it has the same color as a strawberry, or raspberry, or maybe a bilberry, so it must be useful for you. Their designed ultimate objective is to give the consumer passive pleasure while they watch the TV or their favorite movies.

Nature has a lot to offer and teach, it knows the full story from the beginning to the end, it has observed, watched and fed the environment and everything in it since the beginning of time. It is only relatively recently that modern society has started to isolate themselves from Nature and the natural cycles of the seasons. An obsessed western society with blind consumerism and mindless grand scale building projects does not meet the essential needs of humanity and their well being.

Natural Nordic Nutrition.com is a virtual trip to a specific and unique geographic area, it has its own history, story, culture, tradition, and essential ingredients. The early pioneers of the north traveled, explored, lived and interacted daily with Nordic Nature. Much of that environment and nature is still alive today and can be, explored, visited and enjoyed and communicate in the same way as the early pioneers did so many years ago.

You may be an editor, publisher, writer, journalist or tourist. No matter what your role, you may need information and digital images of the Nordic region. Please contact Natural Nordic Nutrition by email to request the images you are interested in purchasing. info@naturalnordicnutrition.com

CHAPTER 7

Bilberries in Finland

(Leinonen, 2015)

Bilberries in Finland are the most favorite summer berries that people forage. The bilberry plant is very much part of the Nordic environment, they can grow in high acidic poor soils as a low growing shrub, (10-50cm) they are found in the temperate and Northern sub-arctic areas. Bilberry plants is a deciduous shrub, the green foliage of the plant changes color to red and pink once the berries have become ripe.

BILBERRY PLANT DROPS ITS LEAVES IN THE LATE AUTUMN-WINTER

The bilberry flowers from May to July and the berries are usually ripe from July up to October. The berry season varies from year to year, there are many variables to consider. Mainly depend on the climatic conditions: the pollinators, as well as the early summer frosts. Lack of pollinators will produce a poor berry season. Also, a late cold during the flowering season can knock out the berry crop of the summer. The flowers are bell-shaped and pink in color, they are susceptible to frostbite. Pollination carried out mainly bees and insects, the bilberry can also self-pollinate.

HOW TO PREPARE THE BILBERRY HARVEST

Bilberry can be enjoyed many ways, depending on where you live and how you obtain the berries. In some temperate areas of Europe the only way to safely enjoy them would be to use them in cooking; as a filling for a bilberry pie, cooked jam, and for preparing the berries for juice extraction. The environment needs to be a clean environment if the berries are enjoyed fresh from the shrub.
The Nordic sub-arctic areas are such clean areas where the berries have grown in a clean environment. The potential threat is from diseases in wild animals, it may be foxes or other mammals or marsupials that carry disease and spread it over the ground cover of the forest with plants and shrubs. This is not a known problem in the Nordic region. Of course, the summer rains wash the berries every so often, but it is always sensible to rinse the berries being harvested before storing them in the freezer.

See Nordic Berry pictures at Face Book. Nordic Berry Pictures.

HOW TO ENJOY THE BILBERRY FLAVOR AND NUTRITION

I like to go berry picking after a summer rainstorm or even when there is a light rain falling, it makes the forest so much fresher, it is more relaxed with crisp, clean berries for the picking. Also, after the storm, there are lots of natural plant and flower scents, with a great natural light tone for photography. Bilberries in a clean environment can be enjoyed fresh from the shrub, they are also great for the breakfast table with cold milk and cereal, traditionally the bilberries were enjoyed during the summer months as a refreshing desert with only using the berries and fresh milk. Most middle age to elderly people in the Nordic region does recall their childhood memories of summers with having enjoyed lots of "Bilberry milk" desserts.

The bilberry pie is equivalent to an apple pie in some other region of the world. They do also make apple pie in the Nordic region, but bilberry pie has been more favored by tradition. It can be a sweet dough base with bilberry filling on top, baked in an oven until the base dough is baked through. The dough recipe varies from a sweet pastry to a non-sugar dough base. Some people like it with a pie pastry that has no sugar included, it could also be so because of potential diabetes sufferers.

JUICING BERRIES FOR WINTER IN THE NORDIC REGION IS VERY POPULAR BY TRADITION

Juicing of many types of berries is done during the summer as the berries ripen, they can be made into a single flavor juice or a mixed berry juice. The berries are put into a large pot with sugar and heated until it comes to the boil, this process will melt the sugar and release more juice from the berry pulp. The pot is taken off the heat and allow to cool down some. Then the hot juice is poured through a strainer to catch the skin of the berries. Depending on how fine the sieve is the seeds of the berries may go through or get left behind. Most of the essential nutrients of the bilberries are in the seeds, but by consuming them alone will not release the compounds, the seeds should be crushed so that the nutrients are released while consuming them. Think of it this way, when a plant flowers are pollinated and grows berries or fruit, the fruit is attractive to lure birds, mammals, and humans to eat them, why? So that they would propagate elsewhere. The berries and fruit are consumed, the flesh and juice is consumed and absorbed in the stomach, but the seeds pass on through and continue on in another cycle of life at another location. The seeds are being protected from the stomach acids by design, they survive it and keep intact ready to start their own life story once they are out in the soil of the natural world.

See pictures of wild Bilberries in Finland. www.Marjamies.fi

CHAPTER 8

Nordic Cuisine

(Leinonen, 2012)

Nordic cuisine definition in this book is all about the natural environment, the fauna, and flora of the Nordic region. I do not

NORDIC CUISINE

subscribe to the pedantic narrow trend's or a extreme pedantic idolatry of a haut-cuisine, that manipulate people into the philosophical funnels of sophisticated marketing strategies, and the coveting social climbers of the envious society elites. Although, I am a qualified chef, qualified in Australia, and has worked in many fine 4-5 start Hotels along the East coast that were very efficient in their food services. However, being pedantic about food, as if it was fine art jewelry, misses the primary connection between food and nutrition. Natural ingredients need to be respected for their nutritional values, colors, flavors, and texture. Narrow minded extremism exists in many areas of art. Finest art forms in are created by life naturally, they do not require human intervention. Life creation is on a much higher level, that provides vital nutrients, clean water, minerals and vitamins for the building and sustaining life in all of the eleven human and animal organ systems.

The problem with a narrow world view and subjective life philosophies that indulge in hedonism is a self-defeating one. It leads away from the beauty and the freedom of a natural environment, where life has evolved naturally, interacting with the extreme elements of nature. For a person to consume food that is like intrinsic fine art, you do not need to pay a high price ticket at a grande cuisine restaurant.

From the Intelligent Design, creation of life perspective, the finest art design samples are not man-made, but rather they are found in the natural environment and they reliving things, plants, flowers, fruits, insects, fish, human beings and animals.

Nordic berries, filled with their natural juices, the berry skin tightly loaded with nutritional value. They present excellence in design, colors, flavors, and aroma. A natural Nordic berry is far more sophisticated in design than any man-made product can match. The Nordic natural environment is unpretentious, slow-paced, traditionally people would spend time in the outdoors to connect with natural life spiritually. The Nordic natural environment offers that experience to those that have the patience to observe the spirit of life in the natural environment.

HAUTE CUISINE

Haute cuisine (French: literally "high cooking," pronounced [ot kɥi.zin]) or grande cuisine refers to the cuisine of "high-level" establishments, gourmet restaurants and luxury hotels. Haute cuisine is characterized by meticulous preparation and careful presentation of food, at a high price level. – Wikipedia.

When I write about the Nordic cuisine, I refer to the unique Nordic natural environment and ingredients that has evolved according to the seasons in proximity to the Northern Arctic hemisphere. It has taken many thousands of years for the natural environment to survive the extremely freezing cold long winters, to get established, and to multiply over various terrains and to produce the ground cover. Fauna and flora, interacting with trees, creeks, rivers, and lakes, that sustain many types of insects, birds, mammals, fish, and plant life. The entire Eco-system works as a unit with the fauna and flora. The Nordic natural environment is unique, it is in most part natural, fresh, and clean. The Arctic winter cold keeps many diseases of plants and animals away that are a nuisance to people in central Europe. Nordic wild berries can be eaten fresh, without the need to cook them to get rid of diseases. Hepatitis A is a notifiable disease at the European Union.

Nordic cuisine, ingredients, and flavors are in many ways a projection of the past 6000 years of the Nordic seasons, the environment of the land, the air, the water of the lakes, the rivers and the Sea. It is the proximity of Lapland to the North Pole that has shaped the flavors of the Nordic cuisine, with the interactions of tradition and culture. Whether humanity has discovered all the flavors of the Nordic natural environment is entirely a different matter. In the past 2000 + years pioneers of the Nordic region have made use of the ingredients that were abundantly available

NORDIC CUISINE

for them, that made the long cold winters of the Nordic regions tolerable to bear. Ethnic cuisine is always in the making for thousands of years before humans ventured into the region, and discovered to experiment with the natural ingredients.

The most abundant and desired ingredients of Lapland history. Big fish of the rivers, lakes, and ponds. Moose, reindeer, and hare. Wild berries, lingonberries, bilberries, cloud-berries, and grand-berries. The Lapland region of Finland and the Nordic cuisine has a strong tradition of using reindeer meat for peoples protein needs as well as the local fish from rivers, lakes, and ponds. There are also many game types of meat in the Nordic cuisine, the most common one is moose, that becomes available during the autumn hunting season. Game birds like wood Grouse, Willow Grouse, Black Grouse, and Hazel Grouse and Pheasants.

Brown bear meat is also available in far north Finland as part of the Nordic cuisine experience for the outside visitors interested in trying out novel meat dishes in Lapland. Tourists all over the world like to try out novel food dishes, whether it is Crocodile or Emu dishes in Australia, or monkey meat dishes in the jungle of Amazon.

NORDIC CUISINE IN THE RESTAURANTS OF LAPLAND FINLAND.

All of the 12 destinations reviews listed here in the Bloggers Guide to Arctic Finland have many restaurants that offer regional Nordic ingredients, prepared in the traditional cultural way. Therefore, it is the foundation of Nordic cuisine in Finland. The natural ingredients of the Nordic region do not need to be redefined, by some modern niche philosophy funnels or sophisticated restaurateurs pushing their marketing strategies onto an ancient culture that has lived and interacted with the Nordic natural environment for thousands of years. The correct order of defining a cuisine is from the bottom up, and not the reverse order. To define a regional cuisine from the bottom up. Starts with the land soil first, and the water of the sky (rain and snow), the water of the rivers, the lakes, and the Sea. And all of the life contained on the land, in the air, the rivers lakes and the Sea. Those entities and elements have existed on the northern hemisphere since the last thaw, said to be some 10,000 years ago.

It is arrogant and disrespectful to natural life to not show respect to the vital elements that yield the produce on the land, the rivers, lakes, and the Sea. It is also arrogant and disrespectful to not respect the indigenous peoples, the pioneers, and the traditional culture of the land, for example, of Arctic Finland. By trying to redefine the Nordic cuisine into something else other than what the region has produced, and the traditional culture have survived on for thousands of years. Ethnic cuisine has deep roots into the traditional culture of the people in a designated region, e.g. Arctic Finland Lapland.

SALLAN TUVAT KIELA RESTAURANT

The Kiela Restaurant near the Salla Tundra mountain does have a good range of ethnic cuisine menu items on their list . Salla Tundra is on the Eastern border of Finland. There are hotels and restaurants in the area that serve the Arctic ethnic cuisine ingredients on their menu item selection.

Salla Tuvat ethnic cuisine menu items at the time when I did some work there as kitchen staff. One regional tasting plate items were dried reindeer meat, local mushroom salad and herbs, smoked reindeer, smoked char, salt-cured salmon with a slice of lemon and dill with baked cheese and local cranberries. On the main plates was tenderloin steak with smoked reindeer, redcurrant jelly and green beans. Regional red meat grilled and pan jus with roast vegetables. Some of the items in this chapter picture collage were taken at the Sallan Tuvat while I was there. Kiela Restaurant does offer an cuisine experience into the ethnic Nordic cuisine of Arctic Finland. Sallan Tuvat East Finland). See the Salla Tunturi website restaurant page from this link. www.Sallatunturi.com

NORDIC CUISINE

NORDIC CUISINE AT YLLÄS LAKE

Spring holiday in Lapland with should include the many opportunities to enjoy the regional food ingredients at the local restaurants. There are many restaurants in the Ylläsjärvi and the Äkäslompolo region that have an excellent selection of regional food ingredients on their menu. One such place is at the Ylläsjärvi, the name of the restaurant is called Pihvi Keisari. I visited the Pihvi Keisari during my spring holiday in Lapland and Ylläs during the March 2012, the service from the personnel was great, really good

Genuine food service. The food dishes that I tried was a regional tasting plate from Lapland (entree). The food ingredients were really fresh and flavorsome, small portions of meat, fish, bread, and pickles/sauce. For the main course I tried the white fish (siika) with a fennel nettle white wine sauce, and regional Lappi puikula potatoes, freshness, great flavors, and texture, I was really pleased with that dish overall. The dessert that I chose was a vanilla ice cream served with strawberry syrup, a refreshing combination of natural flavors.

YLLAS HUMINA RESTAURANT AKASLOMPOLO

Ylläshumina Lodge offers excellent food services for the in-house guests during the peak holiday seasons. There is a good range of breakfast food items on the buffet. Also a buffet dinner service with traditional Nordic items on the menu. Al la Cart menu is also available at times.

See the Yllashumina website from this link.www.yllashumina.com/restaurant1.html

SAARISELKA

Saariselka is a fine destination to sample the Nordic cuisine represented at the many Saariselka restaurants. The raw ingredients of the Nordic cuisine of Lapland are mostly traditional ingredients of the far north of Finland. There are at a dozen Restaurants at Saariselkä that serves traditional ethnic menu items from Arctic Finland region. Lapland Hotel has a genuinely good value for money Hotel food service at the Riekonlinna (Willow Grouse Castle) HotelRestaurant. Buffet, functions and Al la cart.

Restaurant Siberia is a fine dining restaurant service catering more to the top end market. There is also a cafe style service for hot or cold beverages. Many other restaurants to be discovered at the Saariselkä holiday destination,

The proximity to the north cap has shaped the environment and the inhabitants to adapt to the extreme cold of the Nordic winters, and their unique cycles of summer growth and the dormant winter season. Summer season is lush with new growth, mushrooms and many types of berries. The mammals eat berries and mushrooms as nature provides them to be consumed for the fattening of their bodies for the long scarce winter season.

Fine highly prized ingredients from the many waterways like; whitefish, arctic char, salmon, perch, and pike. The salmon from the Barents sea spawn in the river system of the Lapland. During the autumn spawning season the salmon don't feed, they are very territorial and therefore take the fishermen to lure to protect their spawning territory only, but not to feed.

Many of the traditional food items have culturally by default been adopted into the Nordic Cuisine, over many thousands of years by the traditional people of the land. From the early pioneers of Arctic Lapland and Southern Gulf of Finland, the early pioneers explored new regions, the entire land, sky, rivers, lakes, and the Sea was their menu that they gratefully appreciated.

The natural food sources was a primary objective and motivator for relocation. Equally attractive was the knowledge that from the Gulf of Finland to the Arctic Sea the region was sparsely populated 2000 years ago.

Who in their stable, peaceful mind would go to some region like the Mediterranea that was very densely populated by territorial human beings? A hostile reaction would be certain from the locals during the Stone Age, Iron Age and later on down the line.

Human nature is often shaped by the condition and the health of their physical existence and living conditions. Those contributors are reflected onto their living soul functions, Intellect, consciousness, imagination, will, memory, and emotional well being.
People of a tribe, village of a clan, way back 2000 years ago, they had to be well in tune with the seasons, and know the availability of food resources from season to season, year after year. Natural resources availability are not static, there can be a lot of variation from year to year, and season to season.

KAUNISPÄÄ (PRETTY HEAD) SAARISELKÄ AREA TUNDRA SUMMIT.

At the summit of Kaunispää, there is a cafe/restaurant and a souvenir shop, with everything from; postcards, key tags, coffee mugs, woolen socks, jewelry to warm clothing. Customer service is always friendly at the Kaunispää summit. Saariselka hub is a vibrant tourist activity town, that has a consistent international clientele touring the area mostly during the winter season; November-April. Panorama Summit Cafe/Restaurant.

LAPLAND HOTELS BUSINESS NAME

Lapland Hotels as a business name has many hotels and restaurants in the Arctic Finland. They are well established and provide good quality accommodation and food services to visitors and guests.

Lapland Hotels is a Finnish hotel chain with 15 hotels in the province of Lapland and three city hotels in Helsinki, Oulu, and Tampere. The history of the hotels in the chain includes many turns and ownership change of hands. Many of the hotels have been serving customers for decades and have had a significant impact on the emergence and development of the entire tourism industry in Arctic Finland Lapland.

LAPLAND HOTEL COMPANY WAS BORN WHEN TWO FAMILY TOURISM COMPANIES MERGED IN 2002.

Major Hotels at Levi, Rovaniemi, and Ylläs were all owned by the Mr. Pitkästen family owned business. They amalgamated with Mr. Pertti Yliniemi's hotels in Olos, Pallas, Kilpisjärvi, and Hetta.

Later on Mr. Yliniemi company acquisition of Mr. Pitkästen share in the company, they then became the sole owner of the Lapland Hotels chain after Mr. Pitkästen family sold their lot from the joint venture of the 2 companies.

At the same time, Lapland Hotels acquired the entire share capital of Riekkoparvi Oy in Inari, whereby Hotel Riekonlinna was taken over by the chain. Later, Hotel Luostotunturi and Hotel Saaga Ylläs also moved to the Lapland Hotels chain.

The history of Lapland Hotels can be considered to have begun in 1938 when the Finnish Tourism Association built the original Pallas Tunturi Hotel, which is now owned, managed and run by the Lapland Hotels company.

The German military towards the end of World War 2 was hounded out of lapland, during the Lapland War in 1944. And as they were retreating from the Pallas Tundra area they exploded the hotel up sky high. The new hotel building was introduced in 1948 and has undergone several transformations since then. Located in Kilpisjärvi, Hotel Kilpis is also a former Finnish Tourism Association hotel.

The Finnish Tourism Association changed its name in 2001; it had given up its hotels through bankruptcy in the 1990s when several of its hotels were transferred to new owners. The Lapland Hotels

NORDIC CUISINE

chain is not related to these events except by continuing with the former names of these traditional hotels.

Lapland Hotels has 18 hotels, five ski resorts, Kittilä Airport restaurant operations, and program service activities at all destinations.

HERE IS A LIST OF LAPLAND HOTELS IN THE ARCTIC FINLAND.

A website link provided to the Lapland Hotel properties where I have personally worked/dined or stayed overnight as a guest.

1. **Lapland Hotels Kilpis (Kilpisjärvi, Enontekiö) Hotel Kilpis.**

2. **Lapland Hotels Olos (Olostunturi, Muonio) Hotel Olos.**

3. **Lapland Hotels Lumi (Särkijärvi, Muonio)**

4. **Lapland Hotels Pallas (Pallastunturi, Muonio)**

5. **Lapland Hotels Hetta (Hetta, Enontekiö)**

6. **Lapland Hotels Sirkantähti (Sirkka, Kittilä) Hotel Sirkantähti.**

7. **Lapland Hotels Äkäshotelli (Äkäslompolo, Kolari) Äkäs Hotel**

8. **Lapland Hotels Ylläskaltio (Äkäslompolo, Kolari)**

Hotel Ylläskaltio

9. Lapland Hotels Sky Ounasvaara (Rovaniemi)

10. Lapland Hotels Ounasvaara Chalets (Rovaniemi)

11. Lapland Hotels Bear's Lodge (Rovaniemi)

12. Lapland Hotels Luostotunturi (Luosto, Sodankylä)

13. Lapland Hotels Riekonlinna (Saariselkä, Inari) Hotel Riekonlinna

CHAPTER 9

Finland National Flower Kielo

(Leinonen, 2012)

Kielo flower name day is on the 14 June in Finland, Kielo is also the National flower of Finland, since 1967. Lily of the valley flower in English, is called the Kielo kukka, in the Finnish language.

Convallaria majalis, commonly known as the Lily of the Valley, is a poisonous woodland flowering plant native throughout the cool temperate Northern Hemisphere in Asia, Europe and in the southern Appalachian Mountains in the United States. -Wikipedia.

LEGENDS AND TRADITION

The flower is also known as Our Lady's tears or Mary's tears from Christian legends that it sprang from the weeping of the Virgin Mary during the crucifixion of Jesus. Other etiologies it's coming into being from Eve's tears after she was driven with Adam from the Garden of Eden. –Wikipedia. http://en.wikipedia.org/wiki/Lily_of_the_Valley

Other names include May lily, May bells, lily constancy, ladder-to-heaven, male lily, and muguet (French). In Bulgarian and Macedonian, it's called момина сълза /momina.səlza/ and момина солза respectively, meaning "lass's tear." -Wikipedia.

In the "language of flowers," the lily of the valley signifies the return of happiness. Legend tells of the affection of a lily of the valley for a nightingale that did not come back to the woods until the flower bloomed in May.

All parts of the plant are highly poisonous, including the red berries which may be attractive to children. If ingested—even in small amounts—the plant can cause abdominal pain, vomiting, and a reduced heart rate. -Wikipedia.

Here are some scientific terms for the Kielo flower plant.
Kielo (Lilly of the valley flower.
Scientific classification:
Kingdom: Plantae
Clade: Angiosperms
clade: Monocots
Order: Asparagales
Family: Asparagaceae
Subfamily: Nolinoideae

Genus: Convallaria
Species: C.majalis

TRADITIONAL SAUNA VIHTA

Traditional Sauna Vihta making in the spring season.

One of the sure signs of the new spring season is the green leaves on the birch trees. Birch trees get covered up in green leaves early in the spring season, in just two weeks. An essential part of the Finnish sauna tradition during the spring season is the making of a birch tree branch Vihta, alternatively named Vasta.

It is made up of the new fresh birch branches as they appear in the spring season or summer. The branches about the length of an arm that is bundled together, tied with a new branch shoot that forms a tight collar. A single Vihta has about 10 -20 birch branches, tied up with a twig into a bundle.

The use of the spring season Vihta is to whack the back of a person in the hot steaming sauna. The whacking motion fan's steaming hot air. Therefore, concentrated heat is applied to the back of the person. The whacking motion also works like a light scrub or a massage. The green leaves of the branches slapping the back of the person with steaming hot air.

The sauna house gained popularity because of the need to warm up after working and toiling outside during the freezing winters of the Nordic season in Finland. Forestry timber work was backbreaking labor, and it created sweating workers with wet a wet shirt, which eventually (when the action stopped) turned into frozen ice and sore muscles. After a days toil, the Lumberjacks needed to wash up warm up and refresh for the next day toil. The sauna was the ideal remedy for those people of the land in the early years of the 18 century. The sauna was often the first building built when moving into a new area of land for farming or forestry workers campsite.

PICTURES OF THE SPRING SEASON BIRCH TREE VIHTA

There have been many types of sauna's, and various heating methods, fireplaces and the heated rocks that create the steam inside the room. Most of the early ones were heated with the smoke staying inside the sauna room, there was no chimney. After the rocks were hot and ready, a window would be opened to let most of the smoke out, then the bathers could go in, throw water on the rocks and enjoy the hot steam in the heated sauna. The walls of those smoke saunas are always black from smoke, there would still be a visible tell sign if someone had leaned on the wall of a smoke sauna. I'm not sure where/what they sat on, without getting the black soot on their butt.

GRAIN CROPS IN FINLAND

Grain crops are an essential part of the traditional Finnish cultural cuisine, it has been extensively grown/farmed in the region for several hundred years. Initially, grain crops were first planted and cultivated by the Battle Axe tribes-people from the West, that moved along the Gulf of Finland over 2000 years ago. The original Ingria-land people of the Gulf of Finland learned grain crops and farming skills from the visitors to their land.

Grain crops and bread consumption is prevalent, there are many types of bread influence from the west and the east. Wholesome heavy Rye bread and the quick flatbread called "Rieska."

Grain crops were a vital food source for livestock also, e.g., in the days when horses were for transportation, especially during the long winter months. Oats and dried grass/hay would keep the horse's energy level up for hauling heavy loads and transporting people.

BARLEY (OHRA)

Barley is one of the oldest grain crops to been farmed, it was also the first to be planted in Finland. Of the grains listed, Barley has the fastest growing cycle to harvest. One of the first bread to emerge in Finland was a Barley Rieska, it is quick to prepare flatbread. Barley bread is very popular even today.

RYE (RUIS)

Rye (Ruis) is the most important grain crops in the Suomi-land (Finland), the word grain seed was also the synonym for rye. The origin of the word is "rug is" it goes back over 2000 years to Germania. The Rye is suitable for growing in relatively rugged soils and cold climates. Also, the harvesting of a grain crop is straight forward even with a basic harvesting technique. Rye bread and sachet of salt has been used as a symbol of good luck and success, also an ideal symbolic gift for a house-warming party. Dried rye grains were also used as a commodity in the previous centuries. Many gift shops used to sell a gift pack (for show only) with small size rye bread disks and a small sachet of sea salt. The traditional rye bread was about 30 cm diameter flat disks, with a hole in the center. The hole in the center of the rye bread was there for an entirely practical reason. The bread traditionally was prepared and baked in large volume (bulk) then they were hung on the wall of the kitchen to cool down, by a long pole that was hooked on the wall on brackets like a window curtain hanger. There the rye bread could sit on the wall happily and naturally without getting moldy or danger of any rodents. Some old black and white photos of kitchens show that type of bread storage in use.

FIELD OATS (KAURA)

Field Oats (Avena sativa) in the Suomi-land it is "kaura," also a word with origin from the Germania and in the Swedish the word is "havre." By appearance, the oat plants are very similar to that of long blades of grass. The head of the grain has thick a thick husk, and the plant is self-pollinating.

Wheat is one of the oldest and the most essential farmed grain crops plants in the world. It is the most cultivated grain crops in Europe and North America, it is also extensively cultivated in Australia, Argentina, Russia, and China. In Suomi-land, wheat is the most demanding to grow, because it requires a long growing season and a particularly suitable soil. Therefore the ever increasing history of grain in the Suomi-land is relatively short.

SOWING GRAIN CROPS IN FINLAND

The soil conditions and the growth temperatures of the grain crops do vary from the West to East and the South to the North of Finland. Apparently due to the proximity to the north pole and the warm air currents that flow from the south-west of Finland. The grain crops were harvested during the autumn time and re-planted during the same autumn season before the snow falls, and the frost appears in October-November-December with some variation year to year. By planting the grain crops before the winter, that gives the grains a preparation time for the next spring season. Early of the spring season, the fields are covered with snow and ice when the snow/ice melts, and the grounds are soft, wet and boggy which can make it difficult in many cases to plant the grain crop seeds into the soil. So the grain crops seeds spend their first six months covered with snow and ice, and they hibernate in the darkness of the earth, and maybe give some winter sustenance to the field mice and other critters.

NATURAL NORDIC NUTRITION

The Nordic region is distinct by the Natural Nordic Nutrition, and by the unique closeness of the Arctic proximity, and by the vigor of the biodiversity and life that it contains. Norway has benefited immensely from fish stocks of the Arctic Ocean.

The close proximity of the north pole had influenced and shaped the surrounding environment since the early days when the polar cap froze over with snow and ice. It was a tough place to shelter and survive through the raging seas of the Autumn and the long cold dark days of the winter months. The vital links to survival were food, nutrition, good health, shelter, company, warmth, and transport. The Nordic region had treasures of high-quality food and nutrition in the river systems, lakes, ponds, hillsides, valleys, and under the surface of the Barents Sea.

Fishing has thrived in the Nordic region for many centuries, it was the most common source of Natural Nordic Nutrition throughout the year. Fresh fish and seafood in the summer, smoking, salting and curing fish in the autumn time for the long winter months ahead. Fish products have been a great source of nutrition and health for people of all ages.

NATIONAL IDENTITY OF NORWAY

National Identity. By the middle of the nineteenth century, schoolbooks reflected the theme of a distinct, rural Norwegian culture, as did a variety of popular journals. Writers conveyed the notion that everything of true value was found close to home, in everyday life of simple people.....popular enlightenment helped shape the consciousness of a common culture and history. In the national dialogues that followed, national identity was formed, contributing to the eventual dissolution of the union with Sweden.

The Fishing industry is still active today, there is a big demand for fish products, and also the fishing tourism draws a great crowd, year by year to the Nordic region annually.

The Nordic region like many other regions of the world has come under a lot of pressure from overfishing and large manufacturing companies that have Ship-factories going out in a big way to catch large amounts of fish products. Sustainability is a vital hot topic for future generations, and for the excellent health of the waterways and the deep seas. Teno river is one of the rare river systems that have the original gene pool of Salmon, it has not died out from overfishing like most river systems in Europe and the Nordic region.

NATURAL NORDIC NUTRITION EXPLORATION

Natural Nordic Nutrition journey in life is full of new discoveries, this web site attempts to explore the geographical location of the Nordic region, and seek out the features that are unique to the northern hemisphere.

The proximity of the far north to the Arctic has evolved over time to create its unique environment, flora, and fauna. The local biodiversity with food ingredients have developed over a long period, they exist there naturally for a reason, and they support the inhabitants of the area.

The early pioneers were a nomadic people; they grazed, traveled, hunted, and fished to stay alive as nomadic people do. There was deep respect to their environment; the land, the soil, the vegetation, the trees, the climate, seasons, their elders, and their beliefs and mythology.

Life on our planet has changed dramatically over the last 5000 years, even more so in the previous 500 years and also with the current extreme push of technology during the last 100 years.

Some things are constant; the need for food and nutrition, good health and lifestyle are one of them, the importance of knowing Which Food is Good is critical.

A noticeable change that has occurred in the last 5000 years is how people found food, and how and when they consumed the diet that they found. The nomadic people often traveled and grazed during their travels. More so during the summer season, food was much more plentiful during the spring, summer, and autumn season. They would have taken advantage of that natural supply; the bright berry season only came around once in a year similar to other ingredients and food items that peaked at a certain various time of the year.

The modern day lifestyle is a stark contrast to the above, the food supply today is artificially manufactured, stored, and supplied. People are no longer reliant on the natural cycles and natural provisions, the original work, and the seasons. This can be confusing to the human mind at a deep level, and also to their physical being. Artificially fed food, supplied artificially to large storage areas (shops), food created for the pleasure of the experience that diet can provide (restaurants), and not for the nutritional needs and health, that food can supply. Also, the physical activity as being necessary for strength and stamina for everyday travel on foot, and to burn the fuel that is stored on the human body as fat.

Food has always been part of social events and annual celebrations, e.g., as a community, the spring festival and the autumn harvest festival. Also other festivals during the summer, they could have been around anything; the berry festival, the Cod festival, the Baltic Herring festival, the salmon festival, the crab festival or the summer solstice. There has always been the event, occasion, and the pleasure associated with consuming food. It has ballooned exponentially in the last few hundred years, if you consider the contrast between a nomadic tribe feasting on a whole roasted deer, to the indulgence of the French Cuisine aboard the ship Titanic.

The point is this, the essential Nutritional requirements of the human body, with the need for all of the 7 nutritional types. When food was being fished and hunted, picked and foraged, planted and grown, there was a personal investment of time and effort in the involvement of finding, planting, preparing, cooking and storing of food items, and they were also handed down from parents to children. It was very much ingrained in the culture and tradition from one generation to another.

In today's society there are supermarket shelves full of sugar-loaded insulin spiked items, with bright artificial colors and additives, they are colored bright to attract and fool the naive, inexperienced young, and hungry person, that it has the same color as a strawberry, or raspberry, or maybe a bilberry, so it must be useful for you. Their designed ultimate objective is to give the consumer passive pleasure while they watch the TV or their favorite movies.

Nature has a lot to offer and teach, it knows the full story from the beginning to the end, it has observed, watched and fed the environment and everything in it since the beginning of time. It is only relatively recently that modern society has started to isolate themselves from Nature and the natural cycles of the seasons. An obsessed western society with blind consumerism and mindless grand scale building projects does not meet the essential needs of humanity, and they're well being.

Natural Nordic Nutrition.com is a virtual trip to a specific and unique geographic area, it has its own history, story, culture, tradition, and essential ingredients. The early pioneers of the north traveled, explored, lived, and interacted daily with Nordic Nature. Much of that environment and nature is still alive today and can be, explored, visited, and enjoyed and communicate in the same way as the early pioneers did so many years ago.

You may be an editor, publisher, writer, journalist, visitor, guest or a tourist. No matter what your role, you may be interested and need more information and digital image content of the Arctic Finland region. Please contact Natural Nordic Nutrition by email to request the images you are interested in purchasing. info@naturalnordicnutrition.com

CHAPTER 10

Wild Lemmings

(Leinonen, 2012)

Wild lemmings in the Tundra regions of Lapland, Norway, and Finland. Wild lemmings in the natural wilderness of the Nordic Lapland. They are almost everywhere where there are some ground cover and protection from predators. Some of them will give out a warning call when approaching close to them, often it is by their warning call that you find them. Their furry coat is well camouflaged for the vegetation where they live, different shades of brown and black colors make them blend into the environment. While walking in the bush I was often the abrupt-ed by a loud squeal of a lemming close by me, looking around to see where was it, where did the sound come from, it was most times right beneath me in the tusks of grass or hiding among the growing lichen. The lemmings seem to give a warning signal to the others lemmings close by. Wild Lemmings get noticed by the warning call they give to other lemmings. Most times, when I spotted a lemming was after when the lemming had made a loud warning squeal. Only one or twice did I detect a lemming when it was out crossing a road or running past the open back door on the back yard. In the forest there was a good ground cover for them to hide, predator birds do hunt them as well as foxes.

WILD LEMMINGS IN WILDERNESS.

Lemmings presence in the Nordic wilderness varies from year to year, not every year is equal, there are seasons when there are many fold more wild lemmings to be seen, so much that it is impossible to miss them while bush walking in the Nordic wilderness. During my visit in 2011 to Karigasniemi Lapland in north Finland, the abundance of wild lemming was most apparent, and there were lots of them everywhere northwest of the town towards Lake Inari.

CHAPTER 11

Picture Gallery

PICTURE GALLERY

(Leinonen, 2011)

(Leinonen, 2009)

PICTURE GALLERY

(Leinonen, 2010)

CHAPTER 12

Historical View of Lapland

HISTORICAL VIEW OF LAPLAND

Leinonen 2010.

Kuolajarvi village was lost to the Soviet Union in 1939, and the township relocated West some 50 kilometers and given a new name Salla.

Kuolajärvi town also translated as Kola lake in Lapland, in the fifteenth century had eight towns; one of them was called Kola Lake. In the local Sami language, the word Kola is translated to mean; plenty of fish.

Natural Borders. The towns of East Lapland had well defined natural borders; they were not separated by rivers but rather by watersheds, the high ground and by the ridges. The Kola lake Lapland had two gathering groups; each of the towns had eight to twelve mature working males, often grouped together to hunt and to catch fish in the season. The combined population in the kola lake Lapland region was less than one hundred and thirty working males, according to the official tax records.

TRADITIONAL HUNTING

Hunting increased in the fifteenth century, as the Sea traders got access to the White Sea. Karelian and Russian fur traders, Sweden and Denmark extended their trading, the demand for fur increased In Fennoscandia. At Kola Lake Lapland hunting game was; marten, otters, and bears. These items were highly valued, the hunting continued until the early sixteenth century.

The mainstay for a living was from trapping beavers, wild reindeer, and from the fish catch of trout, salmon, arctic char and pike, up until the seventeenth century.

Trading of general goods like tobacco, hemp, butter, and other food ingredients, for the quality furs of the wild Kola lake Lapland.

Reindeer'sat the time were valued for transport, meat supply, furs, and for the antlers. The concept of herding large stocks and the reindeer husbandry had not caught on as it did later on.

Early in the eighteenth century the Kola lake Lapland reindeer population went through many lean years, as the people migration increased from the south, more reindeer were being trapped and hunted, and it could not be sustained any longer. So it brought about a fundamental change, the new concept of reindeer farming was introduced, which would protect and increase the family herds of reindeer for the future.

CULTURAL VILLAGE HUB

The houses were built with timber and peat, built near the waterways, rivers, and streams. Some of the populated areas were at the Naruska River, Kola Peters ridge, and on the town Ridge, west side of the Salla River. Kola Lake was historically a well-established settlement, including antiquity, a hub of the locals, and well known by the traveling nomads and goods traders from Karelia.

By the end of the eighteen century, the population of Kola Lake had increased by some twenty folds to over two thousand. As the reindeer, cattle, horses, and sheep were raised in the Kola Lake Lapland, the natural predators; wolverines, wolves, and bears soon became aware of the new stock, and their stalking of the stock animals became a problem.

SALLA MUSEUM OF WAR AND RECONSTRUCTION.

The Salla Museum, located at the Salla railway station, has a well presented local cultural history on display. Watch the YouTube video by the Lapland Guide on the Kola Lake Lapland. For more information on the history, culture, and tradition of Lapland. Kuolajarvi village Salla stands on the far-East border of Arctic Finland, it belonged to the Kuolajarvi municipality, the Province of Lapland, north-eastern Lapland. Kuolajarvi municipality was established during the Russian Tsar period, in 1857 separating the municipality from the Kuusamo municipality. The name Kuolajarvi was later changed to Salla in 1936. After the Second World war, in the aftermath of the municipality of Salla was forced to cede the territory to the Soviet Union Stalin demands, consequently doing 50 % of the Salla municipality is so-called the "Old Salla" which is now claimed by Kola region of Russia.

The original Kuolajarvi village was an old and beautiful residence about 35 miles from the current Finland Salla border station towards the east and placed at the current Kuola-lake Lower and Upper areas of Kuolajarvi. The village comprised of three parts: Keski-Niemi (lake midpoint/central cape), and the top end of the lake (ylä-pää) and the lower end of the Kuola-järvi (lake). Kuolajarvi the village in 1930 had about 60 houses, and about four hundred inhabitants.

The Stalin aggression during the 1939-45 the kuolajarvi village was handed over to the Soviet Union, with another seven communities of the Kuolajarvi municipalities. Today, the area is marked on the Russian maps as Kairala village and settlements there is only the former Central cape, through which runs the road to Kandalaksha. The Kuola-lake village is often confused with the other uses of Kuola-lake, as in the municipality administrator or as in the kuola-lake township. There are distinctly separate entities in the history of kuola-Jarvi:

KUOLAJARVI MUNICIPALITY

Kuolajarvi, then, was the parish, as well as that of the village name. The Kuolajarvi village Salla name officially changed to Salla in 1936. Today, the use of the name has two purposes, when remembered 'Kuolajarvi municipality,' it often refers to the whole parish of Kuolajarvi. The village use of the name is usually referred to as a "Kuolajarvi village."

CENTRAL CAPE

Central Cape or "Keski-Niemi." Keski-niemi was the Kuola-lake Upper and Lower central isthmus, which was relatively densely populated. This was the center of the Kuola-lake village.

LOWER KUOLA-LAKE

The lower end of Kuola-lake (Alajarvi) had the two sides of the lake well established with a group of houses. The western shore of the lake was almost entirely nutrient-rich and lush covered fields. Numerous dikes could add to the richness of the landscape.

THE UPPER END OF LAKE (YLIPAA)

Kuola-lake southernmost end of the village, Aapajarvi and Central Lake isthmus region and Aapajarvi east side was generally termed as Upper end (Ylipaa). Central Lake region was also called Upper lake (Ylijarvi).

Kuolajarvi village Salla self-sufficiency of the 18 century

Almost every dike ditch had a private water mill, which was used to ground barley flour. Before the Winter War in 1939 Kuolajarvi village had about 50 properties and almost four hundred inhabitants. The town had by that time standards many wealthy houses, and we were practically completely self-sufficient regarding food. The village was cultivated barley, rye, potatoes; many had their own small scale flour mill.

KUOLAJARVI NAME CHANGE

Kuolajarvi name change to Salla 1936. The name Kuolajarvi was changed to Salla in 1936. The name Kuolajarvi is translated to mean; a lake with plenty of fish. The word Salla in the regional Lapp language is synonymous with the words: "groove, furrow, or even being cradled in the lap." The connotation of the word is to "belong," to a place.

As the result of demands made by Stalin during the war, nearly half of the municipality of Salla area (49 %) was extorted by the threat of military war and forced to hand over (threatened with further war violence) to the former Soviet Union. 22 municipality regions were lost, altogether there were 8 villages (Korja, Kuolajarvi, Kurtti, Lampela, Sovajarvi, Tuutijarvi, Vuorijarvi,, Vuosnajarvi) areas and the village of Salla municipal division of the area lost almost entirely.

FOOD TRADITION

Traditionally many common food dishes are still enjoyed today, well known familiar dishes such as saute reindeer, dried reindeer meat soup and mashed butter potatoes. The difference between the present times was the fact that more parts of the animal were used to prepare foods for nutritional benefit.

REINDEER VITAL FOOD SOURCE

Kuolajarvi natural environment and the region produced it's own natural ingredients therefore people enjoyed and made use of the regional natural food sources. Just like any other region of the world they make use of the natural environment and natural ingredients. Most readily available food sources were fish from the lakes, rivers, and the White Sea, and game birds and other edible game meat. Reindeer head soup and kopara stew were made more frequently than at present, and also reindeer abdominal skin was used for food. Reindeer blood was used to make a quick bread.

NORDIC WILD BERRIES FROM NATURE

Nordic berries were collected and stored as much as could be. Bilberries preserved well when dried, ripe Lingon-berries were crushed to preserve them in the underground earth cellars, and Lingon-berries preserve themselves brilliantly through 6 months through the autumn, winter and the spring seasons, without any mold formation.

VILLAGE STORE EARLY 1900'S

The village shops were bought coffee, sugar (toppa sokeria), salt, and other things which were not locally manufactured. Bread and wheat preparation was, of course, prepared at home locally. Such homemade food enjoyment pleasures would have hardly be considered as an opportunity for entrepreneurship business and placing them for sale in a local shop. Today, the use of the name has two applications, when remembered 'Kuolajarvi municipality,' it often refers to the whole parish of Kuolajarvi. The village use of the name is usually referred to as a "Kuolajarvi village."

Before the Winter War in 1939 Kuolajarvi village had about 50 properties and almost four hundred inhabitants. The town had by that time standards many wealthy houses, and we were almost entirely self-sufficient in terms of food. The people of the town were cultivating barley, rye, potatoes; many had their own small scale flour mill. Thank you for visiting Lapland Guide.net website and for reading this Kuolajarvi village Salla article.

Leinonen 2009.

CHAPTER 13

Kilpis Lake Holiday Destination

(Leinonen, 2010)

SPECTACULAR SNOW-COVERED LANDSCAPE VIEWS AT KILPIS-LAKE

Kilpisjärvi literally translated is Kilpis lake. See articles at www.laplandguide.org Kilpisjärvi skiing holiday destination Review. Take a look at my Kilpisjärvi skiing holiday destination Review article and watch the videos from the Kilpis-lake skiing holiday location.

KILPISJÄRVI SKIING REVIEW

Kilpisjärvi skiing Review tells the story of the many fantastic opportunities there are for the various types of skiing, whether it is cross country skiing, backcountry skiing or telemark style skiing in the backcountry of the Lapland. The location of this high mountain plateau lake town named kilpijärvi is in the far North West arm of Finland, at the border of Norway, Sweden, and Finland. The waters of the Kilpis-lake meet all three of the above countries, the East of the Kilpi-lake in Finland, and on the West side of the Kilpis-lake is Sweden and upstream of the Kilpis-lake in Norway. The Kilpis-lake altitude is some 473 meters above the sea level. The exact location of the Kilpis-lake is about 50 km south from the Norway town of Skibothn, and 150 km from Norway Tromssa. 280 North West of Kittilä airports, and some 429 km North West from the city of Rovaniemi. Kilpisjärvi (Kilpis-lake) is excellent for the telemark skiers because of the long winter season; the reason for the cold climate is twofold. The far north proximity, parallel line, the coordinates being: 69°02'57" North. 20°47'40"East.

BACKCOUNTRY SKIING AT KILPIS-LAKE

The kilpis-lake environment offers great backcountry skiing opportunities with the rolling hills of the tundra, there are vast open areas where to ski using backcountry skies. The access to these areas can be made by using the cross country ski tracks to initially get out of the town area or to ski some distance on the frozen Kilpis-lake, and then to go back country when the landscape look suitable for the kind of experience one is after. The daily climate conditions and the time of the season also can determine where and when to go, and how long for. The spring season is most likely to be the most predictable over the autumn and winter seasons. Caution must always be taken, because it is at relatively high altitude, 500-1000 meters, and the weather can change dramatically from one day to the next. Day one may be a brilliant calm bluebird, the following day may be a snow blizzard with no visibility to navigate from the environment, the weather does change from one day to the next, even in the spring season the bright sunny days are followed by clouds, snow falls and winds.

KILPISJÄRVI SKIING REVIEW FOR THE FIRST TIME VISITORS

Kilpisjärvi skiing Review communicates the information about kilpis-lake with pictures from the location, video footage, audio on video and text articles like the one you are reading here. So do watch the videos, there are currently at least 2 of them with content from the kilpisjärvi, like the Kilpisjärvi Holiday Destination video. There is also a picture gallery with picture images from the kilpis-lake, you can see the pictures from this link at Arctic Finland holiday destination.

The cross country ski trails loops are several, there is one that goes on the frozen kilpis-lake to the three border crossing point, from the kilpis hotel it is 38 km two ways. The other one is around the Saana tundra, heading east from the town uphill to get around the Saana tundra and head north to get around it. The total distance around Saana is approx 20 km from memory. The return back to the town is done skiing south on the frozen kilpis-lake for about 5-7 km distance. The other ski trail that I have never been on is the one that goes all the way to the Halti tundra, it is a distance of some 50 km away. It is not a groomed trail, but rather a snowmobile trail that gets also used by the fat bikes. (push bikes with fat tires). The Halti tundra is the highest point in Finland, at 1365 meters above sea level.

(Leinonen, 2009)

As you can see for yourself, the landscape of Kilpisjärvi is spectacular, and the access to the surrounding environment is also accessible, which makes it more user-friendly and safe for visitors to enjoy. The more extreme mountain alps are up north on the Norway side, or further away on the west on Sweden side of the border. In the middle of this high mountain, the plateau is the mountain lake kilpis-lake, which makes the environment relatively flat and easy to access the surrounding rolling tundra hills and fells. Thank you for visiting http://www.laplandguide.org and finding out more information on the mountain lake town named kilpisjärvi. Please do share the video links with your friends and share your likes as well. Have a great next holiday season.

MOUNTAIN LAKE KILPISJÄRVI

A mountain lake kilpisjärvi is up on a mountain plateau about 50 km south of the Norway coastal town Skibothn, at 473-meter altitude, the mountain lake also has a small town on it's Eastern shore bank named after the lake. Translated into English, Kilpisjärvi means Kilpis-lake. The location of the Kilpis-lake is about 50 km south from the Norway town of Skibothn, and 150 km from Norway Tromssa. 280 North West of Kittilä airports, and some 429 km North West from the city of Rovaniemi.

   The Kilpis-lake climate is characteristically a mountain climate, with occasional strong gusts of winds, with thick and heavy snowfalls. The seasonal temperatures also reflect the high altitude. Kilpis-lake enjoys a cool mountain climate, with a long winter snow season stretching out well into the spring season April-May. The sub-zero winter temperatures start in October with the average low temperature for the month being -3.2 'C. The daily mean sub-zero temperatures last for 8 months until June the following year, with average low temperate being 3.6'C according to the Kilpis-järvi climate data.

RECREATIONAL ACTIVITIES AT KILPIS-LAKE

There are a lot of recreational activities at Kilpis-lake at all seasons of the year; currently, it is the spring season in early April, so I will cover the winter snow activities here more in detail.

- Cross country skiing.
- Telemark skiing

- Snowboarding
- Snowmobile safaris
- Northern lights watching
- Ice fishing
- Peaceful cottage holidays
- Honeymoon or wedding anniversaries
- Cross country skiing at kilpisjärvi

The most common style of skiing at Kilpis-lake is cross country skiing, there are ready-made and groomed trails built for the cross country skiers. One such trail is to the three border point, the landmark where the three borders meet. Norway, Sweden, and Finland border. The cross country ski trail from Kilpis-järvi hotel to the three border point (kolmen-tasavallan-raja-tolppa) is 38km there and back combined. The Kilpis-lake is a long narrow lake. Therefore there are many trails along on the frozen ice of the lake, which the snow has covered the ice over time. The other significantly interesting cross country trail is around the Saana Tundra fell, there is also a day hut along the path with fireplace and firewood for the traveler to warm up if needed and to cook something or to boil a cup of water. The cross country trail starts near the Kilpis-lake hotel and heads over the main road towards East, around to the back of the Saana Tundra. There is also a small tundra mountain lake behind the Saana tundra, which is barely noticeable unless really looking for it, because of the thick ice cover and the snow on top of the ice.

MOUNTAIN LAKE KILPISJÄRVI ACCOMMODATION

There are many types of accommodation available at kilpisjärvi, there is one Lapland hotel near the lakeshore west of the town center. Tundrea Lomakeskus (Holiday center) is another accommodation with facilities for caravans and cottage services. Then there is Majatalo Haltinmaa, to name a few. There are also many log cabin style cabins and cottages that can be rented privately or from the Kilpisjärvi and Käsivarren eräämaa. It is translated Kilpis-lake and the Wilderness area of the Northern Finland forearm. A Government organization that takes care of the day huts and the overnight log cabins in the National park. You can visit their Facebook page and make inquiries on the available accommodation on the link provided here, it is also for the summer season. www.facebook – Kilpisjarvi-Ja-Kasivarren-Eramaa

ICE FISHING IS PREVALENT ON THE MOUNTAIN LAKES

The most common fish being sought after are Arctic char and Grayling. The fish are sought out during the winter season and also the summer season. A portable ice drill is being used to bore through ice that may be 75cm to 100cm thick at places. The fishing line with a lure is then dropped into the ice hole and into the lake below, and with some jiggling the fish is being tempted to take a bite of the lure, and in so doing getting caught by the hook, the underlying logic of fishing. For more information on the fishing, expeditions, visit the website Grayling Land. www.graylingland.com/ There are also links to a YouTube channel, where the fish caught can be seen on video and at times by choice being released back into the water.

Mountain lake Kilpisjärvi is indeed a unique location to visit, it is a high altitude mountain lake town, that in itself says a lot about the character of the place and climate. Clean, fresh water in the tundra lakes makes it a very healthy place to live in and to enjoy life in the great outdoors. Yes, the winters are long, from October to May, and the snow starts to fall in November and keeps falling at times until April. It is the beginning of April right now, and there is one meter of snow on the ground so you can tell that the winter indeed has come here to say the full season. Thank you for visiting

Lapland guide.org, and I hope his article has been helpful for the information that you were seeking. For more images of the Kilpisjärvi visit photo gallery Arctic Finland Holiday destination from this link provided.

KILPISJÄRVI SAANA LAKE SKI TRAIL REVIEW

Kilpisjärvi Saana lake ski trail starts from the kilpis-lake near the Kilpis hotel at kilpisjärvi. It is a ski trail loop that can be skied right around the Saana Tundra fell. The location and the coordinates of the Saana tundra fell are 69°02'37"North, 020°51'22"East. The elevation of the Saana dropped at the top is 1029 meters, the Kilpis-lake is at 473 meters, and the Saana tundra lake on the East side of the Saana is at 880 meters. To ski along the other alternative route is to head North, which will take you to the Kilpisjärvi Hiking center, which is about 4 km away on the slope of the Saana fell, east of the Kilpis-lake. Saana lake is located at 69°03'00"North, 20°52'35"East. At the shore of the Saana, the lake is the Saana lake day hut. The weather at kilpis-lake. kilpisjärvi and the Saana lake can change very quickly, it is because of the high altitude, 473m, 880m and 1029 meters at the top of the Saana Fell. Always be prepared for any weather changes, and carry additional layers, wind protection, extra gloves, extra mitten and extra socks, sunglasses and possibly goggles for the windy conditions.

For more relevant information visit website **Kilpis Lake Adventures** http://kilpislakeadventures.com

CHAPTER 14

Ylläs Tundra Mountain

(Leinonen, 2012)

Ylläs Tundra mountain is a great holiday destination with lots of recreational activities and convenient facilities for tourists. It was recognized early in the 1940s a unique skiing holiday destination with the many other Tundra fells near the Ylläs Tundra Mountain.

YLLÄS TUNDRA MOUNTAIN

Ylläs Tundra Mountain has been developed for tourism over many years especially for alpine skiing and snowboarding, and telemark skiing with trail lighting. A large area of the surrounding land also has a network of connecting trails for telemark and cross country skiing. There are many on trail cafe log cabins for short rest meal/snack breaks refreshments and to rest. There are also many snowmobile operators in the region with trained guides for day trips or further overnight stays on the field.

Ylläs Tundra Mountain has been extensively developed for downhill skiing and snowboarding, there are many downhill runs and courses, t-bars, chair lift and a 55 cabin gondola lift for convenient transportation up to the hill. There are two food outlets on the top of the Ylläs Tundra Mountain summit, both cafe style serving mainly coffee & tea, buns/rolls, beverages, snacks, and other food items. There are also food services and accommodation at the base of the east side of the Ylläs Tundra Mountain, it is from the east side that the gondola lift runs from to the summit.

The north side slope has Y1 ski center with many services, the west side of the Ylläs Tundra Mountain is called the Aurinko Rinne (meaning the sunny slope) it has the chair lifts and a cafe at the base. Also on the northeast side, there is the Joker ski slope with cafe food and beverage service at the bottom of the ski run.

On the northeast side slope of the Ylläs Tundra Mountain, there is the Joker ski run with a cafe on the base for food and beverage service. There are many t-bar ski lifts that service all of the ski runs on the Ylläs Tundra Mountain. The Ylläs Tundra Mountain north side ski center is called the Y1.

Ylläs Tundra Mountains a natural landmark that stands out in the Nordic Tundra region, it stands at 719 meters elevation, relative to the Nordic region of Lapland it is a very high altitude, and it is often buffeted by strong winds during the winter and the spring season. The temperatures often dip down to extreme -20C to -30C.

CHAPTER 15

Saariselkä Holiday Destination

(Leinonen, 2012)

Ethnic Nordic Cuisine at Saariselkä town Restaurants. Saariselka is an excellent destination to sample ethnic Nordic cuisine represented at the many Saariselka restaurants. Saariselka at Lapland is located at 68° 25' 15" N, 27° 25' 1.8" E. It is at the far North East part of Finland.

THE NAME SAARISELKA TRANSLATED MEANS "ISLAND RIDGE".

Sariselkä name is a description of the impression of the view from the tundra summit looking down to the lower areas of the township. The view description is a mist covering the lower areas, and only the high points of the ridge are visible above the mist. Therefore giving the impression that the fog is water and the more top points of the elevation are islands surrounded by water.

Visitors to Saariselka will quickly become familiar with the environment of the Saariselkä Arctic town, there are many quality accommodation Hotels with services in the town central hub and also cottage style units available for visitors and guests. It is a busy town during the peak holiday season with recreational skiing and Safari Activity programs made accessible. Visitors to Saariselka for the active Arctic holiday experience, and to be actively involved and interacting with the natural environment. Mother nature does not give hangovers, but diversions do, deviation from good sensible plans reap what they sow. There are no rewards for personal stupidity, only multiplied inconvenience, delays and charges. Prevention is better than cure. Travel wisely.

DISCOVER THE BEST SIDE OF SAARISELKÄ

Lapland Guide Review

Lapland guide can help you to learn more and help you to understand the Lapland Arctic environment.

Lapland does get a large volume of visitors and guest each year, people go to Lapland for five main reasons:

- Romance and the novelty of the Natural Arctic environment

- Home of Santa Claus, meet Santa in Lapland
- Family time with a White Christmas snow experience
- Solitude, peace and rest with an open fireplace, log cabin sauna, after all day outdoors wilderness Safari
- Physical sports training with cross country skiing. Alpine skiing, snowboarding and other recreational activities.

The Arctic Lapland winter environment is unlike other relatively warm climates, there are natural charms and magic about the extreme north winter snow landscape. This experience comes real when going out to the backcountry on a safari trip, depending on what the skill set is. It could be backcountry skiing for the experienced skiers, even skiing on the telemark ski tracks a few kilometers out of town to experience the peace and quiet of the snow-covered forests and sweeping open tundra hills.

LAPLAND GUIDE REVIEW PLANNING IS ESSENTIAL

Planning is always important for any holiday adventure, whether traveling alone, as a couple or a family all things should be considered and planned for so that everyone knows what the time frame of the trip is and how to maximize the opportunity most efficiently making good use of time and resources.

Accommodation in Lapland varies from season to season and from place to place, there is a peak season and there are quiet seasons as anywhere else in the world. Having a plan and knowing what is it that you aiming for can determine where in Lapland is most suited for the purpose and what is the best time of the season to experience Arctic Lapland. Also important to consider all seasons of the year, in so doing you put the location into its full potential perspective. The summer season can be more relaxing and carefree than for example the peak winter Christmas season.

SAARISELKÄ HOLIDAY DESTINATION

Having an open mind for all options can help to decide how to make the most of the holiday experience.

There are at least three categories of accommodation options that are available, it really depends on what is the duration of the holiday and where the destination is:

1. Privately owned Warm log cabins, with an open fireplace, fully accommodated bedding and kitchen, with several rooms with bunks for a family. It may be several kilometers from the town center grocery stores.

2. Large Hotel / Motel accommodation. Fully accommodated with food services for breakfast and dinner, internet cafe, connections, post office and souvenirs shops. Bus services between the Hotel, town and ski center services.

3. Relatively remote location with many conveniences, food services, recreational activities and back-country safaris. Snowshoe hiking, skiing, toboggans, visit Santa Claus, husky dog sleigh, snowmobiles and other recreational activities may be offered.

YouTube Video from Saariselka Resort Town.

Enjoy your holiday and the experience of Arctic Finland Nature at Saariselka.

CHAPTER 16

Skiing and Snowboarding in the Arctic Finland

(Leinonen, 2012)

SKIING AND SNOWBOARDING IN THE ARCTIC FINLAND

Skiing and snowboarding in Arctic Finland are super fun, especially in the spring season. There are many great locations for Alpine skiing and snowboarding. One place to visit for a holiday is the Ylläs Tundra, it is a tremendous big Tundra mountain with lots of facilities and services for Alpine skiers, x-country skiers, and snowboarders. Groomed trails and slopes, t-bar lifts, chair lifts and a 55 cabin Gondola to the summit of Ylläs Tundra.

Skiing and snowboarding in the far north of Finland are great because of the consistent snow conditions. Skiing and snowboarding continue on well into April and May, some variations do occur from year to year.

SKIING AND SNOWBOARDING IS A GREAT SPORT TO BE ACTIVELY ENGAGED

Skiing and snowboarding are physically very dynamic and demanding; there are many benefits to the overall fitness and general good health. Whether x-country skiing, alpine skiing or snowboarding over several days, it will leave a memorial impression on one's muscles and the body, that may be of muscle pain and feeling of satisfaction, in physical fitness it may be true, "no pain no gain."

Skiing and snowboarding at Ylläs Tundra have many services and conveniences to the skier, there are t-bars, chair lifts and a massive 55 cabin Gondola to the Ylläs Tundra summit. Ylläs Tundra mountain stands tall at 719 meters, it gives out a sweeping 360-degree view of the surrounding Nordic Lapland of northern Finland. On a bright, calm day, it is a magnificent sight and a memorial experience to enjoy, especially after fresh snowfalls.

(Leinonen, 2010)

SKIING AND SNOWBOARDING HOLIDAY IN THE YLLÄS REGION HAS A LOT ON OFFER

There is the township on the east side called Ylläs-järvi (Ylläs-lake). Also, the ski resort township on the eastern slope of the Tundra called the Big Ylläs. There is Tundra a grocery shop at the Ylläs lake and plenty of cabins for hire within 2-4 km distance from the ski lifts and slopes, x-country trails are on all sides of the Tundra and snowmobile hire for day trips of further. The Big Ylläs ski resort township has two hotels with accommodation, restaurants, and seasonal live entertainment. There are many cabins for hire on the east side as well for lodging.

SKIING AND SNOWBOARDING ON THE NORTH SIDE AT THE ÄKÄSLOMPOLO TOWNSHIP

There are many shops located there with clothing, equipment, groceries, restaurants and cafe services available. Also several hotels and many log cabins and houses for accommodation services available. Up towards the Tundra slope several km, there is the Ski center what's called Y1. It is a ski center with many facilities and services, ski lifts, lift ticket sales, equipment sales and hire, professional training coaching and advise, clothing sales and hire, safety gear, restaurant food services, and a pub. Ylläs Tundra is a big Tundra mountain in the Nordic environment, there are many slopes to discover and explore, with the weather permitting it has a lot on offer.

SKIING AND SNOWBOARDING AT YLLÄS TUNDRA, OR X-COUNTRY SKIING AT THE SURROUNDING TUNDRA MOUNTAINS

When you are visiting Äkäslompolo town below Ylläs 1, and If you have any equipment requirements for the winter snow sports or summer recreational activities, make sure to visit the Sports Shop at Äkäslompolo. The staff at Sports Shop offer professional advice to any seasonal sports equipment needs, and they are genuinely friendly customer service.

CHAPTER 17

East Border Tundra Town Named Salla

(Leinonen, 2010)

(Leinonen, 2010)

The name Salla is a relatively new name given to the orginal location of an old community trading hub name Kuolajärvi until 1936). Kuolajävi means a lake with plenty of fish. Salla is a municipality of Finland, located in Lapland.

KUOLAJÄRVI (KOLA LAKE) LAPLAND

Most obvious signs of permanent human settlements on the shores of Lake Kola are said to be from around 1500 AD. The inhabitants of Kuolajärvi in Lapland were partly wild-bearers nomadic people free of State borders, traveling freely between Sweden/Finland and the Russian side to the White Sea. The institution focused on rivers and lakes. The lifestyle was influenced by repeated seasonal variations, which can be divided into six different phases. Their historical background extends to the earliest nomadic peoples culture.

The name Salla is a relatively new name given to the original location of an old community trading hub name Kuolajärvi until 1936). Kuolajärvi village was a well-established hub by the lake bearing the same name. A straight forward place name was given to a village next to a lake that contained plenty of fish. It was not until 1933 when the name was changed. It was given the same name as a Tundra Fell name Salla. Another 6 years went by and then came the Soviet Union war against peace, and they took the entire Kuolajärvi region, including the lake.

The people from Kuolajärvi/Salla had to relocate Westwards, some 50 kilometers. Away from the Soviet invasion. Finally, the Finnish military forces stopped the invasion of the Soviets, that had plans to go all the way to Rovaniemi, and kantalahti. Joseph Stalin and the Soviet military generals plan objective was to cut Finland in half. To eliminate the Finland people independence, as they did with Estonia, Poland, Latvia, and Chekoslovakia, and the Soviet military occupied those independent countries for 50 years. That was a horrible phase in history that set the occupied countries back to the Soviet Union level for some 50 years.

There were no legal base for the Soviet Union invasion of the East European independent countries. They were simply acting out with their spirit of lawlessness and anarchy. Total disrespect to the norms of international law principles. The Soviet Union leaders made a Pact with Nazi German leader Adolf Hitler in 1939-1941. And they together invaded Poland 50/50 with Nazi Germany sharing the spoils of war. Therefore the invasion of Finland in 1939, was just a carry on for the Soviets in the spirit of Nazi Germany and USSR Aggression Pact. They went out to invade and pillage East European countries in the one and the same spirit together.

Many historians, especially the egg head theoretical intellectuals, that sugar coat history from the Imperial mother England patronizing viewpoint. They look at the past 100-year history and interpret it similarly as the socialist evolution theory, without looking at the critical immoral evidence, in the light of the basic human rights, right to life, right to liberty and right to property.

There are no moral excuses for justification of the war crimes of the Nazi regime. Just as equally, there are no moral excuses for the justification of the war crimes of the Soviet Union military and their leaders. That is a basic truth on the basis that the German war criminals were arrested and taken to an international war crime court.

The same fate is reserved for the Soviet Russian leadership. Russian leaders today do repress the true facts of history. Russian society has been brainwashed ever since 1922 when the Soviet Union was set up by the Bolsheviks. They repressed the truth and controlled Russian society with State terrorism for 70 years. Not only in Russia but spilled over the borders to the neighboring countries. Tthe Soviet leaders fantasied of a "Global Communist Revolution." It was limited to their evil mind, and power hungry ambition and egocentric dreams.

That was the condemnation from self-respecting moral citizens of East Europe and the Nordic countries. They condemned the Soviet hardcore State Atheism and military totalitarianism, equally as much as they condemned the Nazi regime. There is no favoritism or patronizing impartiality in jurisprudence. The Allied forces were duped by Stalin to compromise moral law, for the sake of Allied forces victors justice. Kuolajärvi is a border town on the eastern border of Finland. It had a direct impact from the Soviet 1939 war against peace. Lost a lot of territories and the people had to evacuate some 50 km westwards. Kuolajävi today means a lake with plenty of fish that the soviet union stole. Salla today is a municipality of Finland, located in Lapland.

CULTURAL HUB.

The houses were built with timber and peat, built near the waterways, rivers, and streams. Some of the populated areas were at the Naruska River, Kola Peters ridge, and on the town Ridge, west side of the Salla River. Kola Lake was historically a well-established settlement, including antiquity, a hub of the locals, and well known by the traveling nomads and goods traders from Karelia. By the end of the eighteen century, the population of Kola Lake had increased by some twenty folds to over two thousand. Like the reindeer, cattle, horses, and sheep were increased in the Kola Lake Lapland, the natural predators; wolverines, wolves, and bears became a problem.

SALLA MUSEUM OF WAR AND RECONSTRUCTION

The Salla Museum, located at the Salla railway station, has a well presented local cultural history on display. Watch the YouTube video by the Lapland Guide on the Kola Lake Lapland. For more information on the history, culture, and tradition of Lapland. Kuolajarvi village Salla stands on the far-East border of Arctic Finland, it belonged to the Kuolajarvi municipality, the Province of Lapland, north-eastern Lapland. Kuolajarvi municipality was established during the Russian Tsar period, in 1857 separating the municipality from the Kuusamo municipality. The name Kuolajarvi was later changed to Salla in 1936. After the Second World war, in the aftermath of the municipality of Salla was forced to cede the territory to the Soviet Union Stalin demands, consequently doing 50 % of the Salla municipality is so-called the "Old Salla" which is now claimed by Kola region of Russia.

The original Kuolajarvi village was an old and beautiful residence about 35 miles from the current Finland Salla border station towards the east and placed at the current Kuola-lake Lower and Upper areas of Kuolajarvi. The village comprised of three parts: Keski-Niemi (lake midpoint/central cape), and the top end of the lake (ylä-pää) and the lower end of the Kuola-järvi (lake). Kuolajarvi the village in 1930 had about 60 houses, and about four hundred inhabitants.

The Stalin aggression during the 1939-45 the kuolajarvi village was handed over to the Soviet Union, with another seven communities of the Kuolajarvi municipalities. Today, the area is marked on the Russian maps as Kairala village and settlements there is only the former Central cape, through which runs the road to Kandalaksha at the shore of the White Sea. The Kuola-lake village is often confused with the other uses of Kuola-lake, as in the municipality administrator or as in the kuola-lake township. There are distinctly separate entities in the history of kuola-Jarvi:

KUOLAJARVI MUNICIPALITY

Kuolajarvi, then, was the parish, as well as that of the village name. The Kuolajarvi village Salla name officially changed to Salla in 1936. Today, the use of the name has two purposes, when remembered 'Kuolajarvi municipality,' it often refers to the whole parish of Kuolajarvi. The village use of the name is usually referred to as a "Kuolajarvi village."

CENTRAL CAPE

Central Cape or "Keski-Niemi." Keski-niemi was the Kuola-lake Upper and Lower central isthmus, which was relatively densely populated. This was the center of the Kuola-lake village.

LOWER KUOLA-LAKE

The lower end of Kuola-lake (Alajarvi) had the two sides of the lake well established with a group of houses. The western shore of the lake was almost entirely nutrient-rich and lush covered fields. Numerous dikes could add to the richness of the landscape.

THE UPPER END OF LAKE (YLIPAA).

Kuola-lake southernmost end of the village, Aapajarvi and Central Lake isthmus region and Aapajarvi east side was generally termed as Upper end (Ylipaa). Central Lake region was also called Upper lake (Ylijarvi).

KUOLAJARVI VILLAGE SALLA SELF-SUFFICIENCY OF THE 18 CENTURY

Almost every dike ditch had a private water mill, which was used to ground barley flour. Before the Winter War in 1939 Kuolajarvi village had about 50 properties and almost four hundred inhabitants. The town had by that time standards many wealthy houses, and we were practically completely self-sufficient regarding food. The village was cultivated barley, rye, potatoes; many had their own small scale flour mill.

KUOLAJARVI NAME CHANGE

Kuolajarvi name change to Salla 1936. The name Kuolajarvi was changed to Salla in 1936. The name Kuolajarvi is translated to mean; a lake with plenty of fish. The word Salla in the regional Lapp language is synonymous with the words: "groove, furrow, or even being cradled in the lap." The connotation of the word is to "belong," to a place.

As the result of demands made by Stalin during the war, nearly half of the municipality of Salla area (49 %) was extorted by the threat of military war and forced to hand over (threatened with further war violence) to the former Soviet Union. 22 municipality regions were lost, altogether there were 8 villages (Korja, Kuolajarvi, Kurtti, Lampela, Sovajarvi, Tuutijarvi, Vuorijarvi,, Vuosnajarvi) areas and the village of Salla municipal division of the area lost almost entirely.

SALLA MUSEUM

The Salla Museum, located at the Salla railway station, has a well presented local cultural history on display. Watch this YouTube video by the Lapland Guide on the Kola Lake Lapland. For more information on the history, culture, and tradition of Lapland.

The municipality has a population of 3,485 (31 January 2019) and covers an area of 5,873.08 square kilometers of which 142.73 km2 (55.11 sq mi) is water. The most prominent Tundra mountain of a Fell is named Salla. Salla Fell has Alpine ski facilities and various types of accommodation. Log cabin cottages and hotel accommodation. The population density is 0.61 inhabitants per square kilometer.

NEIGHBOUR MUNICIPALITIES ARE:

- Kemijärvi
- Kuusamo
- Pelkosenniemi
- Posio
- Savukoski.

(Leinonen, 2010)

CHAPTER 18

Arctic Freshwater Source

(Leinonen, 2010)

The Arctic water source has been identified as the region in the Northern Hemisphere that is most susceptible to the effects of climate variability and change. It is expected to display warming that is more than twice the global average, show decreases in snow cover and sea-ice extent, present further retreat of permafrost, glaciers, and ice-caps, and have increased inter-annual variability in weather conditions.

CHANGES IN THE CLIMATE

Such significant changes/shifts in climatic regimes are expected to have far-reaching first- and second-order impacts on the hydrology and ecology of northern/Arctic freshwater systems by impacting the ability of rivers, lakes, and wetlands to maintain adequate stream flows, water levels and water quality for ecosystem sustainability.

Changing climate is expected to directly impact not only the magnitude and timing of freshwater fluxes but also a range of physical, chemical, and biological processes in northern aquatic ecosystems.

PREDICTING THE FUTURE OF THE ARCTIC WATER SOURCE

It is difficult to project the effects changing the climate, and environmental factors will have on Arctic freshwater systems, partly due to a poor understanding of their interrelationships, and partly due to a paucity of long-term monitoring sites and integrated hydro-ecological research programs in the Arctic.

ARCTIC FRESHWATER SYSTEMS

In light of the need for better understanding of Arctic freshwater hydrology and ecology, through integrated multidisciplinary hydrological, climatologically, and ecological field studies and laboratory analyses. Arctic Freshwater Systems: Hydrology and

Ecology" (Co-Principal Investigators: Fred Wrona and Al Pietroniro) has the research priorities to:

improve our process-level understanding of Changing climate is expected to directly impact not only the magnitude and timing of freshwater fluxes but also a range of physical, biological and chemical processes in northern aquatic ecosystems.

ENVIRONMENTAL FACTORS

It is difficult to project the effects changing the climate, and environmental factors will have on Arctic freshwater systems, partly due to a poor understanding of their interrelationships, and partly due to a paucity of long-term monitoring sites and integrated hydro-ecological research programs in the Arctic.

(ii) develop improved predictive models for freshwater and nutrient flux,

(iii) develop a unique legacy database of freshwater biodiversity (structure and function) and related environmental information on freshwater ecosystems (lotic and lentic) in the Canadian Arctic,

(iv) develop and provide tools and capacity in northern communities for improved community-based monitoring and assessment of the status and trends of the health and integrity of freshwater ecosystems in northern Canada.

For more exciting article reading on the Arctic, freshwater topic visit www.arcticfreshwater.net

CHAPTER 19

Aurora Borealis

(Leinonen, 2016)

Aurora Borealis presented with brilliant colors and starlit night skies over Norway and Finland. This is a time-lapse video of some footage that I shot in Northern Finland and Norway between 1 and 6 January 2013. Aurora Borealis magic over the Arctic skies of Norway and Finland. Incredible video presentation with a time lapse. Enjoy the view from the comfort of YouTube channel, it's not always easy for photographers to be shooting pictures during the light of day and to stay awake during the night in search for the northern lights. My experience has been one of shooting pictures during the early morning, working during afternoon and evening and resting and sleeping during the night time.

AURORA BOREALIS DEFINED

An aurora is a natural light display in the sky (from the Latin word aurora, "sunrise" or the Roman goddess of dawn), especially in the high latitude (Arctic and Antarctic) regions, caused by the collision of solar wind and magnetospheric charged particles with the high altitude atmosphere (thermosphere). www.en.wikipedia.org/wiki/Aurora

Auroras Borealis seen near the center of the magnetic pole may be high up overhead. Looking at the Aurora Borealis from further out they illuminate the northern horizon with greenish glow and at times faint red colors. Aurora Borealis also display magnetic field lines and curtain-like structures, that can flicker and can change quickly within seconds or keep on glowing for a long time, even in hours with fluorescent green colors.

Thank you for visiting this web site www.arcticfinland.org and reading up on this Aurora Borealis and also for checking out the videos. Cheers!

CHAPTER 20

Arctic Treaty Success Model

(Leinonen, 2009)

Arctic Treaty success model, a resolution on Arctic Governance has been passed on October 9, 2009, by the EU Parliament. It has demanded the Arctic Treaty, an international treaty aimed to safeguard the Arctic in the way the Antarctic Treaty system protects the interests of the Antarctic region. Behind the Arctic, the treaty is a proven success model – it is somewhat based on the Antarctic Treaty System, which materialized on 23 June 1961, following ratification by 12 nations which have been active for long in the Antarctic area. Read on to know about the parallels between the Arctic and the Antarctic treaties.

REGIONAL PARALLELS OF THE ANTARCTIC AND ARCTIC

The Arctic region is similar to the Antarctic in various respects, it is covered partially by ice, it is subject to sudden changes in climate and its environment is also vulnerable enough. Not surprisingly then, the demand for a special Arctic treaty was made in keeping with environmental rules.

The climatic necessities and environmental concerns in these two regions are quite similar, which have been reflected in the treaties drawn up for the two areas. Naturally, the treaties for both regions cover similar types of environmental issues.

ARCTIC TREATY SUCCESS MODEL WITH THE SPIRIT OF COOPERATION

The Antarctic Treaty system aims to make sure that the Antarctic region is used only for peaceful ends. It strives to bolster the spirit of international cooperation among various countries in the field of scientific research in all the areas of the region. It also tries to remove disputes regarding the authority of various territories. Likewise, the Arctic treaty aims to promote international cooperation in the field of scientific and military activities among different countries for the improvement of the Arctic region.

CONSTRAINING THE INHERENT HUMAN GREED AND

LUST FOR MATERIAL WEALTH

The real crux behind the Arctic and the Antarctic issue regards to the human occupation and activities can be summed up in three words, greed, lust, wealth. Greed and desire for more material wealth is the force that drives humans to land grabs, conflict, and violence with territorial neighbors and accumulate to wars.
Politics then attempts to whitewash the crux of the human greed problem. The balance can be found by the return to respect for the natural environment and the phenomena of LIFE in general. Corporations are driven by emotional powers that they can't even themselves control. They are driven by forces that they don't even know why? What purpose is it for?

Respecting the natural environment of the planet earth will increase the power of holistic natural living and respect for life. Which in turn will balance the greed problem, and will also allow the remote areas of the planet to be left alone for future generations and for mother nature to heal and take care of and manage the planet environment the way that is more sane and natural.

MILITARY ACTIVITIES

Countries like the US, Russia, and Canada have agreed to come together in the Arctic region for the militarization of the region. There are constant efforts from the nations in using military personnel and equipment for the betterment of the area as well as for search and rescue operations.

The spirit of the Arctic Treaty closely follows that of the Antarctic Treaty, which – although bans all military activity in the area for territorial sovereignty – supports regional cooperation for continued scientific investigations. All the experimental results and observations in the region would be exchanged and shared freely. Both treaties aim to ensure that the areas are used only for peaceful purposes and to promote the freedom of varied scientific researchers for the betterment of mankind.

ARTICLES OF THE ANTARCTIC TREATY

Article 1 – The area is to be used for peaceful purposes only; military activity, such as weapons testing, is prohibited but military personnel and equipment may be used for scientific research or any other peaceful purpose;

Article 2 – Freedom of scientific investigations and cooperation shall continue;

Article 3 – Free exchange of information and personnel in cooperation with the United Nations and other international agencies;

Article 4 – The treaty does not recognize, dispute, nor establish territorial sovereignty claims; no new claims shall be asserted while the treaty is in force;

Article 5 – The treaty prohibits nuclear explosions or disposal of radioactive wastes;

Article 6 – Includes under the treaty all land and ice shelves but not the surrounding waters south of 60 degrees 00 minutes south;

Article 7 – Treaty-state observers have free access, including aerial observation, to any area and may inspect all stations, installations, and equipment; advance notice of all activities and of the introduction of military personnel must be given;

Article 8 – Allows for good jurisdiction over observers and scientists by their own states;

Article 9 – Frequent consultative meetings take place among member nations;

Article 10 – All treaty states will discourage activities by any country in Antarctica that are contrary to the treaty;

Article 11 – All disputes to be settled peacefully by the parties concerned or, ultimately, by the International Court of Justice;

ARCTIC TREATY SUCCESS MODEL

Articles 12, 13, 14 – Deal with upholding, interpreting, and amending the treaty among involved nations.

The main objective of the ATS is to ensure in the interests of all humankind that Antarctica shall continue forever to be used exclusively for peaceful purposes and shall not become the scene or object of international discord. Pursuant to Article 1, the treaty forbids any measures of a military nature, but not the presence of military personnel or equipment for the purposes of scientific research.

www.en.wikipedia.org/wiki/Antarctic_Treaty_System

ARCTIC TREATY SUCCESS MODEL REVIEW

Thank you for visiting the Arctic Treaty website and reading this Arctic treaty success model article, I hope it was informative and helpful. Please do share this website link with friends of the Arctic.

Visit Arctic Treaty FACEBOOK page. www.facebook.com/Arctic-Treaty

CHAPTER 21

The Land

THE LAND

(Leinonen, 2010)

Article source: The Nemesis Book. 2018. (Victor Leinonen)

"The Nordic people were born into a natural environment, with a cultural connection to the land and the seasonal cycles of life. From the early beginnings, the children were raised to learn and interact with the natural environment that stored up lifelong memories of all the seasonal changes. From the hibernating deep snow and ice-covered winters to the awakening sounds of a spring season, with the thousand songs of the migrating birds, singing in the endless sunlight days of the midsummer solstice. People of the land knew what the natural environment was with its biodiversity, and what the habitats had to offer according to the seasons. Their life depended entirely on natural resources. The people moved and traveled like nomads to optimize the seasonal changes according to local knowledge and the wisdom of the tribe leader's collective experience. It was a fascinating life environment to be born into, with the unmistakable signs and the unforgiving extreme cold elements of the natural world in charge of the life cycles, commanding respect from people for life in the natural world. Memorable winter night skies that opened high to the star-filled heaven gates, to a mysterious deep dark universe. There were dancing ribbons of light with pastel-like rainbow colors and sounds, creating the atmosphere of awe and wonder in the inquisitive minds as they watched the extravaganza of the aurora borealis lights in the night sky. The Nordic people did see and experience the extreme powers of nature that were so beyond human and animal reach. Stories and myths were inspired and created based on the visible night skies, the same natural phenomenon, which presented itself ever since the beginning of the ancient people's collective recorded memory. Over the cycle of seasons, from winter to spring season, the starlit night skies put on a memorable starlight display, which is beyond human capability. The minds of the observing people wondered as they looked up high into the shifting distant night skies, but they could not unlock the cause of the ribbons of light dancing up and down and all around the panorama above the snow-covered rounded tundra hills".

CHAPTER 22

Fennoscandia People

VICTOR LEINONEN

(Leinonen, 2010)

The geographical and geological region of Fennoscandia has also been a home for many people groups very early in the history of the area. The people groups settled and made it either a seasonal, temporary home during their Nomadic annual journeys from district to region have left rock art, and cave paintings include indigenous Nomads known as the Sami people from far north Fennoscandia to East Siberia. And as well as the early pioneers that ventured along the Baltic Sea and into the Baltic Ice Lake and the Gulf of Finland after the Ice Age 8000 BC. It needs to be pointed out that the climate at the far north is exceptionally harsh, where temperatures do regularly dip down to -40 C regularly without any abnormality in the environment. So moving from place to place for a favorable region seems logical as the weather is dished out with various wind directions and icy cold blasts of the elements. And the summer season with well-known regions passed on from generation to generation with the storytelling of the food resources would be an attractive destination to travel and look forward to.

FENNOSCANDIA LANGUAGES

The peoples developed their own semantic language over many Centuries, there are different distinctive languages with their various dialects, as with the Sami, Norwegian, Swedish, Danish, Finnish they have their own life history, heritage and story to tell.

The Fennoscandia region consists of the Scandinavian Peninsula, Finland, the Kola Peninsula, and Karelia. When you look at history going back to the most recent Ice Age ended and when the vast glaciers melted some 10,000 BC the melted ice water runoff formed the Baltic Ice Lake. The Ancient pioneers ventured further and further north as the summers came earlier in the year and were noticeably warmer to the previous one.

The early people pioneers of the Fennoscandia came from several directions and regions of Europe and Siberia. There was a DNA study done as the technology was improved with the help of science and computer analysis, many previously made assumptions and written articles had to be rewritten due to the false assumptions prior made. Often false assumptions were made to support their own biases and heresy. Moscow is not the center of the Universe.

FENNOSCANDIA TIMELINE

The logical approach to unravel the mystery of the Fennoscandian history is to look at it rationally, in a sequence of events in the history of the Fennoscandia with a timeline, the gradual process how and where the peoples traveled, settled left rock art and cave paintings and other antiquities and at some places later grew into larger community.

History is often oversimplified, viewed only by the historically most dominant group, and the minority groups that often are the indigenous peoples which are entirely ignored and forgotten. That is ironically the simple one track mind of the club-wielding caveman or a territory hungry conquering foreigner raping the indigenous pioneers of a territory of the ancient elders. One such group and oversimplified were the Vikings, often glorified their warmongering and territory conquests, but not much is remembered of their victims, which may have been peace living indigenous clans.

After several millenniums, the Vikings came to being as the Seafaring traders that ventured far and wide to foreign lands, it was not until around 90 AD that they became a regular sight along the route from the Gulf of Finland, along the Neva River to the Lake Ladoga.

They made use of the water highway that was a connection of Sea Gulf, rivers, and lakes connecting as far as the Middle East. These peoples of Fennoscandia spread over their habitats through forests of Finland to Karelia, the Kola Peninsula as well as the periphery of the Scandinavian mountain chain. They used to make their living by fishing, trapping, and hunting. People of Fennoscandia used reindeer as their food source, clothing, craft materials, utensils, and the means of winter transport. However, in the other areas of Fennoscandia, the Sami homeland started forming up with the expansion of agricultural settlement.

POPULATION INCREASE

The nomadic indigenous Sami peoples of the far north back in history ventured further south during the winter months in the land currently known as Finland. With a smaller population of the early pioneers of Finland that lived predominantly along the shores of the Gulf of Finland and the Karelian isthmus, Neva River and the lake know today as the Lake Ladoga. The population in the region of current Finland was much less than today (5 Million+). So there were open spaces available to which the nomadic made use of and ventured to the softer climate in the south during the winter months. The Nomadic indigenous peoples of the North came south all the way along the west coast, but as the population grew in the land of Finland, the Nomadic indigenous peoples were gradually returning south during the winter less and less.

REINDEER FARMING

Another false assumption is about the Nomadic Sami peoples is that they were reindeer farmers in the early history, with an image of relatively modern reindeer husbandry with flocks of hundreds of reindeer per owner. It is utterly false, similar to the use of grain crops, for many thousands of years globally in the south grain was not farmed. It was picked merely where it grew. Naturally, it took many thousands of years for someone to get the bright idea off the ground.

The grain fields could be propagated, and it would increase the grain crops and ensure consistency and a reliable yield for the winter harvest. The early indigenous Nomadic peoples of the far north had learned to make use of the reindeer in many ways; for food, clothing, craft materials, utensils, transport, and as a pet companionship. The reindeer farming where one family would have more than 3 or 5 reindeer only came about in the Fennoscandia around late 17 century. The Nomadic peoples by nature are not hoarders of material things, they just took what they needed and they traveled light, a large herd of reindeer has a pack will of its own, it takes a significant effort to maintain a large crowd of reindeer and for what purpose? They had no need for it, it was not discovered yet. The world was changing rapidly, including in the far north of Fennoscandia, and their world would never be the same again. See pictures of reindeer from this link.

PAYING OF TAXES

They did not pay taxes until the Swedish Monarchy demanded it. It was after that the Swedish government demanded taxes, and similarly, also the Russian tsar demanded fees to be paid by the nomadic Sami peoples of the north, that merely living self-sufficiently providing for their own families was not enough. Their early tradition and lifestyle as lived out in a Nomadic people without borders, traveling West and East as seasons were favorable. Self-sufficiency and surviving were not enough, now they had to also provide for the government and pay taxes, various items of value could be used to pay taxes, at times it was; reindeer, beavers, moose, bear, fox, or squirrel pelts, and dried or salted fish. At times, they paid tax to Sweden and to Moscow simultaneously. During the 17 century hunting was the most important source of income to the North Finland Lapland district of Kuolajarvi.

CHAPTER 23

Vihta or Vasta?

(Leinonen, 2010)

You may be wondering, what on earth do those strange words mean? Vihta or Vasta?

Vihta may sound like a computer program, but no, it is not a computer program. The words Vihta or Vasta, in Finland means a traditional fresh green leaf whisk that is used in the hot sauna house to whack the back of a person. By doing so, it generates more concentrated heat to the back by fanning the hot steam filled air. The whacking action of the bound bunch of soft birch branches (with green leaves) to the back also works as a light massage effect, with concentrated heat, and the slapping of the green leaves of the birch. Now is the best time to be making a Vihta, the birch branches are fresh and green, they also have a refreshing fragrance. The new branches are soft and easy to shape into a band to hold the birch branches together in a tight bunch.

Vihta can be prepared in bulk during the summer season and stored for winter

Vihta or Vasta can also be made ready and stored in a dry store or a freezer. They are usually stored by hanging them indoors undercover from a line. Before use, they are soaked in hot water for 30 minutes to refresh them. The freezing method works well; also, they do need to be wrapped securely in plastic to protect the leaves from frostbite, otherwise the leaves dry and break up. Even as the drying method, soak it before use in hot water for 30 min.

Awakened and refreshed Vihta does bring the fragrance and the colors of summer back to the hot sauna room during the freeze of winter. A spring sauna birch Vihta in the middle of winter is an excellent reminder of the summer season with fragrance and the next spring season to come. It really is an excellent reminder of the wonders of the natural summer season, during the snow-covered winter months, when there is no green to be seen on the ground for 6 months of the year here In the Nordic region.

Birch trees an excellent source for making craft items

The Birch branches, the bark, and the timber have traditionally been used for many purposes. The flexible white paper, like the bark of a birch tree, was used for making ribbon baskets, shoes, wall decorations, book marks, and many other craft items. Branches also are useful material for crafting baskets, fencing, or fishing trips, along with the branches used to lure the fish during the spawning season. Birch as firewood has excellent qualities, the bark (provided with the wood) is almost like paper, easy to light with a match. The timber blocks split easily into straight segments, the birch timber is very user-friendly, and it is valued highly by the people that live on the land.

(Leinonen, 2010)

CHAPTER 24

Finland Access to the Arctic Sea

(Commons, 2015)

This section Chapter 17 is sourced from my book title, The Nemesis 2018.

REMNANTS OF THE RULE OF LAW

During 1920 the Treaty of Tartu was signed in the city of Tartu

(Estonia) at the Estonian Students' Society building. The ratifications of the treaty were exchanged in Moscow on 31 December 1920. The Tartu treaty confirmed that the Finnish-Soviet border would remain and follow the old border which was established between the autonomous Grand Duchy of Finland and Imperial Russia. (Wikipedia, Treaty of Tartu (Russian– Finnish), 1920)

A WAR BETWEEN THE TWO COUNTRIES 1918

The diplomatic relations between the repatriated Finland and Soviet Russia broke down following the outbreak of the Finland Liberation War. The Council of Russian People's Commissars recognized that the Revolutionary People's Delegation was possibly going to be the future Finnish Government. The 42nd Army of Russia in Finland had also started military operations against White troops, and some of the Russian militaries became Reds military.

There were no significant battles between Finland and Soviet Russia during the Finland Liberation War because the Reds of Finland themselves played a significant role in the battles. Under the Brest-Litovsk Peace Treaty signed in March 1918 between Russia and the German Empire, Russian troops were withdrawn entirely from Finland except for a few volunteers. (Encyclopedia, Treaty of Brest-Litovsk, 1918). The Finnish Senate, as the Government, for the first time declared that Finland was at war against Russia, at the beginning of April 1918, justifying the imprisonment of the Levis Kamenev of Bolsheviks in Åland. Relations between the two countries could not be restored after the Bolsheviks expulsion from Finland war. In April 1918, Soviet Russia appointed colonel Konstantin Kovankon as a diplomatic representative to Helsinki, but the Finnish authorities imprisoned him at the end of May and did not allow his successors to enter the country. After the Finland Liberation War, Finland asked for assistance from Germany to solve the conflict issues of Eastern Karelia and Municipality in the Barents Sea port of Petsamo. After several requests, Germany agreed to host the peace talks between Finland and Russia, which took place in Berlin in August 1918 for three weeks.

Negotiations ended unsuccessfully due to the uncoordinated regional requirements of both countries. Also, Soviet Russia did not accept the Finnish interpretation of the state of war between the two countries, as all Russian state property left in Finland would have been transferred and interpreted as the property of Finland. Over the next two years, the leadership of Soviet Russia declared that it wished to maintain peaceful neighborly relations with Finland for the time being. Usually, diplomatic relations were not possible even though the occasional informal exchange of notes between the foreign ministries of the country. The Finns considered the state of war to continue and held informal contacts with the Russian White Leaders as well.

PEACE NEGOTIATIONS 1920

Peace negotiations over a Peace Treaty began in Estonia, Tartu, on June 12, 1920. The negotiations were held at the University of Tartu Student Organization Eesti Üliõpilaste Seltsi. J. K. Paasikivi led the Finnish delegation. The delegation consisted of the same people as the Committee that had previously prepared the Finnish peace rules. The presidency was initially offered to Carl Enckell, but he refused because he opposed the peace agreement with the Bolsheviks. When the members' views on the need to link East Karelia to Finland varied, the Paasikivi Committee, as a compromise, intended to require the Eastern Karelians to decide by referendum to either side with Finland or with Russia. Foreign Finland minister Holsti, meanwhile, gave the Finnish delegation the goal of pulling the eastern border to the line of Laatokan- Syvärin-Ääninen – the White Sea and linking Petsamo Municipality and the entire Kola peninsula to Finland.

Finland Delegation 1920

Soviet Delegation 1920

Only the requirements of Kirjasalo or Ingria have left aside because their pursuit was not considered realistic, due to the continues Russian expanding city of St. Petersburg. The city had outgrown and ex-pulsed the local population. It was decided to recommend the use of cultural autonomy to the Ingrians. Just before the start of the negotiations, Soviet Russia occupied the area between Murmansk Railway and Finland and announced the establishment of a Karelian Workers' Commune, led by Socialist Edvard Gylling who fled Finland. This was, according to Bolshevik, a demonstration that the people of East Karelia had solved the content of their sovereignty, and no referendum would be needed.

THE COURSE OF THE NEGOTIATIONS

In the beginning, the negotiations stalled in place on regional issues. The Russians insisted on maintaining the borders of 1914, except for the municipality of Repola and the municipality of Porajärvi, which could have been negotiated, as well as obtaining part of the Gulf of Finland Islands and the Karelian Canal. The Finns did not want to retreat from their demands for eastern Karelia because they suspected that Soviet Russia wanted peace as soon as possible with the war in Poland, and the rest of its neighbors and would agree to concessions. The negotiations stalled for several months before the parties were ready to overthrow their demands. When the Red Army in Poland's anti-war invasion near the Warsaw neighborhood in late summer, negotiations with Finland were suspended in mid-July from both sides' wish for two weeks. During the break, President K. J. Ståhlberg lowered demands. Finland still wanted the municipality of Petsamo while the population of Repola and Porajärvi had to decide on their own fate, but the sovereignty of East Karelia could be resilient. After the negotiations resumed, the Finnish Delegation deliberately delayed, as it was expected to clarify the global situation. Finally, on August 9, Foreign Minister Rudolf Holsti allowed Finland's delegates to start negotiations with realism, as Poland had already begun negotiations with the Council of Russia.

(Commons)

The truce was concluded between Finland and Soviet Russia on August in Poland; the Red Army was able to hit back at the Polish border, so the negotiating arrangements began in Tartu to compromise. Soviet Russia was ready to hand over Petsamo to Finland, but it was still waiting for Finland to return the municipality of Repola and Porajärvi, closer to the Muurman railway track the northernmost, year-round railroad to the north of Russia. For Finland, however, two broad areas of the eastern bloc municipality were not as crucial as the year-round ice-free port of Petsamo. From Finland, possession of Repola and Porajärvi was also a way to improve the likelihood of being taken over by Petsamo.

This consensus was contributed by confidential Vaino Tanner, a representative of the Social Democrats of the Finnish Delegation, with Plato Keržentsev, a member of the Russian delegation. Along with Tanner, only Paasikivi knew about these conversations. Tanner suggested to Kerzenville that the acquisition of Petsamo was a priority for the Finns concerning the preservation of Repola and Porajärvi. On the suggestion of Tanner, the Russian delegation presented its last bid to replace these areas, to which the Finns agreed on September 7, 1920. Foreign Minister Holsti, who was pressurized by public opinion, still insisted on keeping Repola and Porajärvi in a hurry, but the Finnish delegation did not want to tear apart the reconciliation that had taken place after months of work. The latest disagreements concerned the borderline in the Fisham fishing island of Petsamo and the fate of the outer islands of the Gulf of Finland required by Russia. On October 2, Vladimir Lenin, the Bolshevik Party's politburo, ordered his representative to conclude peace with Poland as well as Finland as soon as possible.

TREATY OF TARTU 1920

The Treaty of Tartu was between Finland and Soviet Russia. It was finally signed on October 14. 1920. After the negotiations that lasted four months. The treaty confirmed the border between Finland and Soviet Russia, after the 1918 Bolsheviks expulsion from Finland war, and the Finnish volunteer expeditions in Russian East Karelia. The treaty signed in Tartu (Estonia) at the Estonian Students' Society building. Ratification of the treaty was exchanged in Moscow on 31 December 1920. The treaty registered in the League of Nations Treaty Series on March 5, 1921. The treaty confirmed that the Finnish-Soviet border would follow the old border between the autonomous Grand Duchy of Finland and Imperial Russia. Finland additionally received Petsamo, with its ice-free harbor on the Arctic Ocean. As far back as 1864, Tsar Alexander II had promised to join Petsamo to Finland in exchange for a piece of the Karelian Isthmus.

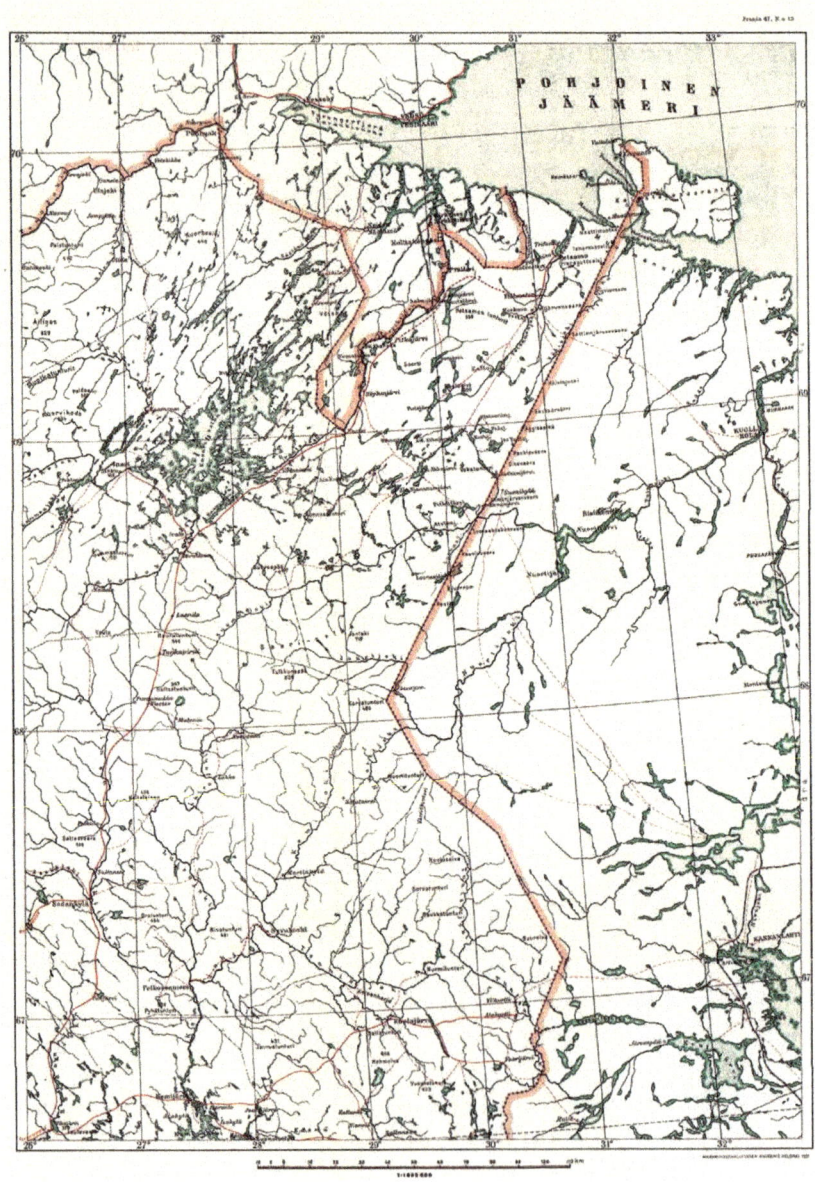

(Wikipedia)

Note: The eastern border of Finland in Lapland has been moved on many occasions over the centuries. The Treaty of Tartu in 1920 was agreed upon, and in 1921, a line drawn by a ruler was taken from the Fisherman's Harbor to Korvatunturi. The 204-kilometer border line was drawn towards north to the Port of Petsamo, together with the Russian delegation. In 1921 the Russian cross border expedition members did not appear in 1921, and so the Finnish cross-border expedition commenced on the marking the border alone. The Municipality of Petsamo was extorted back by Soviet Union dictator Joseph Stalin during the end of World War 2. That is how Finland lost their municipality that provided access to the Barents and the Arctic Sea.

Finland also agreed to leave the joined and the occupied areas of Repola (joined to Finland during the Viena expedition) and Porajärvi (joined during the Aunus expedition) in Russian East Karelia. The treaty also had some articles besides area and border issues, including a Soviet guarantee of free navigation of merchant ships from the Finnish ports in Lake Ladoga (Laatokka in Finnish) to the Gulf of Finland via the River Neva. Finland guaranteed land transit from the Soviet Union to Norway via the Petsamo area. Also, Finland agreed to disarm the coastal fortress in Ino, opposite the Soviet city Kronstadt located on the island of Kotlin. The Finnish outer islands in the Gulf of Finland were demilitarized. (Wikipedia, Treaty of Tartu (Russian– Finnish), 1920)

EAST KARELIAN AGAINST BOLSHEVIKS

The Karelian region. After Finland declared independence from Russia, some Finnish nationalists supported the idea of a Finland expansion Eastwards. It was an attempt to block the Russian encroachment on the Karelian region. The Karelians were much closer culturally to Finland than Russia. More Karelians spoke Finnish than the Russian language. The Finnish culture, the

Karelians, the Ingrians, and the Swedish Kingdom had seen and experienced the push from Moscow since the 17 Century.

In the early days of the calendar years, people lived along the Gulf of Finland, along with the Karelian Isthmus, Lake Ladoga, North Karelia, and the Kola Peninsula. People were living in these areas and speaking their own language for thousands of years before such entity as Moscow or Russia existed. Both Russia and Moscow are latecomers, peoples from the Slav regions migrating East. They have no rightful claims to the Nordic indigenous people's land, only claim it by forceful military conquest. State atheism claims regions that do not belong to them, so they resort to extortion and ruthless totalitarianism and genocide. Every evil deed committed by evil dictators against the Spirit of the Natural Law is felt, seen, noticed, and recorded by the Creator of Life.

Justice will come one day to the millions of innocent lives lost between 1900 to 1991. The soil of this planet never forget the murders, and the innocent lives blood, committed by godless cold heart atheists. The Karelian regions have a long cultural history parallel with the Finnish peoples; they are regarded as Finnish tribes. There was a significant effort by USSR to forcefully remove the people of Karelia and replace the peoples with Socialist Russians, during the 1930 – 1950' s. It was systematic ethnic cleansing with communism obsessed political tactics for expanding the socialist ideals into Europe. 440,000 Karelian were forcefully evacuated by the Soviet Union aggressive warfare in 1939, 40. Some of those evacuees returned back to their homes in 1941 and were forced to leave permanently in 1945.

The forceful evacuation of the Ingrian people in the Karelian Isthmus. Eradicating the Ingrian population and culture from their home region, all because of a war between Sweden and Russia, and Peter the Great started building his new city on a swamp named Petersburg. It was the first established location by Sweden and the Finns, a fortress named Nyenschantz, at the Gulf of Finland shore, at the river mouth of Neva. The Nyenschantz fortress was built in 1611 to establish Swedish rule in the Ingria land, which was initially pioneered and populated by the local peoples, Karelians, Ingrians, and Finns, and later to be conquered by the Novgorod covetousness or the Moscow expansionism further towards Europe.

CHAPTER 25

PRESIDENT OF FINLAND NEW YEARS DAY SPEECH 1940

THE PRESIDENT OF FINLAND KYÖSTI KALLIO.
(1937-1940).

"To Suomi people and friends! "As President of the Republic, it has been a tradition of mine that on the first day of the year to send out greetings message through our radio broadcasts, to create a brief overview of our societies and economic development. This time I have to give up on the practice because now there is only one thing that is on our mind, to rescue our fatherland from the attacker's reach that has struck its claws on our governing body. Our bodies. The old imperialist Russia, throughout history, has been a threat to the Finnish people, once again manifested its old instincts and without the slightest legitimate reason to attack our country.

Russian Tsar Imperialism has collapsed, but the imperialist practices have been inherited to its current rulers, even though their teacher guru Lenin declared when he came into power to be respectful of the sovereignty and self-determination of the peoples on the fringes of the old Tsar territory. In practice, it has turned out to be words only. Initially, the sovereignty of the peoples who had the national strength to rise and watch over their independence, and they did gain independence, but now the Soviet Union leaders appear to be strong enough to demand influence over those countries as well. (growing military strength emboldens Soviet union leaders to demand control of the neighbors).

Such a request even though initially was cautious, was also made to Finland. From the experience of centuries, Finland was aware of what it was all about. Peace-loving-People like Finland, it tried to get the requests presented to us through negotiation, however, the apparent requests of the Soviet Union turned out to be demands on Finland's own security and interest were to be relocated and diminished. The Soviet Union, as usual, made its claim under the guise of security of Leningrad, but in reality, it was the transport connections between the Gulf of Finland and Petsamo fjord control and disposal, weakening of Finland's defense capabilities in the Gulf of Finland, Karelian Isthmus and the Port of Petsamo.

None of the Leningrad's insecurity could have been the truth of the matter because already in Tartu's peace agreement it was agreed that Finland could not fortify Leningrad region, or the islands along the waterway and the shoreline area near Leningrad, nor the Finnish fishermen's island area at the Port of Petsamo. In the negotiations, the Soviet representatives acknowledged these guarantees as sufficient about Finland but required additional guarantees that no superpower could take advantage of Finland's territory in a potential war against Russia. That was also an excuse because Finland is always there openly said that it wanted to stay away from the conflicts between the great powers and laments himself against every foreign power that seeks to offend his sovereignty. Russia's invasion of Finland when the negotiations were still unfinished.

Moreover, they delivered a demand for the appointment of the Communist government to our unconquerable country, shows that it had been presumptuously decided to occupy Finland and at the same time to engulf the country with the spirit of the Bolsheviks politics, when the initial requests as they were, was not granted. Our country was in a state of readiness that Russia did not get us by surprise, even though there is a non-fortified border over 1,000 kilometers. They attacked the border right away in some points, not caring less, and completely ignoring the agreements that we had with them, e.g., the resolution of mutual disputes by peaceful means. Ruthlessly attacking using airplanes on the capital and other settlements by killing children, women and other civilians.

Through these acts, the Soviet Union revealed at the beginning of its agenda. This raw assault brought together the front the whole of the Finnish people, whose national self- esteem and the blood felt love for the liberty of our independence, which every year we are increasingly strengthened. Our defense is intact and indivisible. Our Parliament has unanimously drawn up laws that show its long-awaited consideration today. Defense work does not only involve men but also women who are sacrificing themselves; the versatile operation is of great value. The proportion of women today more noticeable when they are receiving, and part of the refugees and relocating process with incredible pride and with serenity adapted to both sides of the new conditions.

During this great trial of our nation, we have the consolation among us, cooperation and unity. It seems as if the people of Finland in the great distress found themselves. Moreover, that is why we need to rejoice. The sacrifice we now need everywhere is of high divine origin. Sacrifice His work and resources for the neighbor is significant, but to sacrifice himself, the life of his country, and For his people is still much higher. In front of its vulnerability, we are silent, and we humble to thank God for great suffering and sorrows to awaken new life values. We sincerely regret that we have been subjected to warfare that requires victims. But we have no other way to protect our independence than a sacrificial battle for our existence sake. A couple of weeks ago, I had the opportunity to greet our superiors 'officers and crews and express our gratitude to our peoples for the different positions that stand for the protection of our home and the whole motherland.

These two fateful weeks that we have since lived have given us their own for our people and the whole world, new testimonies of the battle readiness of our defense Forces, perseverance and above all the unity and cooperation they have shown on land, at sea, and in the air. On behalf of our people, without mentioning anyone individually, or forgetting anyone, for everyone to our country defenders are heroic and deserves deep praise. This equally grateful greeting is also presented to those wounded at the front lines, laying in the hospitals from their acts of courage. Which I have pointed out they are carrying the hard fate continually remembering their comrades who are on the front lines. However, above all, we take a moment of silence to give respect to the many who have sacrificed their lives for our common homeland. Moreover, you, mothers, fathers, spouses, children, brothers and sisters, who are doing heavy work at home you will know this during this fateful Season, with greetings with the consent of knowing that every hand you know, that this is now about the existence of our nation and the future of which we all are Responsible for. Let us continue to carry our burdens each in place with the same unity and bravery. Every work for the motherland is now essential and necessary."

(President Kallio, 1940)
TheNemesisBook2018 (Kindle Locations 4303-4309).

CHAPTER 26

Santa Comes To Town

SANTA COMES TO TOWN

Leinonen 2012.

The Santa comes to town is a very well known Christmas song, it's creation date goes back a long way. The Santa comes to town song was written by John Frederick Coots and Haven Gillespie, it was first sung on the Eddie Cantor's radio show in November 1934, and It became an instant hit, and caught on everywhere worldwide.

> "You better watch out
> You better not cry
> Better not pout I'm telling you why
> Santa Claus is coming to town."
> "He's making a list
> And checking it twice

> Gonna find out Who's naughty and nice
> Santa Claus is coming to town."
> He sees you when you're sleeping
> He knows when you're awake
> He knows if you've been bad or good
> So be good for goodness sake!
> O! You better watch out!
> You better not cry
> Better not pout
> I'm telling you why
> Santa Claus is coming to town
> Santa Claus is coming to town."

CHRISTMAS IN LAPLAND

Santa comes to town every year for the Christmas day celebrations in Lapland. Christmas in the Nordic Countries has a long tradition in the ideal values of the home and family being in the center of Christmas.

Declaration of Christmas Peace. There is over a 600-year tradition in the South-West coast of Finland, at the city of Turku. It is the declaration the Christmas peace. It has been declared every year since when it began in 1350. It was during the Swedish King Magnus the 4th. The tradition goes like this, In the city of Turku, in southern Finland, large crowds of people gather at the main market square (Isotori) on the Christmas eve, and there have a big band playing live, and just before noon, and after the Turku Cathedral Bell strikes twelve, the Declaration of Christmas Peace is then read.

THE DECLARATION OF CHRISTMAS PEACE:

"Tomorrow, God willing, is the graceful celebration of the birth of our Lord and Savior. And thus is declared a peaceful Christmas time to all, by advising devotion and to behave otherwise quietly and peacefully, because he who breaks this peace and violates the peace of Christmas by any illegal or improper behavior shall under aggravating circumstances be guilty and punished according to what the law and statutes prescribe for each and every offense separately. Finally, a joyous Christmas feast is wished to all inhabitants of the city."

The declaration has become a Finnish Christmas tradition, and it is broadcast over all the radio airwaves and on the TV stations. The ceremony ends with a flourish as the trumpets play the National Anthem. Also, another hymn for the band to play is the, written by Martin Luther:

A MIGHTY FORTRESS IS OUR GOD.

The Christmas season for almost every child in the western world has experienced the good cheer and the festivities that the make-believe belief in the Santa Claus to generously reward children that have behaved well in the previous year. The super magic like the character of Santa Claus that has unlimited powers to travel faster than the Google street view, and also knows more secrets than the NSA.

There are approx 526,000,000 Christian family kids under the age of 14 that are genuinely on the Santa Claus list. But the older people and the parents also get presents, if they celebrate Christmas on December 25th, but maybe some unknown secrets and exceptions, who would know the secrets of Santa Claus. So the Santa has a busy time to deliver over 21 million presents 21 million kids an hour, every hour, on the night before Christmas. That's over 360,000 kids a minute; and about 6,000 a second. And when Santa Claus comes to town, he really does mean business.

How will people learn from the Santa Claus example?

It has been over 2000 years since the demonstrated and prescribed solution was declared to resolve the human core problems of violence, ignorance, selfishness, greed, and loss of direction in life. The complete solution was illustrated step by step how to make a better world that is fair, unselfish, and unbiased.

Now it is a matter of life choice for individuals to learn and to apply from the most significant examples of them all. Making personal spiritual growth more important than taking away from others and especially human dignity.

REFLECTION AND CONTEMPLATION IS GOOD FOR THE HUMAN LIVING SOUL

Human beings need to have objective purpose in life, short term and long term goals that make the journey of life pleasant and rewarding experience. To receive the desirable rewards in life, there need to be goals, that the individual person believes in and works towards. But to achieve desirable life goals can be really challenging at the best of times. There can be obstacles, detours, accidents, distractions, ill health, death and disease. All obstacles can hurt personal motivations, to throw the person off their life long term goals. The human mind is a powerful organ that can be used logically and rationally to design the course of action that one needs to take, so they can plan their way from point A. to point B, and further point C. and point D.

Reflection of past behavior is like having an appraisal on work performance by the employer. It gives reflective feedback on previous work performance and the level of work environment interactions and conduct. Reflecting on the past is also good for the human conscience, human living soul functions require it. Human living soul functions of the mind are the intellect, consciousness, imagination, will, memory and emotions. In reflection, all of the functions of the mind can be allied for self-regulation. To self regulate there needs to an understanding of the right behavior, right information of true lasting moral values avoids the repetition of choosing the wrong choice.

The intellect, consciousness and the will are the primary functions of the mind for understanding rational logic. Moral values are derived from sound reasoning, they can be recognized as being sensible and logical and also morally right. The concept of a benevolent Santa Claus can introduce the child's mind to think in terms of ethical behavior is rewarded. Rewards for good behavior can be a motivating force to empower the child to do the right thing. It leads the child to self-regulation. I do not mean that Santa Claus gifts and rewards are the only belief that can help the children to good behavior. Santa Claus image is internationally publicly acknowledged as being a benevolent father figure, a trustful friend to all children all over the world. It is a projection of a concept, an ideal, of a benevolent father figure. Why is that necessary? It is needed for the sake of all those children that live in broken families and live in environments that are by cause and effect depressing. People can lose the hope of there being anything good in the world. The mind can switch from a positive hope-filled optimist to a negatively skeptical pessimist. Some children go hungry every day of their childhood. Some go without adequate clean water all their childhood. Some are abused, and others are neglected. The Santa Claus figure is much bigger than the unfortunate circumstances of poverty, Santa gives unconditionally, regardless of the child's situation. It may be only one day per year that children meet Santa Claus, but it can be a life long memory of an idea of a Santa Claus father figure decency, that will never be compromised. It is a life long value.

CHAPTER 27

Swans in Finland Mythology and Antiquity

Leinonen 2010.

In the rock art of Karelia, there is a picture outline of swans, the creators of those pictures are sometimes called the "water bird nation" (Fin. Vesilintu kansa). According to the belief of the Karelian people, the white swans not to be harmed, if they were, then the same fate would return to that person as the injured swan. Because when swans are feeding, their heads are submerging under the surface of the water, therefore it is believed that swans have access to the underworld and hades as well. The White Swans inspire Artists, Musicians, and Poets in Finland. Jean Sibelius, (8 December 1865 – 20 September 1957) was a composer, violinist of the late Romantic and early-modern periods. Sibelius fame recognized as Finland's most celebrated composer and, through his music, is often credited with having helped Finland to develop a national identity during the early independence years, to the First World War fighting against Russian Bolshevism and Stalinism. (Jean_Sibelius, 2018)

In the Suite, Lemminkäinen is about a vague concept of a mystical swan swimming around Hades, the island of the dead. The mythological figure Lemminkäinen has been tasked with killing the sacred swan, but on the way, he is shot with a poisoned arrow and dies himself. Eino Leino (6 July 1878 – 10 January 1926) was a famous poet and journalist. Considered as one of the pivotal pioneers of Finnish poetry. His Swan of the Hades poem, inspirational in the symbolism that first started in picture arts. The poem translated from Finnish brings out thoughts like this:

"Oh! The visiting white birds of the Lapland summer, the great ideological beings, Feel welcomed here! Please stay, make the nest there, and tarry, and do go to the lands of the south! Oh, we do a study and learn from the Swans! They leave in the autumn and return in the spring. There is peace on our shores and safety on the breast of the Tundra."

(Leino, 1926)

CHAPTER 28

Christmas in Lapland

Leinonen 2011.

PRE-CHRISTMAS INFLUENCE

The History of the Pre-Christmas holiday celebrations in Finland has evolved over time. It has been forged and shaped by the two opposed traditions and belief systems, that had celebrations at the end of the year. With the natural organic ancient pagan worship, and later on in Christianity. The mid-winter solstice celebrated and recognized in all corners of the world by indigenous peoples. The pagan celebrations at the autumn harvest time, with magic evoking person dressed as the rich yield harvest for the produce of the land.

There were several Christmas day festivals celebrated earlier in history. Later on, the autumn festival was moved to the midwinter solstices and combined. These celebrations have become a regular part of the Nordic countries culture, and very well accepted as a very positive use of the holiday free time. Pre-Christianity, the pagan festival ritual person, would carry goat horns and be personified as a goat of the harvest. According to Mikael Agricolan, kekri was a name given to a god-like mystical figure.

The original meaning for the word Kekri is not certain, whether it was a name for a pagan god or a name for a celebration of the harvest festival. For some kekri was a god-like figure that evoked fear in peoples. Mikael Agricolan. The word Kekri has been used in a mixed bag fashion, used for the All Saints day, or for the Feast of the All Saints Day celebrated in November according to the Catholic Church.

Also used to describe the late autumn sowing of rye seeds, and the word Kekri also used to describe a ghost or a monster. So there is a mixture of religion, heresy, and superstition by those that used the word Kekri for a descriptive term. Early in history, the kekri celebrations had no fixed calendar date. Sometimes it was used for the late autumn festival and other times for the end of summer festivals. It was not until early 1800 that the kekri became known as

All Saints Day of the first day of November, and later it became the first Sunday of November.

PRE CHRISTMAS KEKRI CELEBRATIONS

Kekri celebrations were for the common farm workers celebrations. Kekri celebrations were a time for singing, playing, and dancing in joy. During the 18 century, it also became the departure celebration of farm workers, when they were moving to another property and master. The maids and the farmhands got a two-week leave before starting work again at a different property. They were able to return back to their home town, nearby in the neighbor's district and friends living there.

Because the kekri was at the end of the year, it had similar anticipations of the New Year as today with New Year's hopes and resolutions and predictions for the New Year, so it allowed superstitions and divination. Sometimes the kekri celebrations got an additional activity like a carnival, with the abundant fairy, a monster, and group of jokers went home visiting and door knocking for payments. Where a group would dress up in a carnival manner and people were dressed as a Kekri with goat horns, and they wanted attention and tributes paid for their carnival masquerade and a mixture of celebrations and superstition and entrepreneurship.

PRE CHRISTMAS BEAR HIDE MONSTER WITH HORNS

Masked figures, bear hide and goat horns, the kekripukki was the most feared monster of them all, it could have a bears hide with two men under it and large ladles for horns. It all sounds like they were high on moonshine or magic mushrooms, or just plain drunk by homebrew. Making an extravagant show of letting go, hard years labor, and service to their masters. In a way turning the tables and changing the roles between masters, property owners, and farmhands and maids. The Catholic church viewed the practice as pagan and did not approve of their practices. And in 1729 the Rautalamin clergy got an order to faithfully teach the Gods instructions and to forsake the pagan magic and witchcraft.

Source: www.christmasinlapland.net/pre-christmas/

CHRISTMAS HOLIDAY DESTINATIONS IN LAPLAND

Christmas in Lapland is well worth; considering, sharing with friends, and with professional advice and consultation plan it and finally making it happen. The scope of the holiday destination in Lapland is many. However, the Christmas season is a hectic season in the significant busy destination hubs of Lapland, so it is essential to plan ahead and to book far in advance as humanly possible. Not all destinations are equal in their pre-bookings. Make inquiries to be sure of the suitable accommodation, travel schedule, and the on-ground activity tours at the destination availability.

Depending on your previous experience of the Arctic region in Lapland, if you do have been there previously and if you are well prepared for the extremely cold temperatures, then that won't limit the availability of a suitable destination. The upside of the services provided by the Safari companies is that they provide the services, the cold weather gear, gloves, boots, and overalls as part of the excursion, once you have registered for a particular safari or an outing. They have cold weather experience and know how to provide proper cold weather gear to a specific purpose. It is not 100% fail proof. You still need to have your wits about you and your family and make sure that all the sizes of clothing and boots are correct. And make sure none of the hired clothing or boots are not wet from previous safari use. This precaution is vitally essential when traveling with a family of children, adult supervision is critical. Bring your own suitable mittens for every one of the family, spare socks, beanies and thermal under layers and appropriate Arctic winter footwear. As well as proper outer clothing. Hired clothing is usually only for the safaris and the specified outdoor tours. People travel from accommodation to the events in their own gear and clothing.

ACCOMMODATION IN LAPLAND

Accommodation varies a lot, there are large hotels in the major tourism hubs, townships, and ski resorts. There is also a lot of Nordic styles, privately owned log cabins that can accommodate couples, a family, or a group. The sizes vary from 4 beds to 12 beds, from single levels to multilevel log cabins. There are also Holiday resort villages with a restaurant, sauna, recreational activities and a bar area for beverages. The prices do vary according to the seasonal cycle. The busier the season is more demand there is, and the costs that can go up with the markets.

RECREATIONAL ACTIVITIES IN LAPLAND

- Summer
- Autumn
- Winter
- Spring

There is always the natural environment in nature to see and things to do in Lapland. For most visitors, the Arctic region is very different from many other parts of the world. The fauna and flora of Lapland, the four-season climate impact on the environment, does go through many rapid changes in a relatively short time. Whether it is the splash of bright colors flora during the autumn season, or the bird migration from the south during the spring season, the rain, streams and whitewater rivers, berries, and mushrooms in the summer season. They all give out a unique natural life environment experience, a difference, and contrast to that which follows.

Winter is often dark with short days, and the snow, ice, and cold frost covered ground cover. With only a 5-hour low blue haze light during the day (9:30-14:30). But the winter season also visually surreal with a special atmosphere, often the most favored by the visitors of Lapland during the Christmas season. The Nordic winter is from November to March. The snow cover in Lapland is generally from November to June, some variation from year to year.

More information can be found on www.Christmasinlapland.net

(Leinonen, 2011)

CHAPTER 29

Arctic Ocean Port of Finland

(Petsamo, Liinahamari, 1930).

Arctic Finland Arctic Sea is an Arctic country one of many in the Arctic circle of friends. However, only about 1/3 of Finland geographically is situated within the Arctic Circle. Throughout the Arctic Circle, those that are living above the 60th parallel of latitude are predominantly Finns, with these statics being close to 1 in 3.

Finland is an Arctic country with a historical presence in the cold winter climate of the close Arctic proximity.

The North-East Fennoscandia and now part of Finland area was initially inhabited by the Arctic indigenous peoples. There are cave paintings that go back to 9000 to 6000 BC in the Finnmark region of the current Norway www.en.wikipedia.org/wiki/Norway

It later became under the influence of the kingdom of Sweden In 1533, it became part of Russia. In 1920, the area became part of Finland. The area was later annexed and ceded over in 1944 to the Soviet Union under the World War 2 expansionist ambitions of the Soviet leader Joseph Stalin.

ARCTIC SEA FISH RESOURCES

Arctic Finland Arctic Sea on the shore of the Arctic Sea came about by the Treaty of Tartu.

"Treaty of Tartu (Russian: Тартуский мирный договор, Finnish: Tarton rauha) between Finland and Soviet Russia that was signed on 14 October 1920 after negotiations that lasted four months. The treaty confirmed the border between Finland and Soviet Russia after the Finnish civil war and Finnish volunteer expeditions in Russian East Karelia. Ratifications of the treaty were exchanged in Moscow on December 31, 1920. The treaty was registered in the League of Nations Treaty Series on March 5, 1921. The treaty confirmed that the Finnish-Soviet border would follow the old border between the autonomous Grand Duchy of Finland and Imperial Russia. Finland additionally received Petsamo, with its ice-free harbor on the Arctic Ocean. As far back as 1864, Tsar Alexander II had promised to join Petsamo to Finland in exchange for a piece of the Karelian Isthmus."

www.en.wikipedia.org/wiki/Treaty_of_Tartu

From 1920 to 1939 Finland had access to the Arctic Sea for the natural resources of fishing by the Port of Petsamo. It was blocked by the Soviet Union invasion in 1939 and a few years later became annexed in 1945. Before this, Finland had access to the Barents Sea from 1920 to 1939.

EXTREMES OF FINLAND

Lapland is one of the northernmost provinces in Finland, and there are periods during the summer when the sun does not set for weeks on end. However, during the winter month's, the sun stays below the horizon for weeks at a time. It is during winter in Finland that snow coats the region and rivers freeze completely. The cold and frigid temperatures are nothing new to those living in Finland. Temperatures below 30 degrees Celsius are ordinary during winter, and in the summer season, the temperatures can rise above 30+ degrees Celsius.

SURVIVING ARCTIC CONDITIONS

Those living in Finland have become used to the Arctic conditions that come with close proximity to the North pole, tradition, and culture in the region has adopted the customs to the Arctic conditions over time. In terms of international trade, Finland is often referred to as an island. This is because most export and essential is done by sea. Even though the weather in Finland can be treacherous and unpredictable, that has not stopped Finish ports from being kept ice-free at all times. This allows Finland to be known as the top maritime industry location. Did you know that more than half of the world's ice-breakers are produced in Finland?

ARCTIC FINLAND ARCTIC SEA IMPORTANCE TO FINLAND

Arctic Finland Arctic Sea has sustainable, practical use in the maritime industry integral to Finland, but construction and the mining industry have also become to mine in Finland. The Arctic conditions of this region historically have been manipulated to allow specific industries to succeed in the unique, sensitive Arctic environment.

ACCESS TO THE BARENTS SEA

Finland had access to the Barents Sea fishing by the Port of Petsamo from 1920 to 1939, but the Petsamo municipality and the Port of Petsamo gave access to the Arctic Ocean. The Petsamo municipality that was granted by the Nicholas 2 was revoked the Soviet Union Leader ambitions Joseph Stalin in 1939 and 1944. It is reasonable for Finland to petition for the return of the land that was wrongfully taken away in 1940 and 1944 along the shoreline of the Arctic Ocean. It is a practical gesture that does affect the economy of Finland, natural resources, and energy that Finland provides to the Arctic region, its access is called for and should be granted. The Gulf of Finland was a natural resource of fishing for the people of Finland and Karelia ever since the beginning of the Nomads settling there over 3000 years ago. However, the totalitarian expansion and encroachment of the Soviet Union into the territory of the people of Finland in the Karelian Isthmus came from the ever-growing population of Russian Petersburg and their desire to gravitate towards Europe like it was a cash magnet.

ARCTIC OCEAN PORT OF FINLAND

Wikipedia, Petsamo 1939.

THE LOGIC OF INVASION INTO PERSPECTIVE

"From west to east, the country stretches from Kaliningrad (the exclave separated by the 1990 Re-Establishment of the State of Lithuania from the then-Soviet Union) to Ratmanov Island (one of the Diomede Islands) in the Bering Strait. This distance spanning about 6,800 kilometers (4,200 mi), to Nome, Alaska."

Russia began from the stronghold of Novgorod, Expanded to the area known as Moscow today. From there, eastwards is a massive open space, Russians could have headed that way and made themselves respected in the eyes of the world. But no, their leaders did the opposite, they decided to rob and pillage the territories where other peoples had done the hard work, cleared the farming land, removed boulders from grain fields, build roads, bridges, farms, towns, and cities. Russians went out of their way to steal the property that other peoples had worked for over 2000 years.

"From north to south, the country ranges from the northern tip of the Russian Arctic islands at Franz Josef Land to the southern tip of the Republic of Dagestan on the Caspian Sea, spanning about 4,500 kilometers (2,800 mi) of extremely varied, often inhospitable terrain. Extending for 57,792 kilometers (35,910 mi), the Russian border is the world's longest. Along the 20,139-kilometer land frontier, Russia has boundaries with 14 countries: Norway, Finland, Estonia, Latvia, Lithuania, Poland (via the Kaliningrad Oblast), Belarus, Ukraine, Georgia, Azerbaijan, Kazakhstan, Mongolia, the People's Republic of China and North Korea."

Russian Petersburg had reached over 4 million, the large city population on the shores of Gulf of Finland had degraded the quality of the waters and the health of the fish in the Gulf of Finland. So it is logical and reasonable that the bilateral relations of neighboring countries are respected, and not dictated by some self-centered dictator who has global domination ambitions as Stalin did in 1939, and destroyed the lives of ordinary people of the land by the tens of millions.

Much can be said about the timeline of Russia and the Soviet Union. The pivotal moments in history are telling, from early 1900 to 1922, there was an underground movement called the Bolsheviks, that worked at it like rats to overthrow the Russian Tsar. The Bolsheviks were lawless rebels, they were also anarchists, that hated all ethical values, moral authority over them. They were driven by emotionalism and hatred for the authority figures. They were organized and driven by hatred. The Bolsheviks were handing out the crack pipe of hate against the civil authority, they needed the fix for the dopamine effect, that was highly contagious and spreading the Bolsheviks cause like nothing else could. The Bolsheviks promise to the people was freedom from authority, equality, rights, and abundant resources from the Imperial Russian vaults. The promise of a better future was a deceitful lie, an illusion, and false hope based on rebellion, lawlessness, and anarchy. From 1917 to 1922 the Russian civil war raged, millions died because of the protest movement generated by the Bolsheviks. It was all based on false principles and false premises. The Bolsheviks sowed seeds of lawless and anarchy, they reaped State Atheism from 1922 to 1991. State atheism as the Soviet Unions was a horrible failure model for nation building, with civil order where the rule of law has the authority.

In the end, it all came crumbling down, the Soviet Union was ultimately doomed to fail. Not because of the Russian people, no more than the German people failed that followed the leadership of Adolf Hitler. The Soviet Union collapsed because it was built on dictators political ambitions, and self-centered ego. Stalin wanted to be a higher authority than anyone else. And he completely ignored the Spirit of the Natural Law. Stalin ignored the existence of the Creator of Life. Stalin became a hardcore militant atheist, that destroyed places of worship, burn bibles and murdered millions of God-fearing innocent believers. Stalin got what his hardcore atheism deserved in 1941, the dirty deeds that Stalin did to others came back on him. Katyn forest massacre of 22,000 innocent Polish nationals, in 1940 was murdered in cold blood. It was also an act of genocide on the Polish peoples. The requisition of the genocide was sent to Stalin by the KGP Lavrentiy Pavlovich Beria and approved by the Soviet Foreign Minister Molotov.

"On 5 March 1940, pursuant to a note to Joseph Stalin from Beria, six members of the Soviet Politburo — Stalin, Vyacheslav Molotov, Lazar Kaganovich, Kliment Voroshilov, Anastas Mikoyan, and Mikhail Kalinin — signed an order to execute 25,700 Polish "nationalists and counterrevolutionaries" kept at camps and prisons in occupied western Ukraine and Belarus.[26][c] The reason for the massacre, according to the historian Gerhard

Weinberg, was that Stalin wanted to deprive a potential future Polish military of a large portion of its talent:"
www.en.wikipedia.org/wiki/Katyn_massacre

THE NUREMBERG WAR TRIALS

"The Nuremberg trials were a series of military tribunals held by the Allied forces under international law and the laws of war after World War II. The trials were most notable for the prosecution of prominent members of the political, military, judicial and economic leadership of Nazi Germany, who planned, carried out, or otherwise participated in the Holocaust and other war crimes."

The entire world has heard of the German Nazi war criminals, the Nazi leaders were apprehended and taken to the Nuremberg war trials. According to the Spirit of the Natural Law, a war crime is a war crime regardless of who does it. The German leaders were demonized, and the Soviet Union leaders were let off because the Soviet leaders were members of the Allied Club. It is called a double standard, impartiality, favoritism, and Victors justice.

The war crimes of Soviet Union leadership are still withstanding. At the same time, the Nazi German leadership from 1939 -1945 are hunted internationally, even the frail and aged 90 years old's are being convicted by the International Court of Law. Why is it that the Soviet – Russian are permitted to go without the Second World War trials for the Soviet Union war crimes, and the genocide of the Polish Nationals?

The answer may be found by the principles given in the Holy Scriptures. Proverbs 16:4. Matthew 7:23.

CHAPTER 30

The Early Pioneers

"The early pioneer's many thousands of years ago traveled northwards exploring the unknown, uninhabited Nordic northland. At the same time, nomadic peoples were living along the waters of the Arctic Sea, on the shores of the Barents and the Norwegian Sea. The indigenous people tribes East and West of Siberia, thousands of years ago, have left cave paintings in Norway, that the modern-day scientific dating methods translate the cave painting to be some 8000 years old. The world of the indigenous peoples is very different from the Imperial States colonization. A very long slow history of humanity has been lived out before the industrial revolution, which made way to new concepts to enlighten the human conscience, and how people view themselves and the world that they live in.

The biblical record of the patriarch Abraham goes back some 4000 years, and the days of Moses and the Exodus of Israel takes us back more than 3460 years. The recorded events and dates of the biblical timeline are a reliable source as a reference, because of the context of the five books of Moses are qualified by many generations of spiritual integrity. 2000 years ago, people were living on the shores of the Gulf of Finland, Bothnia Bay, Lake Ladoga, and the Karelian Isthmus. The region later became known as the Suomi-land and the Suomi people. Translated into English as Finland, or Finnish.

The word Suomu translates to the English word is scales, as in fish scales. The alternative autonomy part of a fish is the fin. Therefore, Finland. The original meaning of the word Suomi in Finnish is not precise, but there are several suggestions where the name Suomi originates. The word Suomi is mentioned early in the Treaty of Nöteborg 1323. It was the first settlement between Sweden and the Novgorod Republic regulating their border. A peace treaty of 1323 between Sweden and the Novgorod. (Treaties, 2018)

SOMEWESI. Somewesi was a starting point in the description of the region with a local name, Somewesi or Suomenvesi (Some-wesi, Some-vesi. Translated Fin-land-water). It was describing the area of the Suomi waters in the Bay of Vyborg. The written word Suomi has also appeared at the time of Mikael Agricola (1510 – 9 April 1557) a Lutheran clergyman, who worked pioneered the Finnish literary language. Also, a prominent proponent of the Protestant Reformation in Sweden, and Finland. Several words rhyme with the word Suomi, that can be used as a guide for the origin of the word. Here are two suggestions. Suo = swamp. Finland has over 100,000 lakes and many more swamps. Suomu = scales, as in fish. Clothes made in the early Stone Age years from the skin of fish. The other guide for searching out the meaning of words is anthropology. As in the study of human cultural behavior, in the Finland region nomads, pioneers, language, and societies. The vital clue is found how and why a specific people formed and used their language, and named their geographical region, according to the association, according to what their people valued and experienced at the time. Also revealing the specific cultural values, from 2000 or more years ago. In Lapland there is a town called Kuolajärvi, the word is from the Sami people language. It means a lake with plenty of fish. Similarly, the Sami people have named the Kuolanmaa. Translated into English as the Kola Peninsula. Meaning; a land with plenty of fish. That is the indigenous people's relationship to the creation, food, and life. Food sources gave freely by the Creator of Life. Therefore, the Creator of Life instructions for humanity needs to be taken seriously. Unless people fall onto the wrong side of God's Holy Angels. There is an old cultural connection to the name Suomi land. It refers to the lakes and the fish. From the early hunters and gatherers perspective, what would be the most paramount concern that they had during the summer season? Naturally, the natural resources for food. There were abundant supplies of food provided by the Creator of Life. Moreover, each person could express their soul in gratitude, according to their soul experience, about the provision that they gathered and hunted. In the early days, the salmon and pike skins were so plentiful and practical as a waterproof material, once tanned it is soft and light material to use.

    The Native Inuits of current Alaska also made Salmon skin clothing. The fish skin leather is waterproof, and waterproofing is vital in the extreme sub-zero temperatures. Wet clothing can be life-threatening in the freezing exposed sub-zero temperatures. If the clothing becomes wet, then it will work like a conductor for body heat to escape, the clothing freezes solid once the physical activity reduced and the body temperature drops, the clothing freeze solid and the freezing of skin begins. The fish skin was processed to be durable leather, especially for the outer waterproof layer. The Alaska region Inuits traditionally used it for boots, mittens, and pants. Waterproof hats are practical. A waterproof fish skin roof for a tent may also be practical because they are very light to carry. Once large fish were caught, gutted, skinned, they were scaled and dried. The tanning process cured and manipulated the skin soft. Once the material was tanned, it easily colored with natural colors. The tanned skins made into carrying bags, clothes, and other items with various practical uses. The indigenous peoples were creative, they lived off the land and made use of whatever resources the Creator of life provided them in the natural environment. Many thousands of years ago nomadic people's pioneers traveled towards unknown destinations, due to seasonal changes that caused people to look for new pastures. Ever growing communities, population and stock numbers caused nomadic pioneers to explore further West and south from Siberia until they come across the people that were heading northwards, with the same intent in searching for unconsumed natural resources in the wilderness of the natural world.

The extreme cold Nordic winters did persuade people to find shelter from extreme climate, to warmer regions. Whether it was 100 km, 500km or more distance, they headed south for winter. Few thousand years ago there was plenty of room for the nomads to travel the full length of the country from the Kola Peninsula to the shores of the White Sea, all the way to the Gulf of Finland. There were no Imperial monarchies or ambitious political states lording it over the early pioneers of the lands. The state of Nature ruled the people, and the people were in tune with the natural environment. The early pioneers lived amid a natural environment that provided everything that they needed for survival. The spring season bloomed fresh with many millions of migrating water and land birds arriving from the south, as the new living environment was sprouting and welcoming with a vibrant green environment filled with colorful flower-scented meadows. The summer season was the busiest season for building projects, houses, barns for stock feed, boat repairs and cutting the vital firewood for winter survival. The summer season was the most fun season for children, time for swimming and fishing and foraging for berries. An old traditional Nordic custom, the entire family, would go and forage for wild strawberries, raspberries, bilberries, and mushrooms. The wild berries prepared into conserved jams, concentrated juices, crushed lingonberry barrels and stored in the underground cellars. The summer season was also crucial for the harvesting of building material timber, gathering up for the winter season firewood stocks, and restoring the old and re-building new projects. The autumn season was unique for the grains crop harvesting season and foraging of lingonberries, various mushrooms, net fishing and game hunting for ducks and moose. Planning was the key to survival and healthy living, by keeping ahead of the seasonal changes.

The stock feed was harvested from the open wild grass meadows, to be cut down and dried. Dry grass then gathered and placed inside the log cabin shelter with water and snow resistant roof. The 6-month long winter consumed much stock feed; it had to be sufficiently dry so that it would not go moldy and rot. With the increase in human population, there was more demand, and the old forests were thinned out or cleared. More supply needed for all the stock animals for the cold dark winter months. Life for the people of the land was active and busy even under the most favorable conditions of the natural resources. The children of families grew to be young adults, the young adults mixed and mingled with other young adults of the communities; there was the natural social life, community life, and commitment for new families. Children were born to young parents; new families created. Children had to be raised and cared for, guided and instructed, even educated, in the wisdom of the people of the land elders.

The elements of nature tested everyone's will, intelligence and resolved to keep going, regardless how bitter, cold, how sick, or how miserable, how dark and gloomy the situations turned out to be. There was a strength to be found in the shared values of the community, who respected the Spirit of the Natural Law for the common good. Valued the principles that contributed and ensured survival. Morality is a resource for inner strength when the circumstances change, and the times are uncertain, even when foreign military powers invade to exploit the local resources. War is often a moment for truth, time for a reality check before the Creator of life, and claim the promises made in the books of the Holy Bible, for the believers. For those that respect the Spirit of the Natural Law in words and deeds and obey the instructions. They do not initiate violence or rely on unscrupulous means for selfish gain."

Source: The Nemesis Book 2018 (Amazon Kindle).

THE EARLY PIONEERS

(Leinonen, 2010)

CHAPTER 31

Castle Hills and Fortresses

(Leinonen, 2011)

CASTLE HILLS AND FORTRESSES

The Ingria-land people saw the long boat traffic start, Viking ships entering in and out of the Neva River, starting around at 800AD. They were unchallenged on their journeys to the Lake Ladoga and beyond. They also saw the transformation of the environment that took place over time with the swampland at the mouth of the Neva River. Later on, in 1611AD the Swedish built and controlled the Nyenschantz Fortress, a Swedish fortress built in 1611 at the mouth of the Neva River on the Swedish controlled the water access to the Gulf from Lake Ladoga.

The conflict was rooted in the Viking Age when the Varangians set up a trading outpost in Ladoga and controlled the course of the Neva River. The Slavicization and Christianization of Northern Russia accounted for the deterioration of relations between the Vikings and Novgorod at the turn of the 11th century.

A LIST OF THE PRIMARY 7 CASTLE HILLS AND FORTRESSES

- The Old Ladoga Castle.
- Tiurin Castle (1100-1200AD).
- Vyborg Castle (1293AD).
- Käkisalmi Castle (initially known as Korela castle).
- Pähkinä Saari Castle (1323 AD-Oreshek).
- Nyenschantz Fortress (1611AD).
- Shlisselburg Castle (1702).

LADOGA CASTLE (753-950 AD).

Old Ladoga Castle. According to the legend, a Varangian leader named Ruruk went to the Ladoga in 862 AD and established it as his central capital hub. And two years later he moves to the Novgorod in 864 AD. During the 753 – 950 AD Ladoga was one of the most influential trading ports of Eastern Europe. It was a Water highway from the Baltic Sea up to the Neva River to Lake Ladoga, from there to Constantinople and the Caspian Sea. It is also known as the Trade Route from the Varangians to the Greeks. The original Finnish name of Ladoga was Alode-joki/Alajoki, meaning: the lower River. (Wikipedia, Old Ladoga).

TIVERSKY OR FINNISH: TIURINLINNA

Its heyday happened during the crusades period (1100-1200 AD). Was a medieval Karelian fortified settlement 215–300 meters long and 40–56 meters wide in the Karelian Isthmus. It was situated on an island of the River Vuoksi, which became a peninsula after 1857.

According to the legend, a Varangian leader named Ruruk went to the Ladoga in 862 AD and established it as his central capital hub. And two years later he moves to the Novgorod in 864 AD. During the 753 – 950 AD Ladoga was one of the most influential trading ports of Eastern Europe. It was a Water highway from the Baltic Sea up to the Neva River to Lake Ladoga, from there to Constantinople and the Caspian Sea.

It is also known as the Trade Route from the Varangians to the Greeks. The original Finnish name of Ladoga was Alode-joki/Alajoki, meaning: the lower River. (Wikipedia, Old Ladoga). Tiversky or Finnish: Tiurinlinna). Its heyday happened during the crusades period (1100-1200 AD). Was a medieval Karelian fortified settlement 215–300 meters long and 40–56 meters wide in the Karelian Isthmus. It was situated on an island of the River Vuoksi, which became a peninsula after 1857.

VYBORG FORTRESS

It was started and built in 1293, by orders of Torkel Knutsson, the Lord High Constable of Sweden who made in the 1290s a so-called crusade to Karelia.

The so-called Third Finnish Crusade, actually aimed against Russians. Novgorod. He chose the location of the new fortress to keep the Bay of Vyborg, which was a trading site used by locals already for a long time. From the bay, a riverway goes inland, ultimately connecting the place to several districts, lakes, and indirectly also to rivers going to Ladoga.

KÄKISALMI CASTLE

The center of the hub From the Middle Ages, Priozersk was known as Korela to Russians and Käkisalmi to Karelians and Finns. The Swedes captured Korela twice: in 1578 for seventeen years and in 1611 for one hundred years. The main landmark of Priozersk, Korela Fortress, has historically been the center for the Karelians of the Karelian Isthmus; and from time to time been the northwestern outpost of the realm of the Russians or the eastern outpost of the realm of the Swedes.
 www.fi.wikipedia.org/wiki/K%C3%A4kisalmi
 http://en.wikipedia.org/wiki/Tiversk
 http://fi.wikipedia.org/wiki/Rautu_%28Viipurin_l%C3%A4%C3%A4ni%29
 "The name Rautu meaning (Arctic char) is a former municipality of Finland in the Karelian Isthmus, it was invaded by the Soviet Union in 1944. The original Finnish municipality had an area of 339.6 kilometers ², and its population was 5 989, in 1939."
 "The Rautu name was renamed Sosnovo by the Soviet Union in 1948.

NYENSKANS FORTRESS

In 1611 Sweden built the Nyenskans fortress on the Shore of Neva River, on the bank where the river is at the narrowest point. It was a strategic position for Sweden to control and stop any Russian Battleships entering into the Gulf of Finland.

The fortress stayed in Swedish control until 1703. Later on the Pähkinä-Saari (nut-island) Peace (1323), the border follows the line from Rautu to Hiitola, following the most uniformly populated area along the west coast shoreline of Lake Ladoga, of the border during the Crusades.

On May 1, 1703, during the Ingria campaign of the Great Northern War, the fortress of Nyenskans was taken by Peter the Great and renamed Shlotburg. It was called the neck town, because of the shape of the long narrow channel, at that point in the Neva River. There was geographical funnel shape, a neck or a narrow lane like a chimney. And it was steadily built into a foreign, town center that became a city, and continued to grow around them and eventually become the city called Petersburg. 1713-1728 AD, and 1732-1918 AD.

Petersburg was the Imperial Capital of Russia. The city was built by conscripted peasants from all over Russia; Ingrians, several Swedish prisoners of war were also involved in some years, under the supervision of Alexander Menshikov. Tens of thousands of serfs died building the city.

See the following Wikipedia links for maps:

http://fi.wikipedia.org/wiki/Terijoki
http://en.wikipedia.org/wiki/Viipuri_Province
http://fi.wikipedia.org/wiki/Hiitola

SHLISSSELBURG OR NUT ISLAND

The first fortification was built in 1299 by Lord High Constable of Sweden Torgils Knutsson but was lost to the Novgorodians in 1301. A wooden fortress named Oreshek (also Orekhov) ("Nutlet") was built by Grand Prince Yury of Moscow (in his capacity as Prince of Novgorod) on behalf of the Novgorod Republic in 1323. It guarded the northern approaches to Novgorod and access to the Baltic

Sea. The fortress is situated on Orekhovets Island, whose name, refers to nuts in Swedish and (Pähkinäsaari, "Nut Island") in Finnish and Russian. In 1702, during the Great Northern War, the fortress was taken by Russians under Peter the Great in an amphibious assault: 250 Swedish soldiers defending the fort for 10 days before they surrendered. The Russian losses were 6000 men against 110 Swedish losses. It was then given its current name, Shlisselburg, a transcription of Schlüsselburg. The name, meaning "Key-fortress" in German, refers to Peters perception of the fortress as the "key to Ingria."

http://en.wikipedia.org/wiki/File:Carta_Marina.jpeg
http://en.wikipedia.org/wiki/Shlisselburg

Petersburg was the Imperial Capital of Russia. The city was built by conscripted peasants from all over Russia; Ingrians, a number of Swedish prisoners of war were also involved in some years, under the supervision of Alexander Menshikov. Tens of thousands of serfs died building the city.

The Moscow political powers that formed the Stalinism that followed with its idealistic totalitarian goals and Mega Mania objectives as tall as the pyramids of Egypt. The grand plans of ambitious mega maniac leaders are always in conflict with the values and principles of the local indigenous and rural people. A rural community of people working the soil of the earth that's under the common sky.

They are forced and submitted into slave labour, to realize the dreams and future plans of the militarily power of Russia and the Soviet Union. The reasons being; they were a minority group, a rural indigenous community, they were inconvenient obstacle to the ambitious communist conquerors, but they did have a claim on their land and territory by their indigenous rights. Also because of their roots, their ancestry, belief, Natural law, myths, tradition, and the Christian values. That eventually brought increasing persecutions from the foreign Bolshevik and Stalin ideology. So, the Communist Stalinism of the Soviet Union drove out the indigenous

Inkeri-land people from their ancient homeland by brute force, forced evacuations and cruelty that obliterated their traditional communities.

The Regional Wars, and the Persecutions. Inkeri and the Votes became part of/under the umbrella of Novgorod state; it came to birth during the Viking era after 800 AD. Then the War started over the Ingria-land that lasted for centuries between the East and the West, on the Karelian Isthmus:

NOVGOROD REPUBLIC

Novgorodskaja respublika Old Church Slavonic was a large medieval Russian state which stretched from the Baltic Sea to the Ural Mountains between the 12th and 15th centuries, centered on the city of Novgorod. The citizens referred to their city-state as "His Majesty (or Sovereign) Lord Novgorod the Great" (The Republic prospered as the easternmost port of the Hanseatic League.

The Rus' Swedish: Rus, were a group of Varangians (according to the so called Normanist theory, the Vikings of predominantly Swedish origin). According to the Primary Chronicle of Rus, compiled in about 1113 AD, the Rus had relocated from the Baltic region ("from over the sea"), first to Northeastern Europe, creating an early polity which finally came under the leadership of Rurik. Later, Rurik's relative Oleg captured Kiev, founding Kievan Rus.

The descendants of Rurik were the ruling dynasty of Rus (after 862), the successor principalities of Galicia-Volhynia (after 1199), Chernigov, Vladimir-Suzdal, Grand Duchy of Moscow, and the founders of the Tsardom of Russia.

THE VARANGIANS OR VARYAGS

(Old Norse: Væringjar; Swedish: Väringar; sometimes referred to as Variagians, were people from the Baltic region, most often associated with Vikings, who from the 9th to 11th centuries

CASTLE HILLS AND FORTRESSES

ventured eastwards and southwards along the rivers of Eastern Europe, through what is now Russia, Belarus, and Ukraine.

THE HANSEATIC LEAGUE.

Also, known as the Hanse or Hansa; Low German: Hanse, Dudesche Hanse, Latin: Hansa, Hansa Teutonica or Liga Hanseatica) was an economic alliance of trading cities and their merchant guilds that dominated trade along the coast of Northern Europe.

It stretched from the Baltic to the North Sea and inland during the Late Middle Ages and early modern period (c. 13th–17th centuries). Historians generally trace the origins of the League to the rebuilding of the North German town of Lübeck in 1159 by Henry the Lion, Duke of Saxony, after Henry had captured the area from Count Adolf II, Count of Schauenbur and Holstein. – Hanseatic League. The military battles over the Ingria-land started early in 1200 AD. The Western Baltic Sea States Sweden, Denmark, Germany, and the eastern Novgorod wanted to strengthen their trade links and their political position in the Ingria-land region, as well as the Karelia region and Finland.

During 1500 AD, the Swedish politics of expansionism threatened the Russian interest, and in the Baltic region, there were also other powers wanting to move in and occupy. In the wars that followed the Ingria-land became the focus of destruction. It was during these times that the first resistant movements became to form. They were against the Russian expansion politics over the Ingria-land and Karelia. It is from that time the first recorded evacuation of the Ingria people's to Karelia Isthmus and further north to Finland. Pioneers during the Stone Age. The early pioneers represented by fishermen, hunters and the foraging community that followed, would most likely enjoy relative peace, having arrived at the shores of the Bothnia Glacier Lake.

The seasonal fresh growth in flora and the fauna, during the spring and summer season, it would have been exciting to explore the shores in search for new pastures in the Nordic wilderness and the surrounding land on the edge of the glacier and the white snow and ice of the Arctic.

Most likely the initial endeavors of the pioneers were just an annual spring/summer seasonal event/short term migration along the waters of the Gulf of Finland. Undisturbed environment: waterways, feeding fish along the overgrown shorelines, roaming wild animals, bears, deer, wolves, lynxes, beavers, the overwhelming sights and sounds of the annual flocks of migrating birdlife, white swans, ducks and geese, and the swarms of mosquitoes. The spring and summer seasons that only lasted about four to five months, followed by the chilly winds and the rains of the autumn season. But to stay through to the winter would have required much more planning and many more survival skills. Ultimately it required determination and raw guts due to the harsh, unpredictable, weather of the Nordic winters.

To confront the raw elements of nature for a full winter season, surrounded by winter snow and ice would have required considerable preparation and a suitable environment with constructed shelter, fireplace.

Sufficient supplies, and about 6 months of firewood supply, water, dried fish, vegetables, frozen berry and mushroom supply, a large game like deer/reindeer to hunt down while skiing in knee-deep snow and plenty of animal furs to keep warm during the cold winter days and nights. Relatively comfortable camp and supplies to maintain their health and to keep their spirits up until Mother Nature turns her side at the following spring season, and life on earth starts to smile again. But to stay they eventually did, encouraged by the peace and the quietness of the wilderness, abundance of natural provisions and the ever growing pressure from increasing populations of the south and central Europe. A publication booklet by the Tampere Museum in Finland-Lassi Saressalo: Story of the Inkeri People groups and Cultures. The recent studies have rejected the old theories that the Baltic Finns had come to the shores of the region in waves of migrations in the early part of the first century, from the east/southeast. Results of the research had revealed that the North-European people were of Finn stock (Kanta Suomalainen). Not to be confused with the Finn-Ukraine stock (kantasuomlais-Ugrilaista), as they also moved on the north as the Indo-European people groups became to settle there. They also have a relatively recent history, integrated with the Indo-European Nations.

Similarly, the Baltic Finn tribes and their Nationality are a representation of the local indigenous people of the Baltic Sea, in the same way as the Sami people represent the Indigenous people who found their habitation environment in the south and the far north. The Baltic Sea Finns, the Ingria land people (Inkeriäläiset) also have their roots that go far back in time, at least 2000BC. (Saressalo, 2000) Many Clans, Tribes, and Nations. The first arrivals that went along the shore lines in boats or canoes may have been during the spring season, fishing and searching for nesting swans, geese and duck eggs along the waters of the large inland lake, produced by the melt of the "Big Freeze", their journey during the summer seasons, with the continues light and the midnight sun. Approx 2000 years earlier, (12000BC) the glazier was at the south end of current Sweden. The clear waters from the melting glazier produced a large inland lake with clean water for the fish and the water birds to live and swim in, the distant shore lines that were being engulfed by the rising water covering the land from west to east. Whether they settled on the shores, or went deep into the interior of timber lands is uncertain, but eventually people did settle, during the Stone Age on the Glazier Lake shores, along the river banks and far inside the ancient forest covered land from north of Lake Ladoga to the west as far as the Bothnia Sea. Such tribes and Nations of people are the Sami hunter gatherers

Source: Vesa Leinonen. INKERI-Land (Kindle Locations, 758-773).

CHAPTER 32

Municipalities that were Extorted by USSR between 1940-1945

MUNICIPALITIES THAT WERE EXTORTED BY USSR BETWEEN 1940-1945

(Wikipedia, Commons)

NAMES OF LOST MUNICIPALITIES OF FINLAND:

Antrea (S:t Andree) – was lost to the USSR in 1944
Harlu – was lost to the USSR in 1944
   Heinjoki – was lost to the USSR in 1944
Hiitola – was lost to the USSR in 1944
Impilahti (Imbilax)– was lost to the USSR in 1944,
Jaakkima – was lost to the USSR in 1944
Jääski – was partially lost to the USSR in 1944,
Kanneljärvi – was lost to the USSR in 1944
Kaukola – was lost to the USSR in 1944
Kirvu – was lost to the USSR in 1944
Korpiselkä – was partially lost to the USSR in 1944
Kuolemajärvi – was lost to the USSR in 1944
Kurkijoki (swe. Kronoborg)– was lost to the USSR in 1944
Lahdenpohja – was lost to the USSR in 1944
Lavansaari (swe. Lövskär) – was lost to the USSR in 1944
Lumivaara – was lost to the USSR in 1944
   Metsäpirtti – was lost to the USSR in 1944
Muolaa – was lost to the USSR in 1944
   Petsamo – was lost to the USSR in 1944 Petsamo
Pyhäjärvi Vpl – was lost to the USSR in 1944
Pälkjärvi – was partially lost to the USSR in 1944
   Räisälä – was lost to the USSR in 1944
Rautu – was lost to the USSR in 1944
Ruskeala – was lost to the USSR
Sakkola – was lost to the USSR in 1944
   Salla – was partially lost to the USSR in 1940
Salmi – was lost to the USSR in 1944
Seiskari (Seitskär) – was lost to the USSR in 1944
Simpele – was partially lost to the USSR in 1944,
Soanlahti – was lost to the USSR in 1944
Sortavala (Sordavala) – was lost to the USSR in 1944
Suistamo – was lost to the USSR in 1944

MUNICIPALITIES THAT WERE EXTORTED BY USSR BETWEEN 1940-1945

Suojärvi – was lost to the USSR in 1944
Suursaari – was lost to the USSR in 1944
  Terijoki – was lost to the USSR in 1944
Tytärsaari – was lost to the USSR in 1944
Uusikirkko (Nykyrka)– was lost to the USSR in 1944
  Vahviala – was partially lost to the USSR in 1944,
Valkjärvi – was lost to the USSR in 1944
Viipuri (Swedish: Viborg) – was lost to the USSR in 1944
Vuoksela – was lost to the USSR in 1944
Vuoksenranta – was lost to the USSR in 1944
  Äyräpää – was lost to the USSR in 1944
  Source: Wikipedia.   List of former municipalities of Finland

CHAPTER 33

Petsamo Municipality A Vital Part of Finland

(Karhumäki, 1930)

The Petsamo area, which belonged to the Finnish state between 1921 and 1944, from Korvatunturi (Ear tundra) to the northern tip of the Port of Petsamo Fisherman's Island. It was the result of the last joint area of Russia and Norway as their occupation of the land crossed between 1826 and 1849. As an indigenous population, the area was inhabited by the Skolt Sámi, who practiced a semi-nomadic lifestyle in the areas of their three villages. There was a Russian influence Orthodox monastery, which had been in Petsamo since the 1550s, and was rebuilt in the late 19th century.

The connection of the Port of Petsamo to independent Nation Finland was agreed in Tartu Peace agreement in 1920. The historical background of the Petsamo question was the traditional fishing rights of Finnish Lapland residents on the shores of the Arctic Ocean, Finnish migration to the region in the late 19th century, and the Imperial power politics of the First World War and Finnish plans to build a road from Ivalo to Petsamo.

Petsamo formed its own county in 1921. After that, Petsamo was a municipality and district in the province of Oulu and since 1938 in the province of Lapland. In 1936–1944, in addition to Petsamo, there were also Inari and Utsjoki. From 1922, Petsamo's main government official was the crown of the district. He also served as a signatory until 1936 to assist the nominee with the help of the Petsamo Border Guard (since 1926, the Border Guard of Lapland), which for a long time had customs, post, and other duties. The Customs Chamber and Reserve were established in 1934.

The most important tasks of the Municipality of Petsamo were the care of the poor, the welfare of unemployed, and the health care. Regional society public schools, on the other hand, were administered by the state. The state also owned half of Oy Petsamo Ab, which was founded in 1921 to organize Petsamo fishing and retail. The company's operations were short and replaced by local communities established by the end of the decade, the primary industry of Petsamo the Fishing industry and the Petsamo Cooperative Society.

In the 1930s, the mining industry grew to become the most important livelihood of Petsamo. An English-Canadian company designed a nickel mine in Kolosjoki, but World War II interrupted the project. After the Winter War, the Finnish subsidiary Petsamon

Nikkeli Oy concluded an ore supply agreement with the Germans. Production began at the beginning of 1943.

Before the Winter War, The State Police arrested dozens of Thomamians suspected of espionage for the Soviet Union. The series of events with interrogations, treason, and deaths are known as Petsamo's great espionage, where many questions are still waiting to be answered.

At the very beginning of the aggressive war against peace, the Soviet Union military invaded the municipality of Petsamo and drove the Finns south. There were various military activities along the Arctic Ocean. Under the Soviet war against peace November 1939, the Petsamo population was evacuated West to Norway, and South West to Inari and Tervola, many escaped during the Soviet invasion into chaos, and others were killed or captured as prisoners of war.

In the Interim Peace Agreement, Finland was able to hold together the entire Petsamo municipality. Reconstruction began, and most of the evacuees returned. During the mid-term peace, the Port of Liinahamar served as an important maintenance route for Finland and Sweden and a lively transit point.

At the beginning of the Continuation War, the German Mountain Corps of Norway (36 Corps) was positioned in the Petsamo Municipality. Their objectives were to push back the Soviet positions to the Port of Murmansk and to stop the Allied forces material support supply line transportation by the Murmansk railway from Murmansk to Petersberg. The civilian administration of Petsamo remained in the hands of the Finnish government.

MORE ON THE 1941 GERMAN OPERATION SILVER FOX

In early September 1944, after retaking the lost territory in 1941 to Stalin's extortion demands, with the help of the Allied forces the Soviets returned with a vengeance, and then Finland had no other reasonable choice than to sign a ceasefire with the Soviet

Union dictators demand more territory from Independent Finland. Petsamo had to be evacuated from the Finnish nationals, and the territory ceded to the Soviet demands.

In October, the Soviet troops seized the area. Mostly the Sámi were transferred to the municipality of Kalajoki and were resettled in Tervola in the following years under the Land Purchase Act. The land acquisition was not applied to the Sámi, who left Petsamo, not only the countries and the fishing grounds, but also the reindeer herd. They first settled in Nellim and at the end of the decade, following the settlement plan of the Agricultural Society of Lapland, also in Näätämö. It was only in 1955 that the Skolt Sámi law resolved the land ownership issue.

GERMAN ROLE IN LAPLAND 1941-1945

The German role in Lapland is often misinterpreted generally by too many people, that have not understood the larger world view of the Finland 500 year history. The conflict with the Nordic region and Russia, and the Bolsheviks movement that led to establishing the pseudo-socialism under the pretense of the Soviet Union.

German troops in Lapland were brothers in arms to the Finland State. They served Finland best interest in keeping back the Bolsheviks during 1917-18 Russian revolution that attempted to continue the same spirit of the Bolsheviks into people of Finland territory. With the help of the German military, the Bolsheviks were stopped and driven back to Russia. The Bolsheviks morally were way out of line, they reveled in lawlessness and anarchy against all established rational, the civil rule of law.

The second reason why the people of Finland were grateful for the German support and empathy for people of Finland was the German officers military training schools. Finland had a back of the Nordic woods culture, with very little creative education and training compared to central Europe and America. Finland was a rural environment, peace-loving people that lived close to the land. They had no interest to be consumed by the Imperial mega maniacs, such as the Swedish imperialist glutton or the Russian imperialist wild bear. Early 1914 university students from Finland went to Germany for the military officer training. Finland was under Russian rule until 1917. All military officer training by the independent-minded nationalistic Finns was done secretly in Germany.

The people of Finland over the 600 years have often found themselves between a rock and a hard place. The imperialist power lust covets to exploit small soft targets, that is how they grow, by eating up the indigenous people's territory, and any weak, mindless divided States. Imperialist do not grow by creative, intelligent, altruistic means, they grow themselves bigger by stupid exploitation of peace-loving humanity. This is another reason why small States need to be so much more in tune with the creator of life, they need to petition the Creator of Life to destroy the aggressors that make war against peace, such as the Soviet failed state did during 1922-1991. The Soviet era leaders were dead wrong morally.

The poor and the indigenous people do have an advantage of God. If they stay in tune with God. In the Bible, we can read the facts of life. Stay in tune with the Creator of Life, and the benefit is a spiritual life lived in the will of God.

Some people in Finland and Lapland will criticize the German military role along the East border of Lapland during 1941-1945, for one specific episode. That episode is called the scorched earth policy. The German military indeed used the scorched earth policy when they were hounded out of Lapland by the political backflip Finn leaders, back to German y in 1945.

THERE IS A BACKGROUND TO THAT SCORCHED EARTH POLICY.

"The Moscow Armistice demanded Finland break diplomatic ties with Germany and expel or disarm any German soldiers remaining in Finland after 15 September 1944. "

"Although Finns and Germans had been fighting the Soviet Union (USSR) together since 1941 during the Continuation War, the Soviet Vyborg–Petrozavodsk Offensive in the summer of 1944 forced Finnish leadership to negotiate a separate peace agreement. The Moscow Armistice demanded Finland break diplomatic ties with Germany and expel or disarm any German soldiers remaining in Finland after 15 September 1944."

"The Finnish Army was required by the USSR to demobilize while at the same time pursuing German troops out of Finnish soil. After a series of minor battles, the war came to an effective end in November 1944 when German troops had reached Norway or its vicinity and took fortified positions. The last German soldiers left Finland on 27 April 1945, and the end of World War II in Europe came soon after."

https://en.wikipedia.org/wiki/Lapland_War

The narrative of many people goes something like this, the German soldiers burn down the wooden structures as they left Lapland. Therefore the Germans were vandals, pyre maniacs and arsons. The above logic presumes that the Germans came to Lapland for a holiday. They stayed for 3 years and then got bored and started burning the building down. That kind of interpretation of the crises events mainly causes by external forces, is oversimplified and naive. There is another way to look at the past history, from the German military forces point of view. What were they doing in Lapland between 1941 and 1945? It is also important to consider how their 3-year presence was considered by the Finnish people living in Finland? The German military was warmly welcomed after the cold 1939 Winter War by most people for a very good reason. The Soviet Union leader was a ruthless dictator that could not be trusted. War against peace in 1939 Finland lost too many people lives during the unprovoked war against peace by the Soviet Union military machine.

WAR AGAINST PEACE CASUALTIES:

- 25,904 dead or missing
- 43,557 wounded
- 800–1,100 captured
- 20–30 tanks
- 62 aircraft

TOTAL; 70,000 CASUALTIES.

Over 26,000 died directly from the war against peace instigated by the Soviet leader Joseph Stalin and the Nazi regime leader Adolf Hitler.

The only reason why Stalin and his generals planned the invasion of Finland was because they had similar plans for Poland, Latvia, Estonia, and Czechoslovakia. The Soviet was moving west towards Europe. And they exploited everything beneficial to their communist mega mania utopia. The German military support for the independence of Finland was a lifeline that the Finnish people wanted. The anarchy of the Bolsheviks was abhorrent to the peace-loving society of Finland. Christian values were well established in the civil society of Finland, similarly as the other Nordic countries Sweden and Norway.

So, what was the reason that the German military applied the scorched earth policy on the territory Finland Lapland?

The answer to that question is in the 3 ½ years that the German Mountain Corps commitment, goodwill, and sacrifices that they made during that time along the eastern border of Soviet Union in Lapland.

So, what, when, and who for was the German Mountain Corps commitment and sacrifice in Lapland?

HERE IS A BASIC PURPOSE LIST:

They came to push back the Soviet aggression over independent Finland.
They fought against the Soviet Union from 1941 to 1945.
They provided Finland with critical material support and military assistance.
They lost many lives in Finland territory Lapland.

GERMAN CASUALTIES:

- 23,200 dead or missing
- 60,400 wounded

TOTAL: 84,000.

The German soldiers fighting on Finland territory would have automatically understood that the Finns were the beneficiaries of the German military campaign on Lapland territory against the Soviet Union aggression.

The German military and the Finnish army were brothers in arms.

They had a common enemy. They were the lawless anarchists, the Bolsheviks that murdered the Russian Tsar family, and were hell-bent deterministic on spreading their communist utopia Westwards.

The German soldiers and officers were deeply offended by the Finnish government decided to turn their back on the continuation war brother in arms. Understandably, the German soldiers were offended by such backflip by the Finnish people.

To burn down the wooden structures of Lapland was most likely the least offensive way to get rid of the feelings of hate that the German officers and soldiers had towards the Finns. From the

German perspective, the Finns had betrayed the German military by their backflip.

Could some Finns be so naive as to think that the German military soldiers somehow owned the Finnish people of Lapland favor, by coming to their aid, against the Soviet aggression?

Do the Finns really think that during a World War 2 conflict the Finnish Government could orchestrate the situation along the eastern border with kit gloves on, and behave as a landlord to a tenant during peacetime? To say, yes yes yes, do come, and fight like hell against the Soviets. And when the German military and nation wide is collapsing, at the most vulnerable state, then the Finnish leadership says, get lost, we don't need you anymore? And by the way, do not damage anything as you find your way back to Germany?

The German military did sacrifice 23,200 soldiers lives, and 60,400 were wounded for the sake of pushing back the Soviets threat along the eastern border, more or less.

It contains double standards of the Finnish people to think that the German behaved crudely by burning down the wooden structures. When the Finnish soldiers used the same tactic when they were ordered by their officers to burn down all the wooden structures when they were running out of the Karelian region in 1939 and 1944. Nobody has complained about the Finnish army burning down the Finnish Karelian property during the retreat from the Soviet invasion. The purpose of burning down the wooden building during the withdraw of troops is to make the building useless for the enemy. That may not make much sense during the summer season, but during the extreme winter cold, -15C, or even -30C. Wooden structures with fireplaces are a valuable asset for survival after sustained military contract for recovery of the troops to fight on the next day. Troops to get frostbite on their limbs is a serious hindrance and set back to strategic tactics.

So, what is their point in criticizing the German troops in Lapland? That point is purely from a civilian convenience point of view. Sure, it would have been better for many families if their homes were left standing. But the reality of brutality during a war, the damage of some description is unavoidable. War is often like a brutal thrust into the face of the innocence civilians. By the power-hungry imperial dictator's mad dreams, disguised as peacetime politics. There are always deep undercurrents in politics that are moving hard and fast.

Over 400,000 people were evacuated from the Karelian region after the Soviet communism utopia invasion. 40,000 people were evacuated from the Lapland and North Karelia regions. Joseph Stalin moved Finland's independent border Westwards in 1940, and 1944. A total loss of 10% to the Finland land area. 440,000 people lost their family homes, history, and property. Such is the effect of the imperial dictator's mad dreams for more control, power, money, and influence.

The scorched earth policy of the German military at a sensitive time as the backflip was in 1945, was a small price compared to the German military soldiers sacrifice on the East border of Lapland during 1941-1945.

GERMAN CASUALTIES:

- 23,200 dead or missing
- 60,400 wounded

TOTAL: 84,000

Trees continue to grow, trees are milled into timber, timber is used for building structures, and the buildings were rebuilt after World War 2 was over. There were many other areas of damage, the major structure also to the roads and bridges. Some 200,000 of the German 20th Mountain Army did withdraw fro Lapland Finland.

What was in waiting for them in Germany? Not a positive outlook on the future for them, a lot of bad news from their homeland.

GERMAN FORCES IN LAPLAND

"The 20th Mountain Army had been fighting the Soviet Karelian Front since Operation Barbarossa along the 700 km (430 mi) stretch from Oulu River to the Arctic Ocean. It now comprised 214,000 soldiers, a considerable amount of them under SS formations, led by Generaloberst Rendulic. The number of active troops decreased quickly as they withdrew to Norway. The army had 32,000 horses and mules and 17,500–26,000 motorized vehicles as well as a total of 180,000 t (200,000 short tons) in rations, ammunition, and fuel to last for six months."

THE ARMY WAS POSITIONED AS FOLLOWS:

XIX Mountain Corps (German: XIX Gebirgskorps) in the far-northern Petsamo area beside the Arctic Ocean.

XXXVI Mountain Corps in the area of Salla and Alakurtti, eastern Lapland.

XVIII Mountain Corps was in charge of the southern flank at Kestenga and Uhtua.

"The 20th Mountain Army successfully withdrew most of its over 200,000 men as well as supplies and equipment from Lapland to continue defending occupied Finnmark from the USSR. According to American historian Earl F. Ziemke, "it had no parallel" as an evacuation across the Arctic in winter. The casualties of the conflict were relatively limited: 774 killed, 262 missing and around 2,904 wounded Finns. Germany experienced around 1,000 deaths and 2,000 wounded. 1,300 German soldiers became prisoners of war and were handed over to the USSR according to the terms of the armistice. The German delaying operations left Lapland devastated. In addition to 3,100 buildings demolished elsewhere in Finland, estimates of destroyed infrastructure in Lapland are as follows:"

- 14,900 buildings representing around 40–46 percent of Lapland's property;
- 470 km (290 mi) of the railroad;
- 9,500 km (5,900 mi) of road;
- 675 bridges;
- 2,800 road storm drains;
- 3,700 km (2,300 mi) of phone and telegram lines.

"The reconstruction of Lapland lasted till the early 1950s, although the railroad network was not functional until 1957.[67] In addition to the demolished infrastructure, the Wehrmacht extensively laid mines and explosives in the area. By 1973, over 800,000 cartridges, 70,000 mines, and 400,000 other explosives had been demined in Lapland, a total of 1,142,000 unit devices".

So what were the losses for the Soviet during the 1941-1944 along the Lapland border? Not sure, considering the continuation war border stretched over 1100km's. The entire casualties estimate of the Soviet along the 1100 km border is the follows.

SOVIET CASUALTIES:

250,000–305,000 dead or missing
   575,000 medical casualties (including 385,000 wounded and 190,000 sick)
   64,000 captured

TOTAL CASUALTIES: 890,000–944,000

The casualties of wars are mostly innocent civilians that were inscribed to the military war machine. They would not by choice do such immoral act as start a war on personal whims. The mega maniac dictators do have a habit of starting wars on their personal power hungry egomaniac. Whether it is Joseph Stalin or Adolf Hitler, they went on an immoral limb that folded under them to oblivion.

Power hungry nationalistic politicians are the worst culprits for human destruction. The worst mass destruction of humanity has always been caused by some crazy nationalistic leader that used the State military power to leverage and extend their personal status, to become a big man in the eyes of other humans. It is much better to be great in the mind of humans, and most importantly to be great in the mind fo the Creator of Life through obedience to the will of the Creator of life on earth through peaceful means.

BIBLE SCRIPTURE:

Complete Jewish Bible (CJB)
  Book I: Psalms 1–41
  "How blessed are those who reject the advice of the wicked, don't stand on the way of sinners or sit where scoffers sit! Their delight is in Adonai's Torah; on his Torah, they meditate day and night. They are like trees planted by streams — they bear their fruit in season, their leaves never wither, everything they do succeeds. "

CHAPTER 34

Bothnia Ice Lake

(Leinonen, 2011)

"During the Stone Age when humans ventured along the shores of the Bothnia Ice Lake, according to the scientific dating method it was around 10,000 BC, it was most likely during the spring or a summer season. Traveling on the water by boat or canoes for easy travel and transportation of the animal furs and the meat they caught. Like many other human endeavors searching for food and clothing materials: they went out hunting, fishing, foraging, and trapping into the Nordic/Arctic region.

How far and how long time their endeavors lasted per trip is unknown, within a small community, there was no need to be gone for a long time. Food supplies and clothing materials for a small group could have been serviced within a comfortable radius. During the Bronze Age (4000-3000 BC), the world population rose from 7Million to 14Million and grew further to 30 Million during the 3000 to 2000 BC.

On the center stages of the world civilization at the time, e.g., Iraq and Egypt, the rise of intellectual writings/knowledge and physical architecture often was a source of friction on a political stage. Many rising rulers sought after for more resources and power. Along came leaders with mega enthusiasm and ambitious plans for bigger and better architecture, imperialism, organized absolutism, an internal revolution. The 120+ discovered pyramids, built in Egypt between 3000 BC 1000BC were mostly built and used as tombs for the nation's Pharaohs and their consorts during the Old and Middle Kingdom periods. Grand plans require enormous effort and sacrifice from the labor sources that produce them.

The nomadic tribes that ventured into the Nordic region at the same time were free and naturally interacting with the surrounding environment. It required a strong spirit, alert and observing the surrounding environment, efficient hunters, and many food preparation skills. They needed to find food to eat, cook food, and store the food items, both cooked and raw ingredients. They much depended on their fishing skills, hunting skills, spirit, physical strength, nutrition, health, and stamina. Their purpose in life was not to build pyramids in the heat of Egypt, but to travel and to boat along the unknown wilderness of their Nordic region. At the same time as the Biblical Abraham was a lad, and learning to run like boys do, the young children running around also along the banks of the Ice Lake.

The Baltic Finns had a call of the wild in their blood, and the excitement of adventure, to go out and explore the wild North of the Nordic region. Many real dangers were lurking in the dark of the backwoods of the Nordic region. The flat terrain of the lake country with peat covered swamps and bogs, surrounded by thick forest cover and thickets, spring and autumn fogs, winter darkness, possible early snow falls and the bitter cold, it all increased to the risk of getting lost. The elements of nature and also natural predators; roaming brown bears, howling wolves, and the charge pointed antlers of a wounded deer, was a real life-threatening challenge during the Stone Age, when they faced the wild predators with the burnt sharp tips of the wooden spears, hefty clubs, bone edge knives, and stone-tipped arrows.

Their natural instincts came to the forefront, to search and to hunt, to fish, and to find a suitable protective location where they and family, tribe, and community would survive in relatively comfortable conditions. Their journey along the meandering shorelines of endless lakes, peat bogs, marshes, and swamps. There was a time for chopping down trees, building houses, building rafts/boats, and a time for planting seeds and a season for picking berries and mushrooms. Also, time for catching fish, hunting and trapping fur animals, and exploring the unknown, not knowing what lay on the other side, and making sure to survive at times of danger and through the extreme cold of the sub-Arctic winter. The many islands on the waters would have been an attractive place to go to during the spring and summer season. Freshwater supply, fishing and migrating birds with their supply of eggs, swans, geese, ducks and many other water birds to loot and hunt. Nomadic tribes moving on as nature provided and supply needs to be demanded."

(Leinonen, Inkeri Land, 2010)

CHAPTER 35

Finland Borders of Independence

Quote: The Nemesis Book 2018

IMPERIAL GRAND DUCHIES OF FINLAND

CHAPTER 3

An extended Southwest Finland was made a titular grand duchy in 1581, when King John III of Sweden, who as a prince had been the Duke of Finland (1556– 1561/ 63), extended the list of subsidiary titles of the Kings of Sweden considerably. The new title Grand Duke of Finland did not result in any Finnish autonomy, as Finland was an integrated part of the Kingdom of Sweden with full parliamentary representation for its counties. FINNISH WAR 1808 The Finnish War fought between the Kingdom of Sweden and the Russian Empire from February 1808 to September 1809. As a result of the war, (as the current Finland territory), regarded as the eastern third of Sweden in 1809, established as the autonomous Grand Duchy of Finland within the Russian Empire. The Russian military conquest took the land off Sweden control and claimed to have the right to control and dominate the land and the people of Finland. (Sweden, Finnish War, 2018)

FINLAND BORDERS OF INDEPENDENCE

EMPEROR NICHOLAS II Nicholas II (1868 – 17 July 1918) was the last Emperor of Russia, ruling from 1 November 1894 until his forced abdication on 15 March 1917. The people of the Russian revolution rejected their Monarchy system.

MUTINY AFTER THE 1917 REVOLUTION

After the Russian revolution, the monarchist was hounded, including the organized military, Royal Russian navy ships were in the port of Finland for the winter, Russian sailors mutinied over 100 Russian Navy officers stationed in Helsinki 1917. The Russian revolution fever spiked with the spirit of anarchy. The revolution that started in Russia raged out of control with drunken violence. The spirit of anarchy was contagious, and the fever caught people everywhere, wherever the Royal Russian military was present. It ruthlessly split and polarized the two sides by the lawlessness and bloody violence. There was a protest as early as 1914 as Russian was starting to engage in World War 1. Russia declared war on Turkey on the 2 Nov 1914.

In Finland, by 1917, there was severe poverty, hunger, also the Bolsheviks rebellion, anarchy, and mutiny. There were about 100,000 Russian military troops in Finland, for World War One strategic reasons. Russian leaders feared the Germans, believing that the Germans would go north and land in Finland, and push back the Russian to where they had come from, East side of Lake Ladoga, and east of Neva River.

TSAR RUSSIA TERRORISM

Alexander II Born 29 April 1818 – 13 March 1881) was the Emperor of Russia from 2 March 1855 until his assassination on 13 March 1881. Alexander's most significant reform as emperor was the emancipation of Russia's serfs in 1861, for which he is known as Alexander the Liberator. In foreign policy, Alexander sold Alaska to the United States in 1867, fearing the remote colony would fall into British hands if there were another war.

FINLAND BORDERS AFTER DECLARATION OF INDEPENDENCE

When Finland declared independence on 6 December 1917, the borders remained as they were during the Russian autonomy period. Very shortly after gaining independence the people of Finland wanted more confirmation and freedom of expression for their nation Independence, they wanted to take back what had been taken off them by forceful military subjugation. The people of Finland had been under foreign rule for over 500 years. 400 years under the Kings of Sweden and 100 years under Russian rule.They wanted to share their independence with their kindred spirits in the North Karelian region because the people of Karelian spoke mostly the Finnish language. There were historical ties between the people of Finland and the people of Ingria and Karelia.

2000 years ago, there was no Russia or even Moscow. At the same time, people were living along the Gulf of Finland, speaking the Finnish dialect. The historical facts are that the Finnish speaking people, the Karelian and the Ingrians and some Sami people pioneered the region between around the Gulf of Finland and Lake Ladoga. All the way from the Gulf of Finland to the White Sea and the Arctic Sea. The armed conflicts between the Nordic people and the South/East came from the military invasion of the Slavic Russians. Russian ambitions to conquer the land from the indigenous people has been ongoing for a long time. From the White Sea regions to the Pacific Ocean. From the Black Sea to Siberia.

https://en.wikipedia.org/wiki/Lists_of_indigenous_peoples_of_Russia

Quote:

"There are over 100 identified ethnic groups in Russia. Of them,

41 are legally recognized as "Indigenous small-numbered peoples of the North, Siberia, and the Far East."

"These are the only groups that are legally protected as Indigenous peoples; to meet the requirements, a group of peoples must number fewer than 50,000 people, maintain a traditional way of life, inhabit certain remote areas of the country, and identify as a distinct ethnic group."

"Some groups are disqualified because of their larger populations, such as the Sakha (Yakuts), Buryat, Komi, and Khakas; others are currently striving to get recognition."

"Additionally, there are 24 larger ethnic groups that are identified as national identities or titular nations. These groups inhabit independent states or autonomous areas in Russia, but do not have specific protections under the law."

Source: https://www.culturalsurvival.org/news/who-are-indigenous-peoples-russia

VIENNA EXCURSION

During the years 1918 and 1921–22 Finland voluntary forces tried to unite more of the Karelian people regions to Independent Finland. The so-called Vienna excursion was conducted under Martti Wallenius in 1918, to a region, South of the White Sea called Aunus. In addition, local people from these regions were openly wanting independence from Russia, E.g. the Ingrian' uprising against the Bolsheviks took place in 1919 and the corresponding company of the Eastern Karelians in 1921.

The Ingria peoples also extended to Estonia, which, with the help of the Finns, became largely independent of the Bolshevik power on 24 February 1918. The day will be held on Estonia's first Independence Day. Juho Paasikivi (1870-56) led the Finnish delegation in the peace negotiations in Tartu 1920-21.

The changes made to the Finnish borders by the Finland Independence were small overall. However, for two short periods, the East Karelia merged with Finland: Repola and Porajärvi. In a difficult economic situation and a threat of hunger, two community citizens meetings were held in Repola in August 1918 under the persuasion of the Independent Finns, they decided to join the Independent Finland, and separate from the Soviet Union.

The East Karelian editorial office, established by the Finnish government, then began to deal with the civilian administration of the area, which was also joined by Porajärvi in the summer of 1919. The residents of the area were very pleased with the administration of the Finns, who offered both job opportunities and protection from the internal unrest caused by the Bolsheviks Revolution in Russia.

The border between Russia and Finland became a divisive issue that both sides disagreed upon it. The Bolsheviks wanted to change the Finland border from the previously agreement that the Russian Tsar had agreed to be the Autonomous Finland border. The Bolsheviks had other ideas, they wanted Finland to be further away from Petersburg. In 1920 Tartu Peace Treaty agreed that the border was at Rajajoki. A river that runs Westwards to the Gulf of Finland. Stalin wanted the Finland border to be moved further north, away from Petersburg.

BORDER RIVER MARKER

Raja-joki literally translated as a "Border-River" was exactly that for over 5 centuries. The border river has served as a border between many regions. The river was traditionally considered to have divided Karelia and Ingria. The first use of the River as a border came into effect in 1323 in the Nut Island (Pähkinä saari) peace agreement between Novgorod state and Sweden. In the peace of Stolbova in 1617, the Swedish territory expanded east, but the boundary of the later Finnish region remained on the river. The Border River has been a defining border marker between the West and the East for over 600 years.

The Nordic countries are proud stewards of their land regions. They did not want foreigners invading their land and spoiling the many centuries and generations of hard manual labour that it had taken them to establish the Nordic culture to a well-functioning society.

From early 1900 the Russian Revolution was started by the Bolsheviks, they perpetuated the rebellion, the anarchy to overthrow the Russian Tsar. The Bolsheviks can be compared to rebellious lunatics at asylum that had taken over the asylum management. The reports from 1922 to 1953 prove that Russia leadership went from bad to worse morally and became a totalitarian State that was ruled by the military power.

Soviet State Atheism was their moral code, the human suffering in Russia was horrendous. Political prisoners, persecution of religion, forced labor camps, gulags, and the secret police that used terrorism as a weapon against their own people. Soviet Union leaders moral code was parallel to the hard-core Nazi German officers. Their deeds were also parallel evil deeds. Evil was hidden in the dark, people were not allowed to speak the truth. The truth was a threat, truth shared a ray of sunlight, that the politically ambitious Soviet leaders could not tolerate.

Read more. https://en.wikipedia.org/wiki/Political_repression_in_the_Soviet_Union

CHAPTER 36

The Arctic Sea Route to the Arctic Sea Port of Liinahamar

(Commons, Wikipedia, 2019)

At the beginning of the 1930s, the port of Liinahamar comprised only one quay and a cargo container. The Hamburg-Petsamo line cargo ship arrived once a month. In 1934, a fish processing plant and a factory pier were built, as well as office and magazine buildings. After the Winter War, port facilities were upgraded under the leadership of an engineering team deployed: six docks, 10 oil tanks, a 25-tonne crane and 10,000 m2 of warehouses. The port's daily discharge capacity was then 2,000 tonnes. The engineering team was led by architect Lars Sonck.

WORKERS AND HOUSING CONDITIONS

The large-scale transport operation also required extensive new construction. Thousands of men were assigned to quickly build barracks that would accommodate 100 men per barrack. Service facilities, canteens, and lodgings were built at the Petsamo and along the Arctic Sea Road. For example, the stevedores of the Port of Liinahamar lived in a dozen or so hundred men per barrack accommodation for months, without any washing facilities other than the Arctic Sea.

At the Liinahamari area, a shanty town arose, crime, prostitution and abundant alcohol consumption spread rapidly. In the autumn of 1940-41, the local shantytown was hit by a scarlet epidemic, which was fatal for many children.

The bulk of the transport drivers were self-employed in the transportation of the shipping supplies from the Arctic Sea ports were entrepreneurs of one vehicle who were employed to transport supplies.

They were supervised by the Nordic Transport, but the drivers choose their own schedule. An important incentive was the continuous contract-based service, secure spare parts back up service, and the use of gasoline instead of wood gas that so widely used in Europe in transport vehicles because of the rationing of fossil fuels. World War 2 that was deliberately started in 1939 by Nazi Germany and the Soviet leadership. The Molotov & Ribbentrop Pact was instrumental in the war against peace, these two aggressors ruthlessly invaded Poland, Estonia, Latvia, and Finland during 1939 and 1940.

The Arctic Sea route was a lifeline after only 3 months of the Winter War. It provided paid work for the 10,000 people that were engaged in the project. The most common work in 1940 was mostly related to the World War that was heating up. Work at the time was carpentry, building houses and urgent accommodation for the 400,000 Karelian people that had to evacuate from the Karelian Isthmus due to the 1939 war against peace, and the Finland territory extortion by the Soviet leadership in 1940. 400,000 Karelians had to leave their permanent family homes and relocate in the West.

ARCTIC SEA SHIPPING ROUTE

A total of 1,600 trucks were reserved for land transport, and 3,000 drivers and auxiliaries were hired, and 2,000 were used for loading. There were 1,400 permanent staff and 4,000 part-time road maintenance workers on the road, a thousand men for maintenance of the equipment.

Sweden suffered from the same Baltic Sea blockade as Finland, and some of the port's capacity was allocated for Sweden used. The Swedish organized their own freight transportation with 400 Swedish lorries with Swedish drivers from the city of Rovaniemi to Sweden city of Haaparanta. The cargo was picked up from Haparanda by rail and taken further into Sweden. It is reported that at this tumultuous time in East Europe history the Swedes were also acquiring airplanes by the Arctic Sea route from the USA to Sweden.

One round trip from Rovaniemi to the Port of Liinahamar meant 1 100 kilometers round trip, driving along the gravel surface of the Arctic Sea Road. Some of the transport were trucks with a load of 8 tons, some were smaller 4-ton trucks. Instead of wood gas-powered cars, high-altitude mountainous areas had to use petrol-powered combustion motor engines.

Pillaging and brazen stealing occurred on the Arctic Sea road on slow moving vehicles. The thieves hid and waited in ditches along the banks of the road where the road was going slow uphills. As the trucks climbed slowly upwards the sloping fells, the thieves climbed on the truck tray and unloaded some cargo while the vehicle was moving. The valuable cargo from a slow-moving truck going uphill was an easy target for the unwary drivers. After the initial instances the drivers wised up, the transport was then arranged into the guarded column, and the road was divided into checkpoints every 50 kilometers. The Swedish drivers had also armed themselves.

The biggest difficulties to overcome along the Arctic Sea route was related to weather and seasonal changing road conditions that were often extremely poor during the extreme frost, deep snow or the first thaw, after a winter long deep road surface frost, that kept the ground solid where there was moisture. Equally difficult was the maintaining and managing road safety rules for all.

Before the start of the transport, the road load was estimated to be 400 tons of goods per day, but at worst – or at best – the road transported over 5,000 tons of goods in one day. Thus, it was clear that at times the road softened and collapsed under the trucks. However, road durability was improved during traffic. In addition to heavy loads and hard driving, the durability of the cars was tested in January 1941 by a heavy frost, which intensified between 16 and 30 days between Rovaniemi and Sodan-kylä (war-town) to less than −30 and four days below −40 degrees.

The challenge to vehicle heating and defrosting devices of such cars were completely inadequate for such conditions; there were also no valid anti-freeze agents for the engine cooling system available. The most challenging call on road traffic skills was a long sloping downhill on the north slopes of the Saariselkä fells. It was later left out of the main route. The steep uphill was stressful for drivers going either direction. The drivers ironically named the precarious steep hill, the magnet hill, because of the force of gravity, to quickly get the vehicles unstuck off the surface of the road.

Due to the narrow Arctic Sea road, and the ice-covered stretches along the fells, and the lively traffic, there were many daily hitches on the route. Truck drivers even took conscious risks, from over fatigue, over heavy loads, hurried schedule, and the extra money perk incentives to speed up transportation did not have a positive effect on improving the overall road safety.

Northern Traffic company partly acquired its driver from conscripts who had no previous experience of driving a transportation truck. The Swedish car drivers' habit of driving on the left brought their own added trepidation. At worst, derailments occurred every few hundred meters. According to calculations by Eric Björklund, a Swedish researcher at Petsamo, by the beginning of 1941, 54 drivers had been killed in accidents in the Arctic Sea road; According to this, on the 531-kilometer long road, on average 2 people died due to road accidents per every week for a full year.

The total import tonnage for 12 months was 330,000 Tons. And the Export tonnage for the same period was 200,000 Tons. 200 ships were transporting goods to the Arctic Sea port Liinahamar and Petsamo.

The most general good items transported on the Arctic Sea route was 50 % of the total national wheat, 20 % of the nation sugar, 100% of nation coffee, and 76% of the national petroleum fuels. The Arctic Sea route really was a lifeline for the Finland people during the 1940-1941 Baltic Sea blockade.

There were also Consulate observers from England, Germany, and the Soviet Union at the Liinahamar Port checking the import and export of goods during the 12 months.

After the German war operations moved towards East in operation Barbarossa, the blockade of the Baltic Sea was no longer affecting Finland or Sweden. Therefore the Arctic Sea road ceased the transportation of supplies on June 17, 1941.

BRITAIN SHUTS DOWN THE ROUTE

Finland had allowed German military forces to transit through the Gulf of Bothnia through Finland to Petsamo and to Kirkenes in

Norway since September 1940. The traffic had begun to service and transport the German Air Force and had expanded to include military and equipment and weapon shipments of all types of weapons. A more established network of German troops was developing in the northern Finland Lapland. The foreign powers took notice, Britain enquired from Finland several times as for why and how many German troops were in the country. German activity in Lapland increased in spring 1941.

At the beginning of June, the Germans started massive troop movement into north Finland, preparation for the counterattack of the Soviet aggression and territory extortion of 1939-1940. The Soviet aggression in 1939 was a war against peace. There are no justifiable reasons for the Soviet leadership actions in 1939. Their actions inherited condemnation, immoral, illegal actions of a corrupted leadership in a pariah State. Finland government rightfully resisted the most obvious Russian Bolsheviks lawless archaic worldview, that manifested early in 1917. The Russian revolution was orchestrated by the Bolsheviks spirit of anarchy. No rational thinking, moral person would compromise the most fundamental moral values, the basic principles of reason, as they are taught in the Holy Bible.

Proverbs 14:12 Complete Jewish Bible (CJB)

> There can be a way which seems right to a person, but at its end are the ways of death.

Complete Jewish Bible (CJB)

On 14 June 1941, Britain objected to the Arctic Sea road transportation and cut off shipping from Liinahamar. The Allies forces had sea supremacy, on the Arctic Sea, and any unauthorized freighters according to their understanding would probably have been captured or sunk. By the June 1941 the preparations were well under way for the German Operation Barbarossa, there were already 40,000 German soldiers in North Finland. The Continuation War began on 25 June. The continuation war was a justified war for

Finland. It was a rational payback, to the immoral dictator minded leadership of the Soviet Union.

Joseph Stalin was professional criminal, a hardened rogue. It was not possible to reason with him according to moral rational logic. Stalin's thinking mind was seriously corrupted by immorality. His mind was only capable of thinking according to the law of a jungle. His thinking mind had been seared by his own immoral actions. He was not capable of rational moral reasoning. He had entertained evil, and he was seriously corrupted and destroyed by evil.

The conclusion of the organized Arctic Sea route at the Municipality of Petsamo, the traffic has been identified as a unique collaborative effort by the Ministry of Public Affairs, the Ministry of Trade and Industry, the Ministry of Transport and Public Works, and the Ministry of Défense, along with 10,000 citizen actors involved.

This co-operation served as a basis for a centralized transport system during the Continuation War. In this way, Petsamo's traffic contributed significantly to Finland's defence capability. It also showed for the first time in Finnish history that it was possible for lorries to have an important impact on the national economy. Also the connection with Petsamo to the United States, a "free world", also had great spiritual significance on the people of Finland. A year round traffic, which left the Port of Petsamo and arrived at Rovaniemi with about 130 trucks a day, is still a top performance operation in the circumstances of that time.

Source translated from Wikipedia page: https://fi.wikipedia.org/wiki/Liinahamarin_reitti

CHAPTER 37

Opening Up a New Arctic Sea Route

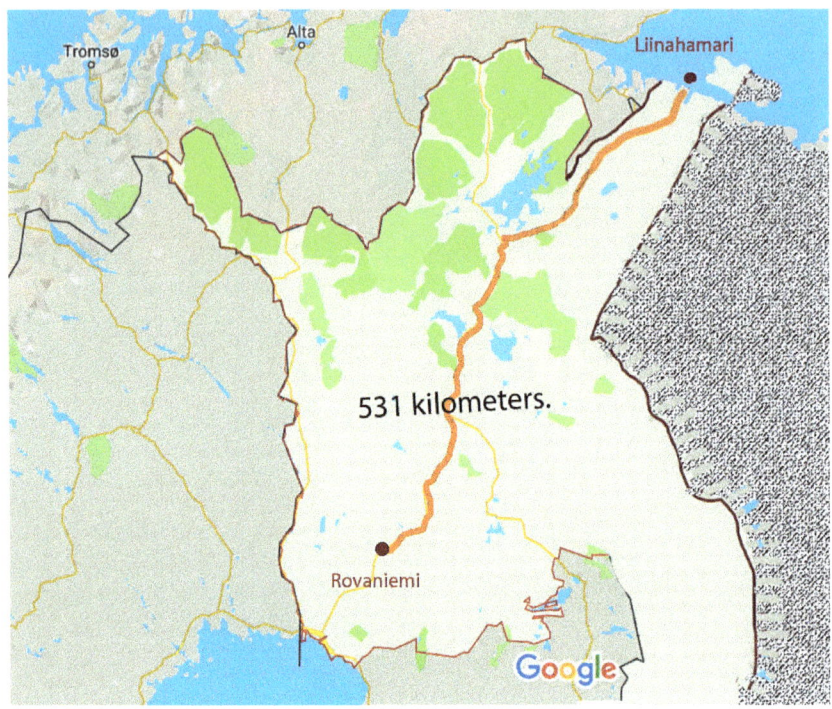

(Google, Maps)

The winding, hilly and the poor unsealed road conditions of the Lapland Arctic wilderness served the Finland nation as lifeline road during the intermediate peacetime between the Soviet war against peace and the continuation war in 1941.

The upgrade of the Arctic road during the Summer month of June 1940, from the city of Rovaniemi to the Arctic Circle Municipality of Petsamo and the Port of Liinahamari, served an urgent role at a vital time for the people of Finland in 1940.

THE GERMAN INVASION OF DENMARK

"The German invasion of Denmark (Operation Weserübung) was the German attack on Denmark on 9 April 1940, during the Second

World War. The attack was a prelude to the main attack against Norway (Weserübung Nord). The term Weserübung means Weser-exercise in English, named after the river Weser in northwestern Germany."

"Denmark's strategic importance for Germany was limited. The invasion's primary purpose was to use Denmark as a staging ground for operations against Norway, to secure supply lines to the forces about to be deployed there. An extensive network of radar systems was built in Denmark to detect English bombers bound for Germany."

https://en.wikipedia.org/wiki/German_invasion_of_Denmark_(1940)

The German invasion of Denmark also closed the Baltic Sea transportation route for Sweden, Finland, and Estonia. At the beginning of the summer of 1940 (June), there was no export shipping of goods coming into Finland or Sweden. Baltic Sea was blocked for transportation at Denmark. The Belts and Sounds going through southwestern Baltic Sea are very narrow, only 5-10 km wide.

(Google, Maps)

The situation in Finland was made worse by the Soviet war against peace from November 1939 to March 1940. The Winter war alone consumed tremendous amounts of general food supplies and the loss for the military defense forces.

The direct casualties of the aggressive war in 1939 against Finland, the Soviet Union leader Joseph Stalin military generals, planning cause the nation of Finland to lose 25,904 soldiers and civilians dead or missing.

Furthermore, 43,557 were wounded directly from the Soviet war against peace. The aggressive winter war of 1939 was deliberate objective in the foreign ministers Molotov & Ribbentrop Pact, between German Adolf Hitler and Soviet Joseph Stalin. There were also prisoners of war, between 800–1100. Material losses caused by the aggressors on Finland were 20–30 armored tanks and 62 aircraft.

The Aggressive Soviet war lasted for 105 days before Finland leadership yielded to the extortion territory demands of Stalin. The territory that the Soviet could not take with their military, then they succeed by the ruthless extortion demands at the peace agreement table in Moscow March 1940. Finland had to cede border areas to the Soviet Union. No supplies were coming through the Baltic Sea in 1940. Another route had to be created for the general supplies to keep importing and also timber export of supplies.

The lifeline for material supplies became the Arctic Sea route from Rovaniemi through the Petsamo Municipality to the Port of Liinahamari. The track had to be widened bridges improved to carry the load of various truckloads of 4-8 tons of supplies per load. The entire distance from Rovaniemi to Liinahamari was about 500 km. The unsealed dirt track needed an upgrade badly that the reindeer herding Sami people had used the route for centuries, seasonal trading of goods, reindeer pulled the sleigh for the mode of transport, between the city of Rovaniemi and the Arctic Sea. Reindeer sleigh works well over a hard packed snow cover, no roads required then.

The road did get prepared by a large team of road builders and laborers, to last the year round trip of supplies carrying trucks that numbered about 2000.

Arctic Sea road from the city of Rovaniemi was 531 kilometers long, all the way to two ports of the Arctic Sea. The Port of Liinahamari and the Port of Petsamo. On this route, trucks handled Finland's foreign trade for more than a year when the Baltic Sea trade route was blocked due to the war. The drivers involved in a huge transport contract tell their stories in the radio program along the Arctic Sea Road.

Finland was in a difficult situation in the spring of 1940. There was a winter war that had been lost to the Soviet Union, and there was a shortage of food from all over the country. The traditional Baltic trade route was closed due to the war that had migrated to Central Europe, and no much-needed supplies were received in Finland.

Fortunately, Finland had access to the Arctic Sea port of Petsamo and Liinahamar in the far north of Lapland. Europe's second deepest port was still open to the Atlantic. The only problem with the Liinahamari Port was that it was located more than 500 kilometers away from the city of Rovaniemi, the nearest railway link.

The Finland government quickly realized the seriousness of the 1939 domino effect events and understood the seriousness of the national situation, and in April 1940 an Advisory Board was established to consider the issue of Arctic Sea route to the port of Petsamo. It was decided to establish a state-owned transport company Oy Pohjolan Liikenne Ab (Northern Transportation), which would take care of the transportation of imports and exports from the Arctic Sea port. Military General Paavo Talvela was the first choice to get the project completed, he was known for his strong grip on a situation, and was placed to lead the company management team.

The radio program "The Arctic Ocean Road" by Olli-Pekka Ihamäki, completed in 1985, tells the story of the furious truck rally of Petsamo amid a mid-1940-41.

In 1920, Petsamo was almost a wilderness area of Finland. On the Rovaniemi side, the road extended to Ivalo, a distanced of 300 km, from there going was much tougher, for the next 330 km distance towards Petsamo.

For many years, the road line had been cleared from virgin forests, over various terrain hazards, rocky outcrops, swamps, peat bogs, sunken mires, and numerous rivers. A road was completed in 1931, but it was very narrow and hilly suitable for family car size transport. It also deteriorated rapidly in a bad condition at the time of the seasonal changes and was awkward to keep open during the wind drove snow blizzards at the slopes of the Lapland fells. For the objective of major transportation exercise the Arctic Sea road required major repairs, as the Finns during the 1939 war against peace withdrawal away from the Soviet aggressive war, the Finnish troops destroyed most of the bridges as they withdrew south.

The problems were many, one of them was the generally poor condition of transportation vehicles, after they were used by the army during the 105 day war. The Northern Traffic company, (Pohjolan Liikenne) started to hire private truck drivers for the Arctic Sea road, but the interest was initially rather slow. The Finnish Northern Transportation company truck fleet was taken into use by the army during the Winter War and the cars were in poor condition. Operators did not want to finally break their ice on the Arctic Ocean. However, traffic started in June 1940 and Finland again had a life hole in the western world.

A WIDE VARIETY OF BENDS ON THE WAY

Before the Winter War, the port of Liinahamari had practically served only fishermen, so much needed construction and renovation work had to be carried out there to start a large freight transportation exercise. The first large cargo ship that arrived at the port was SS Greta, which had transported weapons from Spain, arrived in Liinahamar on April 14, 1940. Finnish soldiers unloaded the cargo and transported it by cars of the armed forces to Rovaniemi, just like all other cargoes in the early stages. The lack of storage facilities in Liinahamar caused major problems and began to be built at a rapid pace. Building, harbor and automobile enthusiasts needed accommodation, and the barracks were built around the daytime of almost one building. Resting places, canteens, and car repair shops were also set up along the route, as there were always 1,400 men on the route, with as many as 4,000 when the conditions got really bad with road surface pits and heavy snowstorms.

After the first ship unloading, Finnish exports started to flow again. Up to 99% of Finland's exports were products of the wood processing industry, but according to Mikko Uola's Petsamo 1939–1944, the wider world also went to the markets. Arabian porcelain products, Karhula glass products, Artek furniture, and Valio cheese. Swedish merchandise also passed through the Arctic Sea port, and also returned with some heavy USA military equipment that was transported on truck platforms to the city of Rovaniemi, and to further Kantalahti railway station.

When the traffic peaked it really was a a sight in the quiet snow covered winter arctic environment. At its peak, there was over 2,000 vehicles operating on the Arctic Sea road. The vehicles drove between Rovaniemi and Liinahamar day and night, and sometimes continues round trip – which at its best lasted for 36 hours round trip, from start to finish. Over tired drivers, hurried by demands, slippery road surfaces, winter darkness, freezing cold, very narrow road, and also the added hazard of the Swedish drivers accustomed to driving on the left-hand traffic caused incidents and near misses. By December 1940, in 6 months over 50 people had already been killed in on the Arctic Sea road traffic.

Source: Translated from Finnish Radio National Audio recording to English text, Mr. Uuno Alaräisänen, and Einari Lehtonen shared their experiences ont eh Arctic Sea road.

CHAPTER 38

German Soldiers Cemetery In the Arctic

(Vuonnala 2017)

Operation Silver Fox: from 29 June to 17 November 1941, was a German–Finnish military operation during World War II. The objective of the offensive was to push back the Soviet defenses along Finland -Soviet border and cut off supply lines and capture the key Soviet Port of Murmansk.

THE OPERATION HAD THREE STAGES:

- Operation Reindeer
- Operation Platinum Fox
- Operation Arctic Fox

In Operation Reindeer German forces advanced from Norway to secure the Finish territory area around Port of Petsamo and its nickel mines. Operation Platinum Fox was an attack from the north by Mountain Corps Norway as XXXVI Mountain Corps and units from the Finnish III Corps, attacked from the south in Operation Arctic Fox to advance and cut off the Murmansk railway.

Operation Arctic Fox was the code name given to a World War II campaign by German and Finnish forces in the Arctic region of Finland, their first objective was to take back the Finnish territory that the Soviets had taken using military force, only 15 months earlier, at the Salla East border of Finland area. Their second objective was to push back the Soviets further back, towards the Murmansk Railway line and the White Sea.

Finland in July 1941. The operation was part of the larger Operation Silver Fox (Silberfuchs; Hopeakettu) which aimed to capture the vital port of Murmansk. Arctic Fox was conducted in parallel to Operation Platinum Fox (Platinfuchs; Platinakettu) in the far north of Lappland. The principal goal of Operation Arctic Fox was to capture the town of Salla and then to advance in the direction of Kandalaksha (Finnish: Kantalahti) to block the railway route to Murmansk.

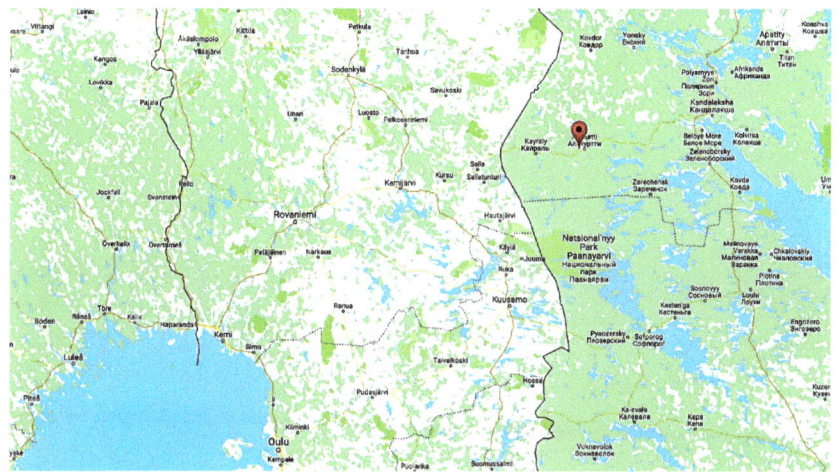

(Google Maps)

GERMAN SOLDIERS CEMETERY IN THE ARCTIC

(Google Maps)

(Vuonnala, 2017).

CHAPTER 39

Being Logical: A Guide to Good Thinking.

In our modern world of digital technology, most people do not understand the history of the last 100 years. They have no knowledge or understanding of the true facts, of why and how the world Wars began in Europe.

There is a lot of biased propaganda loaded material about world war 1, and 2. The Imperialists have created a convenient narrative loop that has been playing over and over from Hollywood for the last 75 years. The Hollywood script on the World Wars, the Allied forces on the moral high ground and the Axis powers on the losing side. The Allied forces formed a Club, for those that joined them privileged and were given favors or let off the guilty and condemned hook.

That was Imperialistic self-centered world view, they set the rules and ruled over others. They made many right decisions when upholding justice for the oppressed victims of Imperial initiated wars. They also made many blunders and completely lost sight of what true justice is and what true justice looks like. It seems that the Imperial powers just cannot think laterally, they are always putting themselves on a pedestal, and expect other smaller nations to be conformed to their Imperialistic Western mindset.

It is common to read the Western Imperial narrative about the World War 2, and how the Axis Powers did a lot of evil, and those were condemned who joined with Germany to fight against the Bolsheviks communist in East Europe. France, England, and the United States just can't get their head around the facts of 1200 years of East Europe history. The Nordic countries knowledge of East Europe history goes much further because that is how long their culture has been impacted by the imperial-minded or despotic minded Russian rulers.

The Nordic people, other than kings of Sweden and their power-hungry imperialism, wanted nothing to do with the self-serving greed of the Imperialist who were always engaged with some power conflict. They were desperately building leverage for their kingdom, to be bigger and stronger than the other kingdom. The power struggles between regional powers started in a big way some 1200 years ago in East Europe. To understand the current day power struggles between the Imperial powers, one needs to go back in time to history. To see what is the entity that their kingdom roots are standing.

Very likely, the power struggles of 1000 years ago are still raging in the high heavens. To understand the last 100-year conflicts, we need to identify the culprits, the aggressors, the lawlessness, and the anarchy spirit that is driving on entities that collide with others forces and cause havoc on humanity.

There are absolutes to be found in the first principles of reason and logic. The greatest human attribute is the intelligent mind capacity to think rationally. Human beings do not need to behave like an archaic wild living beast like cavemen. 2019 is a long shot from the Stone Age 6000 years ago. So why would human continue to use their mind as if they were living in the Stone Ages?

We have much better digital tools off with information that shape the mind to think accurately, rationally, intelligently logically. To help people to navigate through the middle of confusion, indecision, about what is right and what is wrong. Postmodernism and subjective relativism confused minds that says there is no absolute moral wrong or right is a lie. Of course, there is an absolute moral right and moral wrong, the absolute moral wrong is called sin. The temptation of sin is to be avoided, shunned, and rejected from the basis of truth. The first five books of the Bible are also called the Torah in Judaism. Torah is truth according to the Creator of Life, Elohim, Adonai, the First Cause of the Universe. That truth of Torah needs to be studied and understood. Because it is objective truth, it is not subjective truth according to the changes of a human subjective living soul state.

It is not rocket science, but it is scholarly, and it needs a biblical world view. Without a Biblical world view, it is impossible to come to grips with truth and justice. Only with the theological understanding of the Creator of Life, the Creator of humanity, and the First Cause of the universe, can individual humans come to the place of confident trust, in the oracle of God, as it is written in the Holy Bible. Adonai, Elohim. God of Abraham, Isaac, and Jacob.

Once the concept of true justice is based on the Biblical World view, then much of the erroneous information, between cultural, political, and ethnic warring factions. The human living soul is profusely erroneous. The living soul functions of the mind are:

- Intellect (In)
- Consciousness (C)
- Imagination (I)
- Will (W)
- Memory (M)
- Emotions (E)

There are 720 possible permutations for these 6 basic functions or 6 items. IN, C, I, W, M, E.

How does that work? Suppose that a person wakes up in the morning and gets up on the Intellect function-based decision.

Followed by the Imagination function, and followed by the Memory, and then the Will decides to take action.

That set up a sequence for a decision to take specific action during that moment. The next day the sequence may be different. M, E, I, W. = decision + action.

The point of this illustration is to identify the 6 functions of the mind. They are real, and they can be used as objective mind tools to think straight, in line with true facts.

When people are trying to make sense of the world events, especially when humans are being harmed and destroyed by wars, it is so much more critical to know and understand what information true, and which information is full of fabrication and lies.

That, in turn, starts to reveal the nature of the human living soul. What motivates human beings to do the things that they do?

That, in turn, brings out the things that people try to hide and avoid. The inconvenient truth that people often cover up, about themselves or others. Maybe even repress the true facts unknowingly? Strange human creatures? That has the capacity of an intelligent mind, but unaware of its immense power to know truth and reality. Man and woman are made in the image of the Creator of Life, the First cause of the Universe? Almighty God!

Human is often motivated by necessity. For human beings to stay alive, they must meet many physical requirements, for oxygen, water, and food. Temperature relative to the human warm-blooded circular system blood must be within a specific range for the organ systems to function and the person to stay alive.

Human physical structures are intrinsically complex, internally they have 10 organ systems. Each organ system is automated to function on autopilot. There are responsibilities for the person in charge to take care of exercise, rest, drink water, eat nutritious food, and to sleep well.

Individual people have not designed their internal physical organ systems or even the external design of the body. People do have the 6 functions of the living soul, including the freedom of the will to make choices. Conscious free will is real, I can choose to use similar words that rhyme with the will. Such as the hill, with skill, and the mill is still.

Play with words reveals the creative function of the imagination, and the free will to shape decisive action according to the other 5 functions of the mind.

What has the above got to do with the facts of history?

I am leading here to the reality of focused consciousness. Unless there are some mind tools to shape and guide the thinking, then the thinking won't be objective. It makes no sense to try and discuss the facts of history with nothing more than the subjective feelings.

HOW TO GET STARTED ON FACTS.

Learn how to think straight first. Learn the first principles of reason.

Here are the basic principles of logic/reason laid out in a simple way that any English reading/speaking person one can understand. For further reading, there is the source reference to the Amazon Book. Being Logical: A Guide to Good Thinking.

THE PRINCIPLE OF IDENTITY

Stated: A thing is what it is.

Explanation: The whole of the existing reality is not a homogenous mass. It is a composition of individuals, and the individuals are distinguishable from one another.

THE PRINCIPLE OF THE EXCLUDED MIDDLE

Stated: Between being and nonbeing, there is no middle state.

Explanation: Something either exists or it does not exist; there is no halfway point between the two. The lamp sitting on my desk is either really there or it is not. There is no other possibility. We might ask: How about becoming? Isn't the state of becoming between those of being and non being? The answer is no. There is no such thing as just becoming; there are only things that become. The state of becoming is already within the realm of existence.

THE PRINCIPLE OF SUFFICIENT REASON

Stated: There is a sufficient reason for everything.

Explanation: The principle could also be called "the principle of causality." It states that everything that actually exists in the physical universe has an explanation for its existence. What is implied in the principle is that nothing in the physical universe is self-explanatory or the cause of itself. (For a thing to be a cause of itself, it would somehow have to precede itself, which is absurd.) One

THE PRINCIPLE OF CONTRADICTION

Stated: It is impossible for something both to be and not be at the same time and in the same respect.

Explanation: This principle could be regarded as a fuller expression of the principle of identity, for if X is X (principle of identity) it cannot at one and the same time be non-X (principle of contradiction).

Source: McInerny, D.Q. Being Logical: A Guide to Good Thinking. Kindle Edition.

CHAPTER 40

A Worldview and A Life philosophy

A reality-based worldview defended here is logical and rational:

REALITY

Truth based, factual knowledge about human nature and life on earth.

BELIEFS

What is True?

VALUES

What is Right?

BEHAVIOR AND HABITS

What is the right behavior?
   Why is the right choice an intelligent choice? Because, it is giving

space to the priori wisdom of the Creator of life, and it is giving priority to the right outcome. The right result is objectively verifiable. The right outcome is always competed for by many distractions, temptations, and compromise. The need to have absolutes for intelligent decision outcomes for problem-solving. Artificial intelligence also requires absolute values and absolute definitions. Also, for mathematics and geometry. 2 + 2 = 4. A square is a square, and a circle is a circle, they are not equal in shape. Nobody complains that there are absolutes in mathematics, or absolutes in scientific engineering, it makes a whole lot of sense.

Absolute values are also rewarding when purchasing a thing or a machine or flying overseas at 10,000 meters altitude in a crowded passenger jet. Who cares about the absolutes of engineering? The controlled flight maintained by the precision engineering of aviation technology and human knowledge. The most common controversial area where people complain about absolutes is moral ones. They protest the idea that there are absolute values in human conduct and morality. Could it be that their self-determination is heading south? Moreover, the God-given moral law, in the situation, is pointing north? That creates a conflict of interest, a dilemma.

> For where your treasure is, there your heart will be also." Matthew 6: 21. (NIV)

That challenges the individuals living soul core, the intellect, the will, and the heart. Are there such absolutes? Yes, there are. Where do they come from? It comes from the Intelligent mind of the Creator God. Also, human beings made in the image of God. With an Intellect, consciousness, imagination, will, memory, and emotions.

This is how John Locke describes them. "The law of nature constrains what we can do, even when we are free in the state of nature." We are not free to do whatever we feel or desire to do.

There have to be constraints in a multi-people society. What are the restrictions?

> "The only constraint in the state of nature is, that the rights that we have, we cannot give them up, nor can we take them from someone body else. Under the law of nature, I am not free to take them from someone else".   (Locke, THIS LAND IS MY LAND, 2009)

Life, liberty, or property. Nor am I free to take my own life, liberty or property. Where does the law of nature constraints come from? John Locke gives two answers. "For we, being all the workmanship of one omnipotent, and infinitely wise maker, they are his property, whose workmanship they are, made to last during his, not one another's pleasure."(John Locke)

LOCKE AND NATURAL RIGHTS "Locke says to think about what it means to have a natural right, we have to imagine the way things are before the government, before the law, and that is what Locke means by the state of nature."

"He says the state of nature is a state of liberty. Human beings are free and equal beings. There is no natural hierarchy. It is not the case that some people are born to be kings, and others are born to be serfs. We are free and equal in the state of nature, and yet, he makes the point that there is a difference between a state of liberty and a state of license".

And the reason is that even in the state of nature, there is a kind of law. It is not the kind of law that legislatures enact. It is a law of nature. Moreover, this law of nature constrains what we can do even though we are free, even though we are in the state of nature." (Sandel, 2009)

It means that just because we have a consciousness, imaginations, and a free will that enables us to be physically mobile and free, with the ability to determine where and when we move from point A to point B. That does not give license to do whatever, to self or others. The free will is not self-sufficient, it is only as useful with the consciousness, and the intellect is working together.

The will of the mind is a blind mechanism, that needs the other functions of the mind: Intellect, consciousness, imagination, and memory, to bring content, value, and meaning to evaluate the decision, that it intends to execute according to awareness or given instructions.

Human and mammal animal intelligence is extraordinary, highly tuned to evaluate the object, of decision making. How does a pilot of an Air Bus 380 land it on tarmac safely? It requires high intelligence to assess the situation and conditions. Moreover, a free will to optimize circumstances to the desired objectives, under the Creator God laws on the planet earth. The consciousness of the intrinsic human value is vitally important for the development of self-identity, and for the development of the mind.

It provides self-worth and self-respect. If human beings are made in the image of God, then I will make life choices according to God's will. By exercising faith and obedience. Reading good books, the study of scripture, and learning with other believers, how to be a true representative of the Heavenly father that Yeshua represented almost 2000 years ago. A follower of the teaching of Yeshua from Nazareth. Learning to become more like him in life values, priorities, goals, and attitudes with the help of His Spirit of grace.

JOHN LOCKE Fundamental individual human rights. No government, not even a democratically elected government, has the right to override natural rights. However, they can be revoked, by the person's own willful lawlessness.

In rebellion, violating against the Spirit of the Natural Law. No government can override Fundamental rights The natural right to life Right to liberty Right to property. "The Natural inherent rights are not just for the sake of creating a government and a set of human laws for a civil society. Already activated in the Natural State". – John Locke.

"The case for fundamental individual rights. No government, not even a democratically elected government, has the right to override them. John Locke argues that the right to property is not just for the sake of creating a government and political mandate. The right to property is a natural right in the sense that it is pre-political."

RULE OF LAW The term the rule of law is often used all over the world in various countries and states. It may be legitimate law, or it may not be a legitimate law. Just like the currency of money are produced, some are legitimate, and others are counterfeit. The same spirit of corruption and lawlessness is active with the fake currency, and the bogus law. It leads to the same source, the underworld of the Nemesis and the demon host. Law can also be false counterfeit. It depends on the power enforcing it.

Moreover, whether it respects the Spirit of Natural Law. How can one tell the difference between State laws? At the most basic level, to check whether people have the Natural rights: Right to life Right to liberty Right to property.

Most nations have laws; some are arbitrary, the worst-case scenario in the last 100-year European history was the leader's that introduced State Atheism, with the lawless totalitarian military regime, which denied people their right to life, liberty, and property.

Such was the revolution created by the Bolsheviks pseudo socialism in Russia from 1922 to 1991. The Bolsheviks and the USSR roots were a mixed bag from Karl Marx philosophy, Lenin's philosophical theories, and Stalin's ego ambitions for political and military power conquest, as the man of steel. Stalin was not in it for humanity or welfare. Stalin was in it for the sake of power, materialism, and national glory. The Stalinism was doomed to fail, for the same reason Lucifer failed. There is a parallel between the spirit of Lucifer

That is what Locke means by the state of nature". "John Locke says that the state of nature is a state of liberty, human beings are free and equal beings, there is no natural hierarchy, it is not the case that some people are born to be kings and others were born to be serfs, we are free and equal in the state of nature". David Sandell. Harward University. (School of Law).

Consistent with the intrinsic value of human life. "Nor am I free to take my own life, liberty or property. Even though I am free, I am not free to violate the law of nature. I am not free to take my own life, or to sell myself into slavery, or to give someone else arbitrary absolute power over me.?". – David Sandell. Harvard Law School.

Where does the constraint come? By design in the design of the human mind, by the Creator of life. "For men, being all the workmanship of one omnipotent, and infinitely wise maker, they are his property, whose workmanship they are, made to last during his, not one another's pleasure." – John Locke.

Why can't we give up our rights to life, liberty, and property? Why? Because they are not individual rights, to use on self. Because we as humans are the creature of God, in the beginning, God Created a human in His image.

NATURAL LAW

EMMANUEL KANT "Immanuel Kant (1724– 1804) argued that the supreme principle of morality exists as a standard of rationality that he dubbed the "Categorical Imperative" (CI)." "However, these standards were either instrumental principles of rationality for satisfying one's desires, as in Hobbes or external rational principles that are discoverable by reason, as in Locke and Aquinas. Kant agreed with many of his predecessors that an analysis of practical reason reveals the requirement that rational agents must conform to instrumental principles.

He also argued that conformity to the CI (a non-instrumental principle), and hence to moral requirements themselves, can nevertheless be shown to be essential to the intelligent agency". "This argument is based on his striking doctrine that a conscious will must be regarded as autonomous, or free, in the sense of being the author of the law that binds it. The fundamental principle of morality the CI — is none other than the law of an autonomous will. Thus, at the heart of Kant's moral philosophy is a conception of reason whose reach in practical affairs goes well beyond that of a Human 'slave' to the passions.

Moreover, it is the presence of this self-governing reason in each person that Kant thought offered decisive grounds for viewing each as possessed of equal worth and deserving of equal respect". (Stanford, 2018) "Kant's analysis of common sense ideas begins with the thought that the only thing good without qualification is a "goodwill." While the phrases "he is good-hearted," "she is good-natured" and "she means well" are common, "the goodwill" as Kant thinks of it is not the same as any of these ordinary notions. The idea of goodwill is closer to the concept of a "good person," or, more archaically, a "person of good will." (Stanford, 2018) "The Basic function that drives human to become the basic idea, as Kant describes it in the Groundwork, is that what makes a good person good is his possession of a will that is in a certain way "determined" by or makes its decisions by, the moral law.

The idea of goodwill is supposed to be the idea of one who is committed only to make decisions that she holds to be morally worthy and who takes moral considerations in themselves to be specific reasons for guiding her behavior. This sort of disposition or character is something we all highly value, Kant thought". "First, unlike anything else, there is no conceivable circumstance in which we regard our moral goodness as worth forfeiting merely to obtain some desirable object." Which Kant holds to be the fundamental principle of all of the morality". (Stanford, 2018)

Source: The Nemesis Book 2018 (Kindle Location, 1993).

CHAPTER 41

Websites and YouTube Channels.

(Leinonen, 2016)

My name is Victor Leinonen, and I write content for various blogs, such as the following:

ARCTIC FINLAND.

www.arcticfinland.net/

FENNOSCANDIA.

www.fennoscandia.net/

LAPLAND GUIDE.

www.laplandguide.net/

NATURAL NORDIC NUTRITION.

www.naturalnordicnutrition.com/

NORDIC CUISINE FOCUS.

www.nordiccuisinefocus.com/

ARCTIC FRESH WATER.

www.arcticfreshwater.net/

KILPIS LAKE ADVENTURES.

www.kilpislakeadventures.com

NORDIC ART IMAGES.

www.Nordic Art Images.com

WEBSITES AND YOUTUBE CHANNELS.

(Leinonen, 2009)

CHAPTER 42

Finland Centenary 1917-2017

THE 500 YEAR FIGHT FOR THE LAND AND INDEPENDENCE

The Nemesis book 2018 discusses in depth the ancient people of Finland fight for the survival and the independence of the Suomi people over 500-years.

 The 500 years of Finland was constantly harassed by foreign Imperial encroachments and military animosity caused by imperial leaders' ambitions and territorial covetousness. It was not a period protected by human civil values, human self-constraint, fear and respect for the Creator of Life. Lack of respect for the intrinsic human value, lack of respect for the Spirit of the Natural Law. But rather, there was much foreign military force used as an extension to political ambitions, with carnal archaic brute force tactics, invading from the outside. Exploiting the smaller, the weak, the innocent people of the land, and simply a larger force attacking the smaller forces as human predators exploiting soft targets.

One of the most sinister methods that the dictators of the Soviet Union and Russia have thrust upon the people of the land, over many hundreds of years, in their effort to conquer territory, and to subjugate the people of the land, has been the use of false information in their world view propaganda. False information of a false world view.

Forcing the false information propaganda onto people of the land, in so doing brainwashing them to a false reality. The Spirit of the Natural Law is real. It is explained in detail in the first five books of the bible. The Creator of Life has the first word and the last word on truth based world view. Dictators peddle an archaic self-serving world view that is based on rebellion, lawlessness and anarchy.

That is the core reason why the Soviet Russian leaders narrative is most often a false one. They are simply enforcing the Soviet-style Stalin world view. A primitive law of the jungle concept, with no other laws than the law of strength and military power

The entire northern hemisphere has been the target of arbitrary coveting and conquest for 600 years, for conquest sake, as if impersonal bigger is better. State Atheism with Soviet dictators immoral laws imposed onto the people of the land that well knew in their living souls the existence of the Spirit of the Natural law order.

The people of the land knew the Spirit of the Natural Law because they had lived on the land under the Creator of Life for many thousands of years in the Natural State. Concerning the natural laws of the Creator of Life. Their entire existence in the Arctic region and elsewhere dependent on interacting with the natural pallet of life, seasonal changes of the fauna and flora, and the natural cycles of birth and death speak to the human minds collective wisdom. They did their best to ride with the natural laws, not go against them. To go against the Spirit of the Natural Law was to come under the curse of the law. The Spirit of the Natural Law is unlike the counterfeit human-made arbitrary laws, that have no respect for the people of the land, or their ancient history, lived under the Creator of Life. According to the first five books of the bible.

Exactly the same concept of the Spirit of the Natural Law, is explained in the first five books of the bible. It was a spiritual reality to the people of the land, that lived among the works of God, life made manifest in the natural world environment. There was no shortage of information in the interaction between humans and the natural world, they worked, struggled, often trial and error to stay alive, their lives depended on throughout all their generations. Therefore, they talked and shared their knowledge from generation to generation, including the Spirit of Natural Law, specifically on justice and respect for life. Humans being spiritual beings, as spiritual vessels they contain a spirit according to their knowledge, information, and obedience to the Spirit of the Natural Law.

How did the people of Finland defend themselves from corrupted evil dictators that were hell-bent on the conquest of territory and exploitation of peoples? They had to appeal to the Creator of Life. Appeal for justice, wisdom and understanding of what is morally right and what is morally wrong? They very quickly sensed in their spirits that which was contrary to the intelligent Spirit of the Natural Law, that they knew to be the Creator of Life Spirit, much higher above the worst scenario human dictators arbitrary authority.

As people are harassed more and more by ruthless manipulators, they become desperate for truth and sanity in life, amid the cruel mindless human predators that violate all of the human moral qualities that define humans as humane.

After 100 years from the rise of Bolsheviks, and almost 100 years since the creation of State atheism in the Soviet Union, Russian leaders have again returned back to a similar narrative, dictators world view and values as Joseph Stalin. Stalin was desperate for Russian greatness, in the 1930's he said that Russia was 50 years behind the Western industries and innovation. Stalin world view was an extremely narrow one, his model for success was the Western industrial World. He copied the Western model to become great in the eyes of the world. He believed in the dialectic materialism as the way to get ahead. At the same time he rejected the information, the knowledge of the over 3000-year old experiential wisdom books openly shared in the holy scriptures as the oracles of God. A biblical world view is the true world view and life philosophy for contentment in life, from the Creator of Life perspective. Only fools say there is no God. Western freedom was created on the God-fearing principles of respect for the basic human rights, right for life, right for liberty and the right for property. Why respect these basic human rights? Because of the text recordings of the oracles of God. It is written in the first five books of the bible. And later endorsed by the Saviour, the Mediator between the Creator of Life and humanity, a jew with a name Yeshua, from Nazareth.

Stalin life philosophy was that of dialectic materialism. An impersonal First cause of the universe, a world view without an intelligent Creator of life. The head Bolshevik desperately taking the reins of the Russian nation with dictatorial use of military power. Politically ambitious, pushing and scrambling the Russian nation to be equal as the Western world nations, without the Western world foundational beliefs, values and faith in the Creator of Life. To blaspheme and reject the spirit of truth as presented in the Holy Scriptures is nothing short of misguided idolatry.

It is a sin of the worst kind, to destroy the wisdom of the Creator of Life on earth for the sake of an ambitious political dictator. Propaganda was a sharp sword that the Soviet Union used to make their subjects mindless, obedient to the tyranny of the Bolsheviks pseudo-socialism in Russia and East Europe.

This chapter presents the basic principles of the International rule of law. Small independent nations like Finland do not subscribe to the narrative of Soviet Union dictators, or the Russian leaders narrative. Rather small independent nations of East Europe subscribe to the Spirit of the Natural Law. The Spirit of the Natural law is a truthful spirit, that has the best interest of humanity in mind. According to the Creator of Life.

The rational first principles of logic, that help the mind to determine truth from error. But to determine truth, one must love objective truth. The curse of the law is for those that do not love objective truth. The Mosaic law has teeth, it was designed to have teeth. The teeth of the Mosaic law do produce fear of God, because the true fact of the Mosaic law is that it was given by the oracle of God.

The true Spirit of the Natural Law that is presented in the Holy Scriptures of the Bible, by which we can clearly condemn the Soviet State Atheism principles and methods as being evil and gross idolatry. There is no doubt in the revealed truth.

The following article is taken from The Nemesis book 2018.
CHAPTER 6

THE NATURAL RIGHTS

What are natural rights? "Natural rights are those that are not dependent on the laws or customs of any particular culture or government, and therefore universal and inalienable." (Wikipedia, Natural Rights, 2018)

What are the legal rights? "Legal rights are those bestowed onto a person by a given legal system (i.e., rights that can be modified, repealed, and restrained by human laws)." (Wikipedia, Natural Rights, 2018)

The STATE OF NATURE – JOHN LOCKE John Locke reasons that in

the beginning humans lived in the State of Nature. State of nature where there were no overlord State or government to impose the law of men onto their subjects. "The lawbreaker was dealt with one on one, about who broke the law and how. If confronted by a lawbreaker, or catching a lawbreaker doing violence to an individual, then the lawbreaker was punished directly without a third party". (Wikipedia, State of Nature, 2018)

The Spirit of the Natural Law exists first; the natural human rights derive from the Spirit of the Natural Law. In the beginning God, Elohim (Genesis 1: 1). The Natural law first appeared in ancient Greek philosophy and was referred to by the Roman philosopher Cicero. The concept and the Spirit of the Natural Law can be seen in the events of the Bible; it is there as surely as a canvas in a classical oil painting. It is seen in the actions, behavior, manner and the living soul of Abraham, interacting with the Spirit of the Natural Law.

Similarly, Moses sensitivity to true justice, compassion, and mercy for the innocent. Moses teaching in the first five books of the Bible (the Pentateuch) reveals the Spirit of the Natural Law is active. It exists with the presence and the nature of Elohim instructions to humanity. The Spirit of the Natural Law is like a buffer, an interface, that provides knowledge and grace to the human living soul mind. The Spirit of the Natural Law appeals to the human soul mind. It is good to have understanding, to weight up the options. To listen to the voice of reason and wisdom, or to act out on an impulse of the emotions. The human mind and heart can be a receiver, meditating on the Spirit of the Natural Law. God that instructs and guides humanity, according to the wisdom in His word, Elohim.

Natural Law concepts after the fact of bible scriptures. "It was developed in the Middle Ages by Catholic philosophers such as Albert the Great and his pupil Thomas Aquinas." (Encyclopedia, Natural Law, 2018) The

STATE OF NATURE - JOHN LOCKE

John Locke reasons that in the beginning humans lived in the State of Nature. State of nature where there were no overlord State or government to impose the law of men onto their subjects. "The lawbreaker was dealt with one on one, about who broke the law and how. If confronted by a lawbreaker, or catching a lawbreaker doing violence to an individual, then the lawbreaker was punished directly without a third party". (Wikipedia, State of Nature, 2018) The same law principles are written in the book of the Exodus, some 1460 AD.

LAWS CONCERNING PERSONAL INJURY AND HOMICIDE

"Whoever strikes a man so that he dies certainly to be put to death." "If he did not lie in wait, but God let him fall within his reach, then I will appoint for you a place to which he may flee. "If a man acts deliberately against his neighbor, to kill him by treachery, you are to take him to die even if he is at my altar." Exodus 21: 12-14. The State of Nature has a Spirit of the Natural law to govern it, and that law is the reason. Locke believes that reason teaches that "no one ought to harm another in his life, liberty, and or property." The way out of the state of nature is through consent, to join a society is through consent. The consent takes on to the social contract, and to the law of the society/ State. According to the John Locke philosophy of law human's inherent natural rights when they are born. Due to the intrinsic value of human life. Rights can be forfeited, through willful sin. To deliberately flaunt sin, is to disrespect the Creator of life. God is Holy.

THE NATURAL STATE

The building blocks of stable society are illustrated here in the graphic below. The rule of law derived from the Spirit of the Natural

Law. Also, Natural rights in a civil society derived from the Spirit of the Natural Law principles. The right to life, liberty, and property. The Spirit of the Natural Law protects the people in the Natural State, before the population explosion on earth. Since then people have joined the society through consent, and through the social contract. Responsibly, submitting to the laws of that particular society. It is the rational, logical, linear order of native people entering from the natural state, into civil society with the law-abiding society of people submitted to the rule of law. The rule of law is only valid when it depends on the Spirit of the Natural Law; It provides Natural rights to people in society. The right to life, right to liberty, right to property. The natural law protects the people in the natural state, before the population explosion on earth. Since then people have joined the society through consent, through the social contract. Responsibly, submitting to the rule of law in society.

RULE OF LAW

The term the rule of law is often used all over the world in various countries and states. It may be legitimate law, or it may not be a legitimate law. Just like the currency of money are produced, some are legitimate, and others are counterfeit. The same spirit of corruption and lawlessness is active with the counterfeit currency, and the counterfeit law. It leads to the same source, the underworld of the Nemesis and the demon host. Law can also be false counterfeit. It depends on the power enforcing it.

Moreover, whether it respects the Spirit of Natural Law. How can one tell the difference between State laws? At the most basic level, to check whether people have the Natural rights: Right to life Right to liberty Right to property

Most nations have laws; some are arbitrary, the worst-case scenario in the last 100-year European history was the leader's that introduced State Atheism, with the lawless totalitarian military regime, which denied people their right to life, liberty, and property. Such was the revolution created by the Bolsheviks pseudo socialism in Russia from 1922 to 1991. The Bolsheviks and the USSR roots were a mixed bag from Karl Marx philosophy, Lenin's philosophical theories, and Stalin's ego ambitions for political and military power conquest, as the man of steel. Stalin was not in it for humanity or welfare. Stalin was in it for the sake of power, materialism and national glory. The Stalinism was doomed to fail, for the same reason Lucifer failed. There is a parallel between the spirit of Lucifer that led to the fall and the spirit that tempted Stalin to become what he became, utterly given to lawlessness.

"How you have fallen from heaven, morning star, son of the dawn! You have been cast down to the earth, you who once laid low the nations! You said in your heart, "I will ascend to the heavens; I will raise my throne above the stars of God; I will sit enthroned on the mount of assembly, on the utmost heights of Mount Zaphon. I will ascend above the tops of the clouds; I will make myself like the Highest." Isaiah 14: 12-14 (NIV).

It was the spirit of Lucifer that worked the hearts and minds of Karl Marx, Vladimir Lenin, and Joseph Stalin, to the same end as Lucifer, and his demon host. In violent conflict with the Creator of Life. They were all deceived to the wrong side of the angels. It was an aberration of the true Spirit of the Natural Law.

A counterfeit created for the Nemesis, a pseudo-law that twisted and deceived people's minds away from the spiritual truth. It also denied many generations of people the opportunity to have the impartial rule of law, in a respectful, law-abiding, peaceful society.

The pseudo-law did not respect the natural rights, the Natural law, or the Creator of Life. They had ambitiously rejected the Biblical worldview and commenced creating a hardcore State Atheism, supported by narrow-minded subjective relativism. At the very core center where the Law is manufactured for society, the Spirit of the Natural Law should be respected, establishing a moral duty of the government, as being a central core value serving the people.

There was violence done to the Spirit of the Natural Law; the Spirit was evicted out of the national governance by the leaders of State atheism. It was built purely on materialistic life philosophy. Human life had little significance compared to the ambitious goals of the dictators. There the watershed in the worldview and life philosophy, can be seen clearly between the East and the West. It was played out and proclaimed openly by the Satan's State Atheism representatives. Their diabolical lawless deeds were recorded in the historical records, some of them released, others suppressed. How can it be that people generally do not see the evidence of Satan's representatives all over the world history? The reason is that they do not even understand the parables spoken by Jesus from Nazareth.

"Then Jesus said to them, "Don't you understand this parable? How then will you understand any parable?" Gospel According to Mark 4: 1-41.

The dots of history are everywhere, waiting to be joined with understanding. However, there is an obstacle to understanding the truth and facts of life, that obstacle is the deception of the heart and mind. The "deceiver" works in a way that it appears to be in control and ahead of human consciousness time, orchestrating events ahead of manifestation. It is only a matter of perspective, observing viewpoint.

Time is a constant flow; it waits for no man or woman. Humanity cannot do anything to change the flow of time, of the planet earth, the other planets, or the galaxy. The one thing that individual people can change or alter, for better or for worse, is their living soul consciousness. The exercise of the Intellect, imagination, will, and memory. To train their mind, and to exercise the free will selectively. Away from the idiot box, the passive trance meditation on the television, without thinking is all negative as far as the intellect, and the free will is concerned.

The internet is selective, enabling creative use of the mind intellect, imagination, consciousness, will, and memory. If people manage to control the many temptations. People are not equal; nothing is equal in a material world. Individual people with a free will cut their own fingernails, and brush their own teeth. Generally, no one else will do that, which a person can do for themselves. Therefore, the minds of people are not equal.

People will need to exercise and train their minds because no one else will do that for them. People are not even equal physically; some are physically stronger than others. In the animal world, they are not equal, a wombat is not equal to a rhinoceros, salmon is not equal to a marlin. Every artist trains their imagination by the power of their will. Musicians exercise their hearing to distinguish notes, set of notes, groups of notes, scales, modes and their relationship to a given key. To consciously intelligently distinguish notes, major, minor, diminished, augmented, or suspended notes in a chord of notes, is achieved through intelligent consciousness. Consciousness similarly to intelligence is malleable within the personality. Use it, or lose it, applies for everyone.

There are no exceptions to the law of exercise; it can reach anywhere and everywhere. That was already discovered some 3400 years ago; they learned to write and share their life experiences with the following generations. That fact is supported by the need for young people to be educated by teachers and educators. Classical musicians and composers would inevitably develop their hearing sense and the consciousness of listening to music.

That in turn shapes and develops the functions of their mind and the living soul to enjoy and to master their craft in music. To fine-tune consciousness, and to sharpen the mind? Or to blunt it into oblivion? Fine tuning of consciousness with logic and reason, enables responsibility. Responsibility cannot exist without having a keen sense of consciousness, and the knowledge of exercising free will with logic and reasoning. The Nemesis has the advantage of having an army of volunteers for his cause, millions, hundreds of millions of willing volunteers, going blindly with the flow to the more significant (illusion) cause of the Nemesis. Just by volunteering to do lawlessness. That is all it takes; voluntary actions can become habits, that can lead to sin. Sin and lawlessness is the only reward that is offered for those that offer their will to serve Satan's will on earth.

There is a rational and a logical explanation of the conflict, the very core reason for the conflict, it is visible, from history for everyone to see. It has manifested again and again, also been recorded for thousands of years. Only those people that deny the Spiritual reality and their minds are under the deceitful power of Satan, deception by convoluted explanations and philosophies, which defend immoral actions and lawless deeds. They fail to see and understand the profound spiritual nature of the Spirit of the Natural Law. It requires a personal relationship attitude to the Creator of Life. Technology is God's mercy and grace to humanity, Satan would not have allowed technologies to advance from the dark ages. No text printing of the Good News Bible. No global transport for distribution. No medical breakthrough would serve the purposes of Satan. No communication devices serve the purposes of Satan, the dark ages with heresies, sickness and disease, black plague, and other horrendous diseases that are some of the Nemesis ointments to put on God's creation and humanity.

What are the benefits of digital technologies for dictators? If there were no global communications? No public reporting of atrocities. No Spiritual light from the lantern to the dark corners of spiritual darkness. The evidence of this reasoning can be seen in the Iron Curtain, and the Bamboo Curtain. The internet does not serve the purposes of Satan on earth primarily; there are counterfeits for everything good and useful for people to grow and become educated for a better world, with less suffering.

"Neither do people light a lamp and put it under a basket.

Instead, they set it on a lampstand, and it gives light to everyone in the house." In the same way, let your light shine before men, that they may see your good deeds and glorify your Father in heaven." -Yeshua. Matthew 5: 15,16.
   TheNemesisBook2018 (Kindle Locations 1915-1917).

(Leinonen, 20112)

PART II

BOOKS BY THE AUTHOR

BLOGGERS GUIDE TO ARCTIC FINLAND 2019

This book content is a compilation of my blog articles, from blogs that started way back in 2009. My first blog was named Nordic Cuisine Focus. The blog content covered many areas of the Nordic region that I really enjoyed to visit, photograph, and write content on and publish. The articles were focused mainly on the natural Nordic environment, Finland, regional produce, ingredients, nature, traditional culture, and cuisine.
BLOGGERS GUIDE TO ARCTIC FINLAND 2019

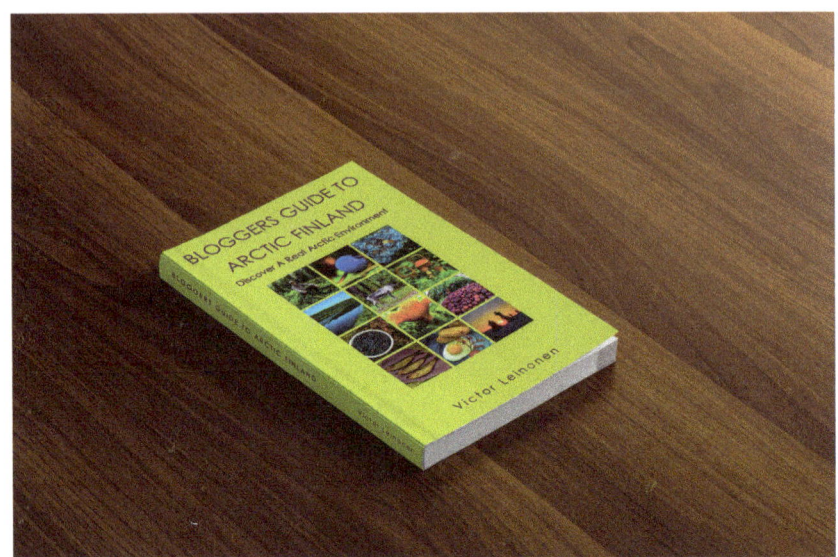

A CLAIM FOR A TRUE WORLDVIEW 2020

A Claim For A True Worldview is revised, edited and upgraded version of The Nemesis book 2018. With some chapters and content removed and new content and new chapters added. Including upgraded with new maps and new pictures.

THE NEMESIS 2018

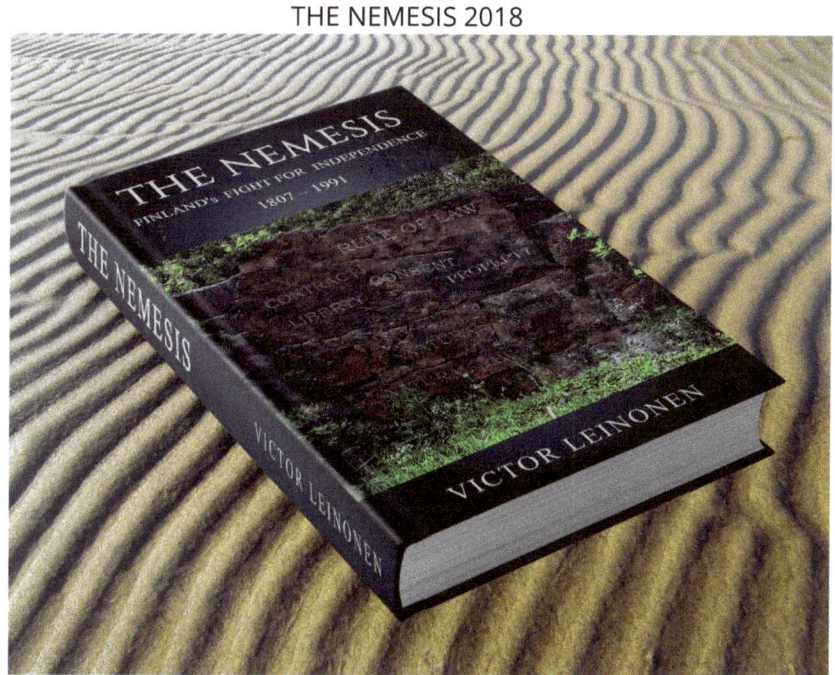

THE NEMESIS 2018

The Nemesis Book discusses the nature of the fight for the survival and the independence of the Suomi people as its central theme. However, the relatively short 500-year period of Finland was not short of foreign Imperial encroachments and animosity caused by covetousness. It was not a period protected by human self-constraint, respect for the intrinsic human value, or respect for the Spirit of the Natural Law.

Before the King of Sweden started taking an interest in the

territory of Finland around 12th Century, the indigenous tribes from Lapland's nomadic Sami peoples regularly visited and lived along the shores of the Bothnia Sea, the central lakes, and Lake Ladoga. During the early common cultural formation years, people living in the areas along the shore of the Gulf of Finland to Karelian Isthmus, North Karelia, shared a common culture and they were communicating in a similar language, which became known as the Suomi language.

Religion came with the messengers, and the reformation started by Luther in the early 16th century reached the people of Sweden and Finland. The Reformation enlightened the people's minds and gave rise to the Finnish written language development. Mikael Agricola (1510-1557) brought the Reformation to Finland and developed the Finnish speaking language into written text. The New Testament translation into Finnish in 1548. The entire Bible appeared in the Finnish language in 1642.

The Spirit of Natural Law is the essence that inherently provides the right to life, right to liberty, and right to property. The Natural Law protected the spiritually intuitive people in their Natural State before the population explosion on earth. Following Imperialistic slavery and totalitarianism, people have joined civil society willingly through consent to accept a social responsibility contract.

The news of the Russian revolution reached Finland in 1917. The majority of the law-respecting people in Finland were horrified by the Russian revolution's rebellion, lawlessness, and anarchy—by the spirit of the Nemesis overtaking the rule of law. Because the spirit of grace spiritually enlightened the people, they understood the significance of the spirit of the Natural Law, and the meaning of the rule of law. It is a profound spiritual truth for a stable society, a foundational truth in all of the stable law-respecting societies of the world.

Author VICTOR LEINONEN. All Copyrights Reserved 2018.

Link to the Amazon Kindle The Nemesis Book.

INKERI LAND 2010

Preface.

The current Inkeri Coat of Arms presents the historical conflict of the Inkeri region particularly clearly, the wide flowing water border of the Neva River, travel, transportation, and trading. Defensive castle walls of the two opposing sides, the North and the South, covered with red blood. The idealistic hope for a Judgment by the Wise old King (God), with a Golden Crown with jewel stones embedded. "AD. 1300. Sweden built a fortification at the mouth of River Okhta in 1299-1300 AD; they called it the Crown of the land. According to the author of the Novgorod Chronicle:

"The same year the Sven came from beyond the sea in great strength into the Neva; they brought masters from their own land, and they brought a special master from great Rome from the Pope."

"They established a town at the mouth of the River Okhta on the Neva and strengthened it with indescribable strength, and placed battering rams within it. And the accursed ones boasted, calling it the "Crown of the land." For they had a king's lieutenant with them named Maskalka; and having placed special men in it with the Voyevoda Sten, they went away, the Veliki Knyaz not being then in Novgorod." (Forbes., 1914)

The original Inkeri peoples inhabited the land that the Neva River cuts across which is only about 15000 square kilometers. The history of Ingria the political power plays that took around it and the constant warring which took place in the area since the year 1200 AD, it paints a clear picture of how desperate, irrational, ruthless, cruel, sick and warmongering the human race can be. When small and massive violations happen over property, when there are encroachments to traditional hunting/fishing grounds by foreigners, and when insults/violence follow suit, the people resort to ramping up more force to resist force, and use political power of a group to build a bigger group, to ensure the selfish land grabs, and paybacks. The "leaders" in history often lusted for political power that would satisfy their selfish desire for even more power over the smaller/weaker, at the expense of thousands of innocent, hardworking rural people who lose their homes, property, families and even their lives, so that the political leader's objectives were realized. People were subjugated, and the material wealth contained/consumed. The word Inkeri or Ingria is used in two ways in this book: To describe the geographical area. The people of Inkeri/Ingria community. Because the history of the Inkeri is so eruptive, tumultuous and destructive, it is easy to lose the thread of the original meaning and the original spirit of the Inkeri Baltic Finns community. For the following reasons: They were free, independent tribe and part of the regions pioneering rural community. The initial Inkeri/Ingria community was made up from the Baltic Finns, Votes and Izhorians. They grew together and shared the Finnish language with the Chuds, Estonians, Izhorians, Vepsians. Vikings and the Swedish & Novgorod Wars, and the formation of Russia and the totalitarian Stalinism that followed.

The King and Country of Sweden fought the Russians and gained control from; 1580-1595, and; 1617-1702. Russian, Denmark, Poland, Germany attacked again in 1700 and re conquered Ingria-land 1702. Stalinism was ruthless in uprooting any community that did not comply with their doctrine. Their values and political views were not of the same mind as the Soviet Union communism which eventually destroyed the Inkeri people.

The point is not about who/what/where it is done, but that when it happens it is morally wrong, criminal, and to be condemned as guilty, no matter who does it. The indigenous Ingria-land community was roughshod over by Imperial power politics. The early beginning of the nomadic people settling on land that nobody else was using, because there just wasn't that many people on the planet, it is estimated to being at 30 million during the 2000 BC.

And because of the recent Ice Age, the Nordic region during the Stone Age just wasn't that attractive for the hunter fisher gatherers, not the same as going to some Mediterranean city or a remote island, the Black Sea, or some tropical palm island on the Pacific. So there was plenty of free space in the Nordic and Fennoscandia region for some time to go around during the 2000 BC to 800 AD time period.

Vesa Leinonen. INKERI-Land (Kindle Locations, 293-309).
Link to the Amazon kindle Inkeri Land Book

VISIT THE REAL ARCTIC ENVIRONMENT

LAPLAND
ALL SEASONS
WWW. LAPLANDGUIDE.NET

About Author

BLOGGERS GUIDE TO ARCTIC FINLAND

(Leinonen, 2014)

Thank you for taking an interest to explore this book about Arctic Finland. I hope the book content has been informative and useful.

I have a keen interest in the Nordic environment, regional produce, and the local farmer's markets, having worked in the food industry for over the 20 years I have come to respect all regional food produce and natural regional products. Here are some specific topics that get my time and attention.

- Nutrition and ingredients
- Nordic environment
- Food & Health
- Life and vitality
- Intelligent Design
- Traditional and culture
- Travel and holiday destinations in the Nordic region
- Stock photography and sales of digital images.

ABOUT AUTHOR

I am a qualified chef, worked with many high caliber professional chefs over 20 years in Australia. Worked in many 5-star hotel banquet kitchens, and a restaurant owner-operator with 2 stars Michelin chef.

Menu planning worked, photographed, traveled, trekked the East coast of Australia, from Tasmania to Cook town.

Also worked in Arctic region of Finland, mostly seasonal work during the winter season. And lived on the West Coast of Finland.

To all those who enjoy the Nordic country climate and the environment in Finland, and planning a holiday, or considering relocating there to study, work or to live permanently should find

Bloggers Guide To Arctic Finland book refreshing with the content of regional photography presented in collage style images.

There are also website and YouTube video links to experience many locations in Arctic Finland.

The Bloggers guide to Arctic Finland presents the Nordic region, the land, the climate, the seasons, the natural ingredients, the food, the people, and the challenges that come with the territory.

I have worked in commercial kitchens of hotels, resorts, and family lodge Restaurants in Australia from 1990 – 2008. I moved to the Nordic region of Finland in 2008 and worked many seasons in restaurant kitchens in Arctic Finland. Also spent a lot of time skiing and snowboarding, and going on day trips, and capturing the experience for sharing.

The summer season was mostly used up foraging for wild berries and exploring the environments. Captured wild berry flowers to the berry harvest time and selling them at the local farmer's markets. The Clean Nordic environments make it possible, to forage berries from the forest with the knowledge that they are safe to eat. Unlike the large parts of southern Europe where natural ingredients from nature are not safe to eat without boiling them first.

The Nordic region has a unique natural environment, the cycle of seasons, and proximity to the Arctic North Pole.

The natural Nordic ingredients, history, the people's cultural interactions with the environment are also unique. The Nordic region is a truly interesting place to visit, to live, to explore, and to enjoy. To enjoy the Nordic region comes naturally to people that enjoy winter sports and enjoy spending time in the Nordic natural environment during the Spring and Summer season.

Seasonal changes are really apparent.

After the 6 months of snow and ice, the days start to get longer, from 6 hours of daylight to 12 hours and 24. Summer season is great to go outdoors and see, feel, and listen to the sounds of summer. The experience of listening to the birds singing their songs all night, even after midnight, is so strange at first for those that are customed to experiencing the darkness of night time.

When the first phase of the summer berry harvest ends (bilberries), then it is followed by the Lingonberry harvest. In autumn it is also the mushroom season. There are many varies of mushroom in the Nordic environment. The grain fields are harvested around September. From then on, the snow usually arrives in November, December and continues until the middle to the late month of March, then the warmth of spring weather melts the snow and the new growing season begins.

There are about 6-7 months without any cultivation/harvesting being done.

Specialties: Chef work, menu planning, photography, videos, and Blogging.

Favorite photography and video subjects: Natural environment, farmers markets, local producers, ethnic cuisine, traditional culture, modern history, world view discussion, and Biblical philosophy.

2017 I relocated back to Australia, and currently living in the Riverina district of NSW. I enjoy studying history, culture, and article writing. See Ezine-articles under my name for more articles with information on Arctic Finland.

WATCH A VIDEO PRESENTATION ON ABOUT NORDIC CUISINE FOCUS.

YouTube Channel: Natural Nordic Nutrition.
Video in English and Japanese languages.
http://naturalnordicnutrition.com/
http://nordiccuisine.eu/japanese-intr... / ラップランドフィンランドのブロガーガイド　ラップランド北極圏環境は、物理的に北極環境を体験する機会を持っていない可能性があり、友人や家族とユニークな本当の北極環境を共有するための素晴らしい方法写真撮影のための優れた環境です。北極圏の環境は季節の極端な変化を経験します、そ

して各季節は経験するのにユニークに素晴らしいです。　夏から秋への体験。　北欧のラップランドの夏のシーズン温度の気候は、ツンドラの丘を転がり、新鮮な北極の淡水スプリングをバブリング、小川をドラグリング、川、穏やかな湖を実行しているの開いているビューで、トレッキングのために温帯です。　秋のシーズングランドカバーの鮮やか鮮やかな色。針葉樹と落葉樹、様々な落葉ワイルドベリーの低木、および苔に覆われたグランドカバーからの風景の上に色のスプラッシュは、あります。ラップランドの秋の色は、緑オーバーン、ブルー、オレンジ、赤と黄色のアレイです。　冬の経験　雪に覆われた冬のワンダーランド、真冬の夏至の暗い日。穏やかな天候や日のために上に行くことがあり、一定の降雪。2月の周りの春シーズンは長い日と日光で開きます。凍結黒夜の空気中北部ライトのきらめく星との回で干満と時折完全に晴れた夜の空。朝の澄んだ青い空と、数時間持続する上に、雪の皮と白い雪に輝きます。　春シーズンの経験　春の日差しは、丘陵やツンドラ山に沿ってバックカントリーを旅行中に体験する喜びです。　夏の季節はまた、長い間寒い冬から湧き出る新しい人生と共に、自然環境においても素晴らしいです。渡り鳥はしばしば来て、夏の確かな証拠、新しい生活にあふれアップスプリング落葉樹にも新たな成長です。　どこ北極圏フィンランドでの休暇のために行きます　ホリデーシーズンに季節の活動の拠点を持っている少なくとも12個の領域があります。　ここに記載されているそれらのいくつかはあります。　1.キルピスヤルヴィ　2.稲荷　3.イヴァロ　4.サーリセルカ。5.ピーヘア/ルオスト　6.エカスロンポロ　7.パラス。　8.イェラス　9.サッラ　10.ルイ　11. カリガスニエミ　12.ロヴァニエミ　番号が付けられているこのリストは特定の順番ではなく、各地域はそれ自身の歴史、文化、施設、そして文化的伝統によってユニークです。ラップランドの目的地ハブの規模と近代化の順序では、ロヴァニエミ、ルウィ、サーリセルカ、ユラス、ピヘア/ルオスト、サラ、キルピスヤルヴィ、イヴァロ、イナリ、そしてパラスから始めることができます。

Bibliography

Retrieved from Postileimat: http://www.postileimat.com
Arkisto. (2019). *Petsamo*. Retrieved from Arkistojen Portti: http://wiki.narc.fi/portti/index.php/Petsamo
Commons. (2015). Retrieved from Wikipeida: https://commons.wikimedia.org/wiki/File:Petsamo.png
Domain, P. (2010). Retrieved from https://commons.wikimedia.org/wiki/File:Map_of_Lapland,_Finland-fi.svg.
Google Maps. (2019, June 27). Retrieved from Google: https://www.google.com/maps/place/Rovaniemi
Karhumäki. (1930). *Liinahamari Hotelli*. Retrieved from Postileimat: http://www.postileimat.com/kuvat/petsamo/P62017.htm
Leinonen, V. (2010). Inkeri Land. Amazon Kindle.
Leinonen, V. (2012). *Picture Collages*.
Leinonen, V. (2018). *Nordic Art Images*. Retrieved from Nordic Art Images: http://nordicartimages.com
Leinonen, V. (n.d.). *Arctic Finland*. Retrieved from Arctic Finland: http://arcticfinland.net
Petsamo. (1930). *Harbor of Liinahamari in Petsamo,*. Retrieved from Wikipedia: https://commons.wikimedia.org
Räisänen, O. (2010, July 17). Retrieved from Commons.wikimedia.org: https://commons.wikimedia.org/wiki/File:Map_of_Lapland,_Finland-fi.svg

Vuonnala. (2017, September 8). *Autumn Visit*. Retrieved from Salla Seura: http://sallaseura.fi/

www.ingramcontent.com/pod-product-compliance
Lightning Source LLC
Chambersburg PA
CBHW062021290426
44108CB00024B/2729